False Economy

A Surprising Economic History of the World

ALAN BEATTIE

PENGUIN BOOKS

PENGUIN BOOKS

Published by the Penguin Group
Penguin Books Ltd, 80 Strand, London WC2R ORL, England
Penguin Group (USA), Inc., 375 Hudson Street, New York, New York 10014, USA
Penguin Group (Canada), 90 Eglinton Avenue East, Suite 700, Toronto, Ontario, Canada M4P 2Y3
(a division of Pearson Penguin Canada Inc.)
Penguin Ireland, 25 St Stephen's Green, Dublin 2, Ireland (a division of Penguin Books Ltd)
Penguin Group (Australia), 250 Camberwell Road, Camberwell, Victoria 3124, Australia
(a division of Pearson Australia Group Pty Ltd)
Penguin Books India Pvt Ltd, 11 Community Centre, Panchsheel Park, New Delhi – 110 017, India
Penguin Group (NZ), 67 Apollo Drive, Rosedale, North Shore 0632, New Zealand
(a division of Pearson New Zealand Ltd)
Penguin Books (South Africa) (Pty) Ltd, 24 Sturdee Avenue, Rosebank,
Johannesburg 2196, South Africa

Penguin Books Ltd, Registered Offices: 80 Strand, London WC2R ORL, England

www.penguin.com

First published by Viking 2009
Published with revisions in Penguin Books 2010

10068 56545   1

Printed in Great Britain by Clays Ltd, St Ives plc

A CIP catalogue record for this book is available from the British Library

ISBN: 978-0-141-03370-9

www.greenpenguin.co.uk

Penguin Books is committed to a sustainable future
for our business, our readers and our planet.
The book in your hands is made from paper
certified by the Forest Stewardship Council.

To my parents

Time, that gives and takes our fame and fate
and puts say, Shakespeare's features on a plate
or a Persian poet's name on a Tandoori
can cast aside all we commemorate

and make Lot 86 or Lot 14
even out of Cardinal and Queen
and bring the holy and the high and mighty
to the falling gavel, or the guillotine.

Tony Harrison
The Blasphemer's Banquet

Contents

Acknowledgen

A book, particularly a first book, doesn't com   ⸱ce
without a lot of help.

An assortment of people read sections at variou⸱ stages and
gave me helpful comments and encouragement: Richard Baldwin,
Ha-Joon Chang, Simeon Djankov, Damon Green, Ed Luce, Kirsty
McNeill, Todd Moss, Moisés Naím, Marcus Noland, Adam Posen,
Pietra Rivoli, Dani Rodrik and Razeen Sally. Sathnam Sanghera
gave me advice and guidance at the critical early stages, and sagely
pointed out that if he could write a book, so could I.

My editors Mary Mount and Geoff Kloske took a big a chance
on me in the first place and have displayed remarkable patience
and persistence, especially during the ongoing drama of the Great
Title Hunt. As an agent, Jonny Geller has proved to be absolutely
everything he was cracked up to be.

The *Financial Times* has been my employer for a decade, and I
am grateful for the time and space it has given me to pursue my
obsessions. Particular thanks, especially for help and inspiration
during my first and rather nervous months, are due to Chris Adams,
Richard Adams, Lionel Barber, Robert Chote, Stephen Fidler and
Martin Wolf.

For support and help in recent years I owe thanks to an indis-
pensable group of friends: it would be invidious to single any out,
but they know who they are. For as long as I can remember, my
closest supporter of all has been my brother, John, a judicious
guide and a resolute ally. And finally, my debt of longest standing
is to the people to whom this book is dedicated, who brought me
into being, who taught me to read and then read the first things I
ever wrote, who have been reading me ever since and who have
always given me boundless and unconditional love: my parents.

Preface

Franklin Delano Roosevelt, perhaps the greatest of all of America's presidents, loved stories about himself. One of his favourites went like this. During the Great Depression of the 1930s, one Wall Street commuter had a daily morning ritual. He would buy the newspaper on the way into the train station. He would glance only at the front page and then, without taking another look, hand it back to the boy on the newspaper stand and board the train. Eventually, the newspaper boy got up the courage to ask him why he only ever read the front page. The commuter explained that he bought it solely for the obituaries. The newspaper boy pointed out that the obituaries were at the back. 'Boy,' the man said, 'the son of a bitch I'm interested in will be on page one.'

At the time, Roosevelt was busy trying to save the US economy in the face of a colossal global dislocation. He was working to preserve the most powerful engine for creating wealth in the history of the world. To do so, he expanded radically the frontiers of American government. And a decade later, at the end of his presidency and his life, he would help to create the institutions that led a global economy shattered by war and by misguided isolationism back on the route to openness and prosperity.

And yet he was vilified by some, like that New York commuter, who would continue to benefit from the success that he helped to restore. Roosevelt was trying to save capitalism from itself, and some of the capitalists were resisting. Knowing the right thing to do to enrich your nation and the world is hard enough. Bringing people with you to get it done is even harder.

The financial crisis that started in 2007 and exploded across the world was a reminder of how fragile and reversible is the history of human progress. But it should also remind us that our future is in our own hands. We created this mess and we can get ourselves out if it.

To do so involves confronting a false economy of thought — that our economic future is predestined and that we are helplessly borne along by huge, uncontrollable, impersonal forces. To explain the vast complexity of the economic history of the world, there is a rich variety of fatalistic myths on offer: that some economies (the US, western Europe) were always going to get rich and that others (Africa) were always going to stay poor; that particular religions are intrinsically bad for growth; that market forces are unstoppable; that the strutting vanguard of globalization cannot be routed and driven into retreat.

The aim of this book is to explain how and why countries and societies and economies got to where they are today: what made cities the way they are; why corruption destroyed some nations but not others; why the economy that fed the Roman empire is now the world's biggest importer of grain. But it will reject the idea that the present state of those economies, countries and continents was predetermined. Countries have choices, and those choices have substantially determined whether they succeeded or failed.

Economic history is a challenging thing to explain, and to read, for two reasons. First, it involves forcing together disciplines that naturally fall in different directions. History in its most traditional form lives on specifics and particularities — what the historian Arnold Toynbee (disapprovingly) called the study of 'one damned thing after another'. It stresses the importance of narrative in the way that countries develop, the role played by chance and circumstance and the influence of important characters and events. Economics, by contrast, seeks to extract universal rules from the mess of data that the world provides — offering reliable and testable predictions that economies run in a particular fashion, or starting off from a particular point will end up a particular way. Both approaches have dangers. If history can become the undisciplined accumulation of a random heap of facts, economics risks descending into the pseudo-scientific compression of a complex reality into a simplistic set of fixed categorical moulds.

Second, economic history is vulnerable to fatalism. Any study that takes as its endpoint the present day is always liable to argue backwards from the conclusion. History is so rich in scope and detail that it is always possible to pick a particular constellation out of the galaxy of facts to explain clearly and precisely why things are as they are. Yet such reasoning is frequently proven wrong by subsequent history. Or it completely fails to explain why other, similar, countries and economies came to a different end.

If we are going to learn from history rather than just record it, we need to stop reasons becoming excuses. Drill too far down into explanations of how things turned out the way they did and you risk hitting a bedrock of determinism. There are plenty of reasons why countries have made mistakes. Often their decisions are driven by a particular interest group, or a coalition of groups, whose short-term gains stand at odds with the nation's longer-term benefit. But such interests can be overcome. Similar countries facing similar pressures can take different decisions. Most nations that discover oil and diamonds in their ground suffer as a consequence, but not all do. Some interest groups have captured countries and dragged them down; some have been resisted. Islamic beliefs have proved a drag on certain economies at certain times, but they do not have to. Some economies have managed to capture great benefits from the globalization of markets in goods and services; some have missed out.

History is not determined by fate, or by religion, or geology, or hydrology, or national culture. It is determined by people. This book is not a whimsical set of disconnected stories. It is an explanation of how human beings have shaped their own destiny. It also shows how decisions being taken now are determining our future.

Nothing can call back the finger of history to cancel even half a line of what has been written. But still we can compose the script for the remainder of our lives and beyond.

1. Making choices

Why did Argentina succeed and the US stall?

Everyone remembers the horrendous, world-changing events of the morning of 11 September 2001. Everyone remembers the planes commandeered by terrorists slamming into the twin towers of the Centro Mundial de Comercio in Buenos Aires. As the richest country on earth and the modern world's first global hyperpower, Argentina was a prime target for malcontents revolting against the might of the Western capitalist order.

Fewer recall the disaster that befell the United States of America three months later. Fewer recall the wrenching moment when the US federal government, crushed by the huge debts it had run up borrowing abroad in pesos, announced it was bankrupt. The economic implosion that followed, in which thousands of jobless, homeless Americans slept rough and picked through trash tips at night in New York's Central Park, shocked only those still used to thinking of the US as a first-world country.

Well, no. It happened the other way around. But that was not inevitable. And the crisis that hit the global financial system in 2008, threatening to plunge the world into another Great Depression, should be a dark warning. The US could have gone the way of Argentina. It could still go that way, if the painfully learned lessons of the past are forgotten.

The strong likelihood is that in the long sweep of history, the global financial turmoil will be seen as a crisis of capitalism but not its terminal crisis. The world economy – and particularly the US – has recovered from financial crisis and economic recessions, indeed depressions, before.

Each time, similar lessons have emerged. Countries do not get rich by accident. They make choices that determine the path their economies take. It is not always clear which is the right path at any given point, though some general rules can be drawn. But the countries that succeed are those that are flexible enough to learn from experience, and which do not come to be captured by groups whose interests are sharply at odds with those of the country as a whole.

The US and Argentina took different paths. Yet that was not inevitable. A short century ago the US and Argentina were rivals and started off in similar places. Both were riding the first wave of globalization at the turn of the twentieth century. Both were young, dynamic nations with fertile farmlands and confident exporters. Both brought the beef of the New World to the tables of their European colonial forebears. Before the Great Depression of the 1930s, Argentina was among the ten richest economies in the world. The millions of emigrant Italians and Irish fleeing poverty at home at the end of the nineteenth century were torn between the two: Buenos Aires or New York? The pampas or the prairie?

A hundred years later there was no choice at all. One had gone on to be among the most successful economies in history. The other was a broken husk. Inept, corrupt governments had time and again stolen the savings of their own people. When the flesh of that fruit was sucked dry they stole from foreign investors foolish enough to recall the promise of the distant past and forget the failure of the present.

Perfect hindsight encourages us – and historians – to imagine that the two countries were fated to diverge in the way they did, that one was bound to fly and the other destined to stall. A superficial similarity over a hundred years ago might have been enough to fool desperate Italian and Irish emigrants, we might think, but surely we can see clearly the fatal flaws that were to be found beneath?

History invites us to think we are explaining and analysing when in fact we are retrospectively rationalizing. Things that happened were always going to happen, and the proof that they were always going to happen is that they did happen. Since we know that Argentina was going to fail, we can always pluck some fundamental elements out of the vast thicket of geographical, social, environmental and political influences that make up its history to show that the failure was inevitable.

An old saying of historians is that until lions learn to talk, history will always be written by the hunters. There is some truth in that, though not a universal truth; the losers of history have their modern champions as well. Less recognized is the tendency to assume that the roles of lions and hunters were irreversibly assigned at the beginning. This book will argue that the paths taken by different countries largely reflect the decisions that they made, even if they were unaware that they were making them.

Imagine the US had followed the arc that Argentina did, falling from the first world to the third. How many factors from earlier in its history, fundamental and superficial, would now triumphantly be adduced as evidence that it always would have done? America was a nation whose forebears travelled across an ocean to establish a colony of religious absolutism, a country whose birth was induced by the rejection of a colonial power, whose revered first president warned against 'foreign entanglements', which insisted even on playing sports alien to the rest of the world. While successful Argentina imported political liberalism from Europe along with the grace and artistry of association football, the isolationist, insular US invented its own brutal and violent version of each. Clearly the US was always going to make the fatal mistake of rejecting the opportunities offered by the international economy and turning in on itself. Wasn't it?

Almost as unhelpful as historical fatalism is trying to nail down a single turning point when a country, an economy or a society went one way or the other. The human desire for a story means it is usually possible to find symbolic events that fit the need for narrative moments of crisis and resolution. But tightening the focus pull of causation on a single event itself invites the misleading if-only feeling that had a close-run thing gone the other way, the entire direction of subsequent history would have been different. The old saying has it that for the want of a nail, the shoe was lost; for the want of a shoe, the horse was lost; for the want of a horse, the message was lost; for the want of a message, the battle was lost; for the want of a battle, the kingdom was lost. The nail assumes critical importance. But a kingdom that had grown vulnerable to the loss of a single messenger was, perhaps, not long for this world no matter whether that message got through.

Harper Lee's wonderful novel *To Kill a Mockingbird* starts with the endpoint of the narrative it tells. Scout, the narrator, recounts that her older brother, Jem, had his arm badly broken at the elbow when he was nearly thirteen. Within the novel they dispute the cause. Scout identifies the key event as being a couple of years previously, when the man that attacked him came into their lives. Jem, four years older, reaches back years further to a first encounter with a new friend who conceives of meeting the recluse who eventually saves Jem from the attack.

Their father, wisely, pronounces both of them right. There was no individual event at which Argentina's future was irrevocably determined or its path set on a permanent divergence from that of the United States of America. But there was a series of mistakes and missteps that fit a general pattern. The countries were dealt quite similar hands but played them very differently.

The similarities between the two in the second half of the nineteenth century, and in fact up to 1939, were neither fictional nor superficial. The 'lords of the pampas' – young Argentines strutting the salons of Europe between the wars – pop up in accounts of the time as an equally prominent type as the swaggering Americans playing at European decadence in Berlin and Paris.

For a long while the two countries were on parallel paths. Unlike most African and Asian colonies, those in the Americas generally gained early independence from European empires. The states that later became the US declared independence in 1776 and became a new nation in 1789. The vice-royalty of Argentina, part of the Spanish empire that then reached across the continent to Peru, was overthrown in 1810 by rebels inspired by the American revolution who were then emboldened by the repulse of two British attempts to seize Buenos Aires, the capital. In 1816, Argentina became an independent republic.

Both faced an internal struggle between those that wanted a centralized nation and those that wanted power reserved for the individual states or provinces. In the US, the separate colonies had existed long before the idea of uniting them and it was not guaranteed that the republic would actually happen, nor that it would succeed once formed. The negotiations that led to the writing of the constitution were long, tortuous and often bad-tempered, and the different denominations, traditions and constitutions of the previous colonies all too evident. Only five of the thirteen founding colonies, later states, even bothered turning up to the first drafting meeting, in 1786. Virginia, the most populous colony, wanted a strong central government with directly elected representatives based on population size. New Jersey, one of the smaller ones, wanted equal power for each state. The US Congress to this day reflects the compromise: a lower house elected roughly by population and an upper Senate with two representatives per state.

The idea that an American identity sprang fully formed from the adoption of the constitution is a comforting thought for a country that sees itself as the embodiment of great and universal principles. It is, however, something of a myth. Battles had to be fought to make flesh the national motto 'E pluribus unum' ('out of many, one'). That motto appears today on US coins, but at the time of independence in 1789 dozens of different currencies were circulating – the 'continentals' printed by the continental congress, the governing body of the independence movement (and the forgeries of same issued by the British to destabilize the war effort), and currencies issued by states, cities and foreign nations. A national bank and a single 'national debt' – making the federal government responsible for the debts of the states – were not created without fierce opposition. Some of the most prominent of the new republic's founding fathers, particularly Thomas Jefferson, believed too much power was being pulled into the centre.

In Argentina, it took decades of struggle between centralists, who wanted all tax to pass through the hands of the national government, and federalists, who wanted it reserved to the provinces. A constitution was adopted in 1853 with a system of sharing tax revenue between the centre and the provinces. But there remained continual tensions, which were not settled until the suppression of an armed uprising in the province of Buenos Aires in 1880, at the cost of 2500 dead and wounded, handing more power to the centre. Domingo Sarmiento, who had tried to forge an Argentine national unity while president between 1868 and 1874, said he would settle for an Argentina whose inhabitants were not killing each other. Instead of the French Revolution's rallying-cry of 'liberty, equality, fraternity', he said, he would be content with 'peace, tranquillity and liberty'.

On the face of it the economies of the two countries also looked similar: agrarian nations pushing the frontiers of their settlement westwards into a wilderness of temperate grasslands. In both nations, the frontier rancher – the gaucho and the cowboy – was elevated into a national symbol of courage, independence and endurance. But closer up there were big disparities in the way this happened. America chose a path that parcelled out new land to individuals and families; Argentina delivered it into the hands of a few rich landowners.

From the founding of the colonies, America was fortunate enough to have imported many of the farming practices of northern Europe and the aspirations of its people. The farmers of 'New England', the densely populated states of the north-east, came largely from Britain, Germany and the Netherlands – all countries with a lot of people and not much land. They brought with them the tradition of skilled farmers on small homesteads. Argentina, by contrast, had a history of a few rich landowners on great estates left by the Spanish and the aristocratic elitism that came with it. It also had a labour shortage. Mass immigration to Argentina came later in the nineteenth century, but the country had to push forward its frontier with a skeleton staff.

Both countries opened up the west, the US to the Pacific and the Argentines to the Andes, but not in the same way. They faced similar problems. The vast distances and unfamiliar terrain were weapons of great value for the native Americans in both halves of the continent. The westward expansion could not be blocked indefinitely, given the gulf in technologies. Rifles and revolvers would in time defeat axes and bows and arrows. But the resistance they encountered helped to shape the settlement.

America favoured squatters: Argentina backed landlords. Desperate to push westwards and short of cash, Buenos Aires found the best way to encourage settlers was to sell in advance large plots in areas yet to be seized from the native Americans, or to promise them to military officers leading the charge. This was an extreme form of performance-related pay: no win, no farm. But once the battles were won the victors were exhausted, good farm labourers in short supply and the distances from the eastern seaboard to the frontier vast. Most of the new landowners simply encircled wide tracts of grassland with barbed-wire fences and turned them over to pasture. Raising cattle or sheep required relatively little hired help, but it did not leave much scope to increase productivity with fertilizer and machinery. Nor was that initial misstep much rectified.

Thus was privilege reinforced. A small number of wealthy and powerful landowning families controlled vast amounts of sparsely populated pasture. Argentina's land conquests did little to change its nature. European emigrants to Argentina had escaped a land-owning aristocracy at home only to re-create it in the New World. The similarities were more than superficial. In the early decades of agricultural commercialization, the 1860s and 1870s, the land-owners regarded rural life and the actual practice of agriculture with disdain. Many lived refined, deracinated lives in the cities, spending their time immersed in European literature and music in cloistered salons rather than bothering to run their farm estates themselves. Even when a number of new immigrants made it into the elite, they still acted as though their blood had been blue. The closest they came to celebrating country life was elevating polo, an aristocratized version of a rural pursuit, to a symbol of Argentine athletic elegance. Even then it took an elite and exclusive form: the famous Jockey Club of Buenos Aires, founded in the 1880s. This elitism worked, too; by the end of the nineteenth century some were sending sons to Eton, a school at the apex of British aristocratic privilege. A few were even accorded the ultimate accolade of being permitted to marry into titled European nobility.

Though it regarded what it termed the 'manifest destiny' of expansion with imperious, and almost imperial, ambition, America's move westwards was more democratic. The government deliberately encouraged a system of smaller family holdings. Even when it did sell off large tracts of land, the potential for a powerful landowning class to emerge was limited. Squatters who seized family-sized patches of soil had their claims acknowledged, which created an incentive for westward migrants to follow en masse. Its cattle ranchers did not spend much time boning up on the entrance requirements of elite English schools. And as well as raising cattle, the western settlers ran higher-productivity arable farms growing wheat and corn. The massive westward move of America opened up a vacuum in the coastal east of the country, which soon filled up with emigrants sucked in from the poverty and desperation of Europe. By the 1850s, the US was importing a quarter of a million immigrants a year.

Immigrants came to Argentina as well, and later made up a bigger proportion of the population than in the US. But they came later and with fewer skills. Even from across the Atlantic, the wages offered for lowly farm labourers did not always look enticing. Low productivity meant low wages, for which, in the main, only the poorer and less well-educated Europeans were prepared to emigrate in large numbers. The surge of immigrants into Argentina, largely low-skilled Italians and Irish, came in the last few decades of the nineteenth century. In 1914, a third of Argentina's population was still illiterate.

The European migrants to Argentina had been pushed as much as pulled. A rising population and inefficient farming – which, appropriately enough, was undercut by cheap agricultural produce exported by the US and Argentina – drove Italians off the land in their home country, while the Irish were escaping the famine of the potato blight. America imported the special forces of British agriculture, and in addition a large number of literate, skilled workers in cloth and other manufactures. But while there was an English-speaking aristocratic landowning clique at the top of Argentine society, the only British farming colonists of any note in Argentina were the Welsh who pitched up deep in the southern Argentine province of Patagonia – poor, isolated hill farmers swapping one cold and remote land for another.

Nor were many immigrants gripped by an Argentine version of the American dream. A lot of the immigrants were 'swallows' (*golondrinas*) who came from Italy or Spain for the harvest season and then returned home. Between 1850 and 1930, only 5 per cent of immigrants even became Argentine citizens. Italy won the 1934 football (soccer) World Cup with three Argentine players in its squad. Since they were of Italian descent, it considered them essentially Italians and simply poached them ahead of the tournament, to the fury of Argentina's football fans. It is hard to imagine England getting away with requisitioning American athletes of British descent.

Still, America's openness to immigration was not a given any more than it is now. The Plymouth colony founded by the Pilgrim emigrants of the seventeenth century was intended not to extend freedom and democracy but to give a different denomination the ability to impose its own religious purity. America's low church Protestants had left Catholicism and its near neighbour, Anglicanism, in Europe. Many had no wish to let them follow on behind.

Associations of American-born workers arose to oppose more immigration. With an unconscious gift for self-satire, one powerful political movement in the middle of the nineteenth century styled itself the 'Know-Nothings' after the response they were required to give when asked about their half-secret gatherings. The Know-Nothings wanted Catholics and foreigners banned from public office. There were riots in New York against the incomers. But in the end the exigencies of economic growth won out. There was no point fighting over shares of the pie when it became evident just how rapidly it was growing. America was not a zero-sum game.

Meanwhile Argentina was heading down the wrong track. It

had more land than it could efficiently work with too few home-grown or imported labourers to work it. But it was well into the twentieth century before the rot in the foundations became apparent. Its faults were for a long while masked by a great and unearned gift.

Hyperbole about the 'unprecedented' nature of the twenty-first-century globalized economy is misplaced. There was huge integration in markets for goods, capital and (particularly) people during the first 'Golden Age' of globalization, roughly dating from 1880 to 1914. Peace in Europe coincided with the growth of cities and with them urban consumers. A global trading system developed with astonishing speed. Transport costs dropped sharply. In the middle of the nineteenth century, wheat cost more than twice as much at destination in London than it did at source in Chicago. By 1913 they cost about the same. Most leading countries fixed their currencies to the price of gold, meaning that they would be sure how much their export earnings would be worth.

It was a great time to be a New World farmer. American and Argentine farming had a big competitive advantage (relative to other countries) and a comparative one (relative to the New World's other industries). A canning industry already existed, boosted by the American Civil War. Soldiers, particularly of the Southern armies, had had to fight a long way from reliable sources of fresh food. Fray Bentos, long famous in Britain as a brand of glutinous tinned meat pie, is a town in Uruguay near the Argentine border. Canning was now supplemented by new industrial processes invented elsewhere, such as freezing and refrigerating meat. American and Argentine farmers saw the markets of Europe open wide and clear in front of them. This, after all, was the way specialization was supposed to work in a global market. The New World did farming: western Europe did machines.

Along with Australia and Canada, Argentina and the US formed a clutch of efficient, profitable, export-oriented New World farming countries. Production expanded massively, seizing on the new technologies. Fresh American beef appeared with frequency on the tables of Europe. The growing market and established supply chains meant that concentrating production in a few items like beef and wheat seemed the logical thing to do. By the end of the nineteenth century Argentina's economy, per head of population, was higher than that of France and a third higher than Italy's.

A British visitor to Argentina in 1914 wrote:

one cannot go through the country and see its fecundity, go into the killing houses of La Plata and Buenos Aires, watch the ocean liners, with the Union Jack dangling over their stern, being loaded with many sides of beef, visit the grain elevators at the ports of Bahia Blanca and Rosario pouring streams of wheat destined for European consumption into the holds of liners, without the imagination being stimulated when standing on the threshold of this new land's possibilities.

Wisely used, the benefits of the export boom could have kept Argentina up in the pack chasing the US. But much of the money was captured by the owners of huge swathes of pasture, not their badly paid employees, and they generally either spent it on imported consumer goods or bought more land with it. Argentina needed to import more than just technology to benefit from the commodity boom. It needed to borrow the money from abroad as well. At this time it hardly seemed to matter. The British were on hand. They poured money and expertise into railroads that opened up the pampas just as they had opened up Australia, Canada and the US.

If Argentina looked like it was following the American route, it was doing so by rote, not by understanding. Argentina borrowed money from the British, but America learned from its experience as well. Economies rarely get rich on agriculture alone. Britain had shown the world the next stage, industrialization. Crudely put, labour-saving inventions increased farm output, created surplus profits and reduced the demand for labour. The savings were used for investment in industry. The displaced farmers went to the towns to work in the factories.

The same benefits that boosted American farming also helped it industrialize. Sometimes it helps to be second on the scene: the

US could follow the track that Britain had already beaten down. Two advantages in particular were familiar from its agricultural revolution: one, the technologies of smelting iron and so forth already existed; two, it could tap some of Europe's, and particularly Britain's, large pools of money looking to invest abroad.

America learned quickly. Though it benefited from the farm trade in which it also had a comparative advantage, and from British investment, it never became as dependent on either as its southern counterpart. Its most significant import from Britain was neither money nor goods but ideas. In particular, it grasped that building a manufacturing industry would allow it to benefit from better technologies, while half-heartedly trying to squeeze a little more wheat out of the same fields would not.

American business owners wanted to invest their own money in industrializing their country. Although it was the world's fastest-growing importer of capital, thanks to its size and rapid development, it also did a lot of its own saving. Foreign capital accounted for no more than 10–15 per cent of investment in America, compared with more than a third in Argentina.

It was not as if Argentina consciously and visibly rejected the same course. It could scarcely avoid growing its own manufacturing industry unless it copied the remarkable Chinese decision earlier in the millennium to retreat from the world and regard foreign technologies with suspicion. But when the industrialization did come, the prevailing prejudices ensured it was limited and late. The elites of Argentina rejected the mentality (and actions) that industrialization required. Safely milking the golden teat from their farming, they saw no particular reason to risk their status and livelihoods in the fickle and dangerous world of industrialization. Conspicuous consumption was a far more attractive proposition than tying up money for a long time in an uncertain project that might in any case harm rather than help their farming interests. And despite the large inflows of immigrants at the end of the nineteenth century, Argentina still suffered from a chronic labour shortage. There were not enough new Argentines to fill factories.

Argentina brought the same conservative and oligarchic tendencies to industrialization that it had to the ossified agricultural sector, preferring cosy, safe monopolies protected by government fiat and regulation to the brutal riskiness of competition. Nascent Argentine industry was, in essence, carried by the rest of the economy. It had little momentum of its own.

Argentina's development during the Golden Age was rapid but precarious. Its well-being rested on farm prices continuing to hold their own against the prices of manufactured goods, and on global markets remaining open. A boost from new technology and new export markets was a very different thing to a secure place on the escalator that would take the economy past agriculture and into manufacturing.

Many of the manufacturing industries that did spring up were adjuncts to the farming business, such as the Fray Bentos canners. They became not replacements for farming but offshoots from it; they did not lead but were towed behind agriculture. Argentine manufacturing was small-scale – handicraft workshops rather than factories – and used imported capital and technology. Its labour force was unskilled and remained that way. The wealth and status of the Argentine elite, while it also owned some service industries like banking and transport, was still based on landowning. Manu-facturing was regarded as a little vulgar.

Often, or at least often in the narratives of historians, there was a symbolic pivot when it became clear that the investors and industrialists of the cities would be the future rather than the landowners and farmers of the countryside. In Britain, the de-fining moment was the repeal of the Corn Laws in 1846, the import tariffs that had protected British grain from foreign com-petition and artificially raised the value of land. In America, it was the Civil War, in which the industrial North defeated the agrarian South. The closest Argentina came was the burning down of the Jockey Club by urban supporters of Juan Perón (of whom more later), more than a century after Britain had repealed the Corn Laws.

If the South had won the Civil War and gone on to dominate the North, America might have looked a lot more like Argentina.

The antebellum Southern states would have been very familiar to an Argentine: large estates with a few rich landowners and some badly paid labourers. (Thanks to the low productivity that could not attract enough labour, they also had a lot of slaves.) They exported crops, particularly cotton, to the rest of the world, but with little ability to expand and diversify. The cotton went to Liverpool to be made into textiles in Lancashire; the South did not make clothes itself.

Though the war itself was a pretty close-run thing, in reality this is one of the what-if turning points ascribed more significance than it deserves. A Southern victory in the Civil War might have slowed and skewed American industrialization but not halted it. Even if the North had lost, and failed to bring the South back into the Union by force, it would most likely have gone its own way, building an economy based on manufacturing and commerce and leaving the South to wallow in its victorious stagnation. Manufacturing and finance were supplanting farming. No country was going to keep up with the leading pack by remaining in agriculture.

The American commerce–finance–business establishment got another scare in the 1890s. Farmers from both Northern and Southern states, seeing their prices drop because of global over-supply, wanted in effect to print more money by fixing the dollar to the price of more plentiful silver rather than, as it was, to the price of gold. The 'Populist' political movement arose to press their case. The investors and business community regarded the link with gold as essential to the country's position as a financial and trading hub. It ensured that the dollar kept its value both against other leading currencies such as the pound sterling, which were also fixed to the gold price, and in terms of what it could buy. The limited amount of gold in the world also meant that all currencies linked to it were kept in short supply, keeping a tight lid on inflation at the cost of large swings in output and employment. The presidential election in 1896, which largely turned on the issue, was close, but the supporters of the gold standard won.

But though the central demand of the Populists was defeated, the discontent they reflected was not ignored. This discontent had arisen in the last decades of the nineteenth century for a reason that will seem all too familiar today. Unregulated finance capitalism appeared to be enriching a powerful minority while subjecting everyone else to the vagaries of a volatile economy. The US learned that this was not sustainable. And because it was a democracy, however imperfect, it reacted.

The Progressive movement arose to restrain the excesses of the first era of globalization. Theodore Roosevelt, president between 1901 and 1909, showed that America was capable of maximizing and redistributing the harvest of golden eggs without killing the goose. Campaigns of trust-busting broke up exploitative monopolies and new legislation protected consumers from impure food and medicines. Later, the US constitution was amended to allow a national income tax and to guarantee women the vote. Confidence in the government remained. By adapting, the US system survived. Argentina, by contrast, remained stuck in old ways. Economically, it had a single world-class sector dependent on demand from abroad and on imported capital and technology. That turned out to be a poor choice.

The twentieth century was a time of change and cataclysm, of markets opened and snatched away, a time that rewarded rapid and flexible reactions to unprecedented and unforeseeable events. Buenos Aires got a glimpse of the future in 1890 when Barings, one of the best-known British banks, nearly collapsed after over-extending loans in Argentina. The Argentine government, dependent on overseas borrowing, had to declare a moratorium on repaying debt in 1891. (As a child of the Spanish empire, Argentina was following a family tradition: Philip II, king of Spain in the sixteenth century, was history's first serial sovereign defaulter, failing to honour his debts four times.)

An economy like America's, with a nimble and productive industrial sector, was well placed to take advantage. An economy like Argentina's, grown fat and complacent endlessly borrowing foreign money to pump out grain and corned beef to foreign markets, was not. By the end of the nineteenth century, pretty much all the fertile land had been taken. There were no more frontiers to be pushed forward, and hence, apart from the steady upward grind of a rising population and increasing agricultural productivity, Argentine farming had, to all intents and purposes, taken the country as far up the league table of nations as it could.

America may have entered the twentieth century as a country whose defining myth of self appeared still to be the amber waves of grain stretching from sea to shining sea. But in reality its immediate future lay in the dark industrial huddles of Chicago, Pittsburgh and Cleveland, just as Britain's had been in Manchester, Sheffield and Glasgow.

Like the US Civil War, the First World War is an obvious candidate for historians casting about for a marker post for the end of the first Golden Age. Certainly the international flows of capital and trade peaked in 1914 and were sharply lower between the First and Second World Wars. But with money and guns suddenly in short supply the war itself was a good time for countries with the trifecta of capital, factories and peace. Standing lucratively aloof from the mud in Flanders until late on in the war, the US did rather well out of it. Constructing a neat system of vendor finance, it lent Europeans the money to buy its armaments exports with which to kill each other. By the end of the war, American industry had decisively become the best in the world and the country had moved with striking speed from being a borrower of European capital to being a net creditor.

The European countries themselves sold off assets around the world, facing the cost of a long and inconclusive war and, particularly for France, having to write off investments in Russia after the 1917 Bolshevik revolution. The US picked up some of them cheaply, its decades of higher savings paying off. Argentina did not. It had been so dependent on foreign borrowing that a decline in international investment, and particularly a sell-off of assets by the British, was a threat rather than an opportunity. In 1914, half the fixed capital in the country – railways, factories, the telegraph, meat-packing plants – was owned by foreigners. The previously submerged question of exactly who was paying for Argentina's infrastructure suddenly surfaced. After five decades of narrowly focused foreign investment and exports Argentina was a glorified export zone, not a global financial power.

The stresses of the interwar years and particularly the Great Depression after 1929 revealed how America and Argentina had entered different camps. At the time the Depression appeared to be a crisis of the whole of capitalism rather than any single variant. American and Argentine cities were both encrusted with reminders of economic dislocation – the shanty towns known as Hoovervilles in the US, after the hapless Depression-era president Herbert Hoover, and as *villas miserias* in Argentina.

Many in the US and in Latin America drew the same conclusion: that a crisis transmitted so rapidly through international markets for goods and money showed the foolishness of relying on global entanglements. But the political systems of America and Argentina reacted in critically different ways. The Depression drove a wedge between them that would later cleave into a wide gulf between democracy and dictatorship.

Between 1880 and 1914, the US political system was reacting to change, absorbing new ideas and addressing the demands of the discontented, even if only in limited fashion. But Argentine politics remained dominated by a small, self-perpetuating elite. The American equivalent might have been a dynasty of former Confederate officers permanently camped in the White House and on Capitol Hill after their victory in the Civil War, with politics limited to a series of internal spats. When the philosophy was tested to destruction in Argentina, so were its champions. Although politics was often conducted with great drama, the political spectrum was stiflingly narrow.

A country can inoculate itself against political extremism by allowing a weak version of the virus to circulate freely. Nations thus strengthened and confident were always more likely to be able to cope with the extraordinary challenges thrown up by the aftermath of the stock market crash of 1929 that began in Wall Street and spread instantaneously to Europe. The very fact that the economic crisis sprang from the collapse of stock prices in New

York, one of the world's biggest financial centres, raised fundamental questions about the worth of liberal democracy as well as
free-market economics. But America could (and still can) absorb
new ideas like government intervention in the economy without
fearing that it meant the end of democracy itself. The American
response to the crash was intended to save market economics, not
to bury it.

How much threat there ever really was to private enterprise as
the defining feature of the US economy is debatable. But Franklin
Delano Roosevelt, the president elected amidst crisis and despair
in 1932, was taking few chances. Roosevelt, scion of an established
political dynasty and a distant cousin of Theodore, saw that reform
was needed. He met the Depression aggressively head-on with a
somewhat experimental set of policies distinctly at odds with the
hands-off doctrine of the Golden Age – government intervention
to shore up the banking system, a campaign of public investment
and a limited federal deficit to let government spending take up
some of the slack in the economy. As if to underline that an era
was over, the US also left the gold standard.

Given the tiny size of the national government in the economy
at the outset – federal public spending was just 3 per cent of
national income in 1929 – the New Deal, as the package of
measures was called, could not return the US rapidly to full
employment, not least because of a premature return to the orthodoxy of balanced budgets in 1937. It was not until the build-up to
war in 1939 revived demand for factory output that the economy
truly recovered. But the political impact of the federal government's efforts was undoubtedly felt. The system was capable of
absorbing new ideas. The system could renew itself. The system
did not crash.

Yet achieving even such limited gains was not straightforward.
To pass the New Deal, including creating Social Security, now
one of the most popular government programmes in America,
required overcoming the mistaken opposition of those, particularly
in Wall Street and business, who believed that any amendment to
the system meant ruin.

There is a remarkably simple rule about how political systems reacted to the Depression, reflecting what happens when an international financial system freezes up. Countries that owed money were now cut off from more lending, saw no virtue in continuing to depend on an international system that had let them down, and moved towards economic isolationism and political authoritarianism. Countries to whom money was owed sustained smaller economic damage and remained wedded to democracy and the international economy. Even within continents and between neighbouring countries the rule held. France, which still held significant assets abroad, remained a democracy even through repeated political crises in the 1930s; its indebted neighbour Germany, despite the initial success of the interwar Weimar Republic, rapidly succumbed to fascism.

Argentina was no exception. By contrast with America, it suffered a deep crisis that ran throughout its narrow and exclusive political class. The electoral franchise had been extended in 1912 and a new party come to power in Argentina in 1916, but in practice it made little difference. With a pathological dislike of anything that smacked of socialism, it appeared paralysed by the slump. Exports of beef and wheat, products in which it had an advantage, were particularly hard hit. A crisis in farming and a glut of produce everywhere were compounded by the fact that the consumption of beef, as a relatively luxurious food, was the first to be cut. By the end of the 1920s, meat exports to continental Europe had fallen by more than two thirds from their level in 1924. In 1932, the champion bull at a famous annual livestock show in Palermo, Buenos Aires, fetched the lowest price for twenty-five years.

Only now did the foolishness of betting on the indefinite willingness of foreign capital and foreign companies to produce and sell large quantities of a few exports become so evident. Without even perhaps realizing what it was doing, Argentina had staked its all on red, and not only did black keep coming up but the roulette wheel itself was being removed from the table.

Failure to use the system meant the system was replaced. The

Depression brought FDR and a more active federal govern-ment to the US. To Argentina it brought dictatorship. Even had Argentina's elite grasped the nature of the problem, it would most likely by the 1930s have been too late. Because it was still a big borrower, not a creditor, slamming controls on the banking system would merely have scared away what few foreign investors had not already taken their money and run. Having neglected to prepare or to respond, the whole establishment suffered a failure of credibility. It had predicated its legitimacy on the basis of a simple model, borrowing from its food shoppers, which had collapsed.

The traditional politicians had taken a republic and turned it back into a colony, but without even the benefits a true colony might have received. London reacted to the crisis in international trade in the 1930s by granting 'imperial preference' – allowing in imports from its remaining overseas possessions and keeping out those from the rest of the world. To maintain its meat exports to Britain, Argentina had to sign a treaty that made a host of con-cessions to British companies, including making it easier to take their profits out of Argentina.

When export demand plunged again as a result of the Second World War, the game was up for Argentina's experiment with liberal democracy. In 1940, one of the brighter government minis-ters of the time, Federico Pinedo, proposed a smaller-scale Argen-tine version of America's New Deal, including extending credit to manufacturers and cutting import tariffs on the raw materials and other basic inputs they needed. But it died in petty infighting among Argentina's uninspiring political elite.

Liberal democracy and liberal economics seemed to have failed, just as they had in the Weimar Republic. The result was similar in direction if not in extremity. The president was kicked out with the help of the army, and something close to political chaos replaced him, with the military having to suppress disgruntled workers protesting in the streets. Nationalism and self-sufficiency became attractive, while hapless democratic governments passing power ineffectually between each other did not. The new authoritarians wanted the country to take back its destiny into its own hands.

The man who came to embody the new doctrine, Juan Perón, was from the army, the natural home of authoritarians. One of the leaders of a military coup which replaced a civilian government in 1943, he became president in 1946. His direct style contrasted sharply with the patrician sophistication – or sophistry – of the civilian politicians. Perón's populist appeal was helped by his rise to prominence through the army, one of the few Argentine institutions that could reasonably claim to promote talent rather than privilege.

Perón projected an assertive, disciplined nationalism for the new Argentina. Though his power was confirmed in an election, faint overtones of fascism grew stronger once he was in office. He encouraged a cult of personality to grow around him, quite unlike the faceless elite that had run the country in the past. He also urged Nazi-style economic self-sufficiency and 'corporatism' – a strong government, organized labour (under strict limits set by the state) and industrial conglomerates jointly directing and managing growth.

These ideas came to the US, too, but few took them seriously. Like Argentina but unlike Europe, America, little unionized, never had much time for socialism or communism. Roosevelt managed to co-opt all but the most radical labour activists into the coalition that supported the New Deal. There was widespread discontent with the international economic system, but belief in US democracy held firm.

Had America gone the same way as Argentina, it is not hard to see where the equivalent of Peronism might have come from. Strains of thought in movements like the America First Committee, formed to argue against the US joining the Second World War, had a similar horror of what George Washington had referred to as 'foreign entanglements'.

Like Peronism, such campaigns attracted men who viewed themselves as embodiments of uncompromising action, not weasel words, and who frequently harboured unpleasant prejudices. The

America First Committee's best-known advocate was the national hero Charles Lindbergh, the first pilot to fly solo across the Atlantic, who partly blamed the Jews for trying to get the US into the war. There were isolationist demagogues like Father (Charles) Coughlin, a Catholic, 1930s version of a talk radio shock jock. Coughlin's weekly broadcasts attracted audiences of millions listening to his denunciations of both free-wheeling finance capitalism and communism in favour of a socially cohesive economy run by big companies and big labour unions. He, too, showed rising admiration for Hitler and Mussolini, and his broadcasts became increasingly anti-Semitic.

But though the America First Committee and its like managed to keep the US out of the Second World War for two years, until the attack on Pearl Harbor in 1941, it never became a serious political force. Its modern-day defender is Patrick Buchanan, a populist blowhard whose frequent excoriations of foreign entanglements rarely gain enough support to make a discernible impact.

America is a militaristic society, as democracies go, but its soldier-politicians (Dwight D. Eisenhower, Colin Powell) have gone into politics within the democratic system, not threatening to challenge it. The only senior soldier directly to challenge a president was Douglas MacArthur, the commander of UN troops in the Korean war of 1950–53, who spoke out against Harry S. Truman's decision to negotiate an end to war. MacArthur might well have had the authoritarian part of Peronism down pat: he had earned some notoriety for having used teargas to suppress a demonstration of army veterans in Washington in 1930 protesting against cuts in pension payments. But after Truman relieved him of his command in Korea, he soon saw his immense personal popularity dissipate under the pressure of public attention.

There is a great deal of ruin in a nation, as Adam Smith, one of the modern creators of economics, had it. Even during the two lost decades between the wars, Argentina was one of the ten richest economies in the world. It would not remain so for long.

Argentina after the Second World War knew only one big thing:

that relying on the outside world for money and markets had been a mistake. The instinctively defensive reaction to the troubles of the 1930s solidified into an ideological carapace. Having won independence from European colonialists once before, it was only natural to declare it again.

Peronism meant corporatism, not a free-market or a socialist economy. It argued that Argentina had been devastated by the anarchy of free markets in goods, people and money, which had brought the misery of the Depression. Now a strong and confident country would build its economy through the patriotic cooperation of labour, the government and the owners of industry.

The self-sufficiency of the new order, an idea that gained adherents across the world, was given a name: import substitution. Argentina believed that its travails had been caused by becoming an economic colony even after it had ceased to be a political one – exporting low-value commodities and importing higher-value manufactured goods. There was some truth in this, but the solution, to industrialize at the cost of cutting off the economy from the rest of the world, was not the right answer.

Argentina sealed off its manufacturing companies behind a high wall of tariff protection. It could argue that it was only following the pattern set by many other countries, including America, that had climbed clear of their agrarian origins. But not only had the US had a much bigger domestic market to generate economies of scale, but having raised infant industries to adulthood it eventually unleashed them to seek out markets around the world. Argentina wanted manufacturing not to build a base to conquer export markets but to keep out imports. And its companies were coddled and shielded not only from the outside world but also from domestic competition by hefty state intervention in the economy.

It helped, too, that much less drastic versions of the same philosophy were gaining ground even in market democracies. As the countries of western Europe rebuilt their shattered economies, many expanded the role of government by nationalizing big industries and promising their people generous welfare states. Some of the money to rebuild, naturally, came from America, completing its transition from being Europe's borrower to being its banker, though it was noticeable that the US government itself displayed rather less enthusiasm for occupying the commanding heights of its own economy through nationalization.

But in reality the similarities between democratic Europe and Argentina were superficial. While government took a bigger role in both, it led the economy in different directions. Argentina had a visceral fear of free markets, and the government was running the economy not to direct but to replace them. In Europe, government was there to correct the failures of the market, not to abolish it entirely. Capitalism in Argentina was caged: in Europe it was merely leashed. Europe and the US turned back towards each other, not in on themselves.

In 1944, a meeting at Bretton Woods, New Hampshire, created the eponymous system of fixed exchange rates and controls on capital. The freebooting globalization of the Golden Age was not to be repeated. The footloose money of speculators was to be subordinated to the production of real goods and services. To oversee the system, the conference created the International Monetary Fund – an institution which, as we will see, later achieved demonic status in the eyes of Argentina. The US and the Europeans also began the first of a series of global talks to reduce barriers to trade, starting to undo the effects of panicked protectionism during the Depression.

Argentina was heading blindly off in the other direction, defiantly rejecting the tenets of open trade. Perón referred to foreign capital as an 'imperialist agent'. There was little to stop him. These ideas were common across the developing world, particularly in African countries escaping the colonial yoke. American capitalism evidently did not prove a sufficiently compelling counter-example. In any case, as the Peronist movement developed its defiant nationalist ideology, anti-Americanism became a useful tool. America's leading role in the Cold War made it easy to portray as a bully.

You did not have to be one of the many psychoanalysts enduringly popular among elite Argentines to see this as a badly disguised form of envy. Argentines were used to seeing themselves as the

US's equals. With every dollar by which the gap in income between the two of them grew, this became a harder and harder thing to believe. Argentina found it easy to be self-righteously disdainful of Europe's wealth and stability, built on the historic exploitation of colonies like themselves. The presence of the US as a rich and successful New World country spoiled this excuse for economic stagnation. It had, after all, gained independence from Europe not long before Argentina.

Writing in 1961, Federico Pinedo, he of the abortive recovery plan of 1940, mourned that Argentina was not a founding member of the Organization for Economic Co-operation and Development, a club of rich countries. Indeed, it was one of the unfortunates that the rich nations (including of course the US) thought they needed to help. 'Among the countries deemed capable of giving aid we find not only little Denmark, a seller of meat and butter, but also others with a predominantly rural population and a make-up similar to ours, such as Australia, New Zealand and South Africa,' he wrote. Indeed, the OECD contained European countries whose people, a couple of generations earlier, had emigrated to Argentina in search of a better life. Pinedo concluded: 'This is a humiliating aberration.'

Meanwhile, Japan, the first of a stream of east Asian countries to industrialize, was starting to show what was possible with growth led by exports. Simon Kuznets, one of the first academics to study the economics of poor countries as a subject in itself, used to say there were four kinds of countries: developed, developing, Japan and Argentina.

Rather than face the reality of its own problems, the elastic Argentine sense of victimhood stretched to include successful economies in its own continent, like the US, as well as those across the Atlantic. Argentine politics became dominated by an unpleasant and destructive discourse, mixing self-pity and arrogance in equal parts. Each of Argentina's frequent failures had a prefabricated excuse; each of its occasional successes represented the indefatigable spirit of the Argentine nation overcoming adversity.

This attitude endures. One of the more bizarre evenings this author ever spent was at a dinner at the World Economic Forum in Davos, gathered to discuss the economic crisis following Argentina's debt default of 2001. Of the several dozen or so attendees at the dinner there appeared to be only a non-Argentine handful – including me, another journalist and a New York bond lawyer – who regarded Argentina's fate as primarily of its own making rather than the effects of a malign and capricious world.

It has been said of solipsistic nations which persistently make wrong choices – India, before its recent economic revolution, chief among them – that part of their problem is that they only ever compare themselves with themselves. Argentina was even worse. It compared itself with its deluded vision of itself, and found the contrast too painful to bear. There is a traditional reciprocal dislike between Argentina and its neighbour, Brazil, and the standard Brazilian joke is that the best deal in the world is to buy an Argentine for what he is worth and sell him for what he thinks he is worth.

Argentina's obsession with itself was shared by few. The US attitude was one of neglect and condescension. Once it had satisfied itself that Argentina was unlikely to ally itself with the Soviet Union, the US turned its attention to preventing other Latin American states going that way – generally with success, though at considerable cost to its reputation as an incubator of liberal democracy.

Just as in the First World War, the US emerged from the Second with both moral and financial credit from Europe. For thirty years after the Second World War it anchored one corner of the global monetary system, the dollar being the hard currency on which the Bretton Woods arrangements rested. The US economy, safely on the right course, was raised by the tide of trade, technology and growth that lifted all the western European countries together. Some referred to the three decades after 1945 as the second Golden Age. The world economy was less integrated than during the first one, but the benefits of growth were more widely and sustainably spread.

Meanwhile Argentina was pursuing industrialization within one country. Massive tariff walls were erected around its newly favoured industries. Tariffs averaged 84 per cent in the early 1960s, at a time when barriers between the advanced countries in Europe, and between Europe and Australia, the US and Canada, were being sharply reduced towards single figures. As well as taxing imports, it also taxed exports: Argentine goods were for Argentines. Having been one of the most open economies in the world in the late nineteenth century, Argentina increasingly turned in on itself. By contrast, the US progressively undid the effects of protectionism during the Depression and trade grew faster than national income.

Peronism was largely an urban movement. Even before industrialization Argentina had still acquired a large urban population, pushed by the lack of opportunities in the countryside as much as pulled by the opportunities of the towns. The economic recovery at the end of the 1930s and during the war did not eliminate the *villas miserias* from around the big cities. Originally a symbol of the Depression and the failure of international capitalism, they now became a permanent reminder to Perón of the constituency on whom his power depended.

But it was as much the impoverishment of the countryside as the success of the cities that produced the appearance of industrialized modernity. Argentina's farmers and landowners paid for industrialization. Their own incomes still depended on the vicissitudes of international prices of commodities, while the prices of their tractors, their cars and even their clothes were kept high by import taxes. Perón also imposed price controls on food, an even more blatant transfer from the countryside to the towns.

As far as Perón was concerned, this merely meant the lords of the pampas were being deservedly knocked from their privileged perches. For him, Argentina's oligarchic aristocrats were of a piece with the foreigners trying to do the country down. Perón's populism went by the name of *justicialismo*. In 1951, he declared: 'The defense of justicialismo is our fight. Outside, against imperialism and reaction; inside, against political and oligarchic treachery.' The traditional landowning classes were hammered by new laws fixing rents, which forced many to sell land to their tenants. Yet long after many had seen their estates broken up in the 1940s and 1950s they were still firmly fixed in the public mind as the epitome of reactionary gilded decadence, and Peronists continued to demonize them.

The payback for retreating from the world was facing retaliatory tariffs in Argentina's export markets. This angered the farmers, who remained competitive by world standards. Agricultural trade protection across the world stayed high, and remains so to this day, one of the sources of righteous self-pity that so animated my dining companions in Davos. But it did little to upset the urban masses, who wanted Argentine products kept for Argentines, not sent out of the country.

Shortly after coming to power, Perón raised the export price of linseed, one of Argentina's internationally competitive agricultural products, which was bought by US manufacturers to make paint. American importers complained. Perón was unrepentant. 'If they want linseed, let them bring their houses to Argentina where we'll have them painted,' he said. Instead, the US started to plant its own linseed, and Argentina had lost an important export market.

Peronism endured, and indeed endures: Argentina's current president calls herself a Peronist, and so did her predecessor, who happens to be her husband. One reason is that, in a limited way and under its own distorted terms, it succeeded. The state had become strong. The government owned and ran not just natural monopolies like water and electricity but anything that looked big and strategic – steel, chemicals, car factories. The economy did industrialize. Imports of consumer goods tailed off and were replaced, if at all, by homemade equivalents – 'import substitution' at work. By the 1970s, the share of manufacturing in GDP and in employment was around a third, close to that in the US or Europe.

In truth, the achievement was nothing like as impressive as it appeared. Argentina may have industrialized but it was still falling behind. During its burst of agricultural growth in the nineteenth century, the Argentine economy was catching up leading countries like the UK. During its industrialization it dropped back, growing at around 2 per cent per head per year, well below the world average. In 1950, Argentine income per head was twice that of Spain, its former colonizer. By 1975 the average Spaniard was richer than the average Argentine. Argentines were almost three times richer than Japanese in the 1950s; by the early 1980s the ratio had been reversed. Argentina's was a fragile and superficial progress that masked relative decline. Like the elegant Italianate architecture of central Buenos Aires, it looked like an impressive symbol of national achievement only if one ignored the far larger *villas miserias* encircling the city.

Argentina was not in fact following the American path of industrializing behind tariff barriers and going on to let its companies loose on world markets and expose them to more competition. The import substitution model was designed to distance Argentina from the rest of the world economy, not to prepare Argentine companies to compete in it.

The use of import tariffs to help the first stages of industrialization is known as 'infant industry' protection. In America, the protection was temporary, though it did persist for decades. In Argentina, the infants knew at the beginning that they would never have to leave the nursery, or at any rate that their mewling could become voluble enough to ensure that the door remain closed. American capitalism was quickly Argentinized, turned into a cronyish, corrupt game where access to protection and subsidies from the state were more important than competitiveness. Its cars cost twice as much as American cars, and frequently broke down. Its washing machines and radios were clunky, expensive and unreliable.

After a while, it became evident from country after country that the whole model of import substitution was flawed. Import substitution economies sputtered and stalled. Although consumer goods imports were blocked, raw materials and components for industrial production had to be admitted, and at prices elevated by taxation as they passed through customs. Since exports had been discouraged, and in any case were often not competitive on world markets without hefty government subsidies, this meant

Argentina again and again ran into balance of payments problems, its exporters failing to earn the dollars the economy needed to buy imports.

The country's political development followed its frog-march industrialization. Perón himself was forced out in 1955 (he would later return) but Peronism survived. The strains on government spending from the lavish promises of social welfare that Perón had made to the urban workers meant that the government was often in deficit. Frequently it printed money to escape the problem, and rising inflation eroded the value of the debt it owed its own people. And when the stability of the Bretton Woods system broke down in the early 1970s as even the US struggled to make its budget balance, Argentina's defining trait came to the fore. Argentines might not have known how to build, but with expertise stretching back to the 1890 Barings crisis and beyond, they most certainly knew how to borrow.

No countries except net exporters of oil did well in the 1970s. Even America had double-digit inflation as the terms of trade turned decisively against its economy and in the direction of Arabia. But at least the US, being a creditworthy country, could continue to borrow in dollars. (It still can today, one of the saving graces of America during financial crisis.) New York City nearly went bankrupt in 1975, but the federal government rescued it. The Watergate scandal shook, but did not destroy, the stability of the republic. Gerald Ford may have sounded more confident than he felt when he said, on taking over from Richard Nixon: 'This is a government of laws and not of men. Here, the people rule.' He was, though, largely right.

Argentina had gone much further towards losing trust. In fact, it was surprising and, perhaps, ultimately unhelpful, given that lenders gave Buenos Aires more and more rope with which to strangle itself, that so much trust remained. Despite its turbulent history, Argentina was regarded more favourably than many other developing countries. To a casual observer it looked like a European country. Its metropolitan sophisticates were urbane and educated. As used to be said of the Republic of Ireland before its recent economic boom, Argentina had the credit rating of the Netherlands with the economy of Jamaica.

The pretence that Argentina was still a first-world country should have disintegrated in the 1970s. Swelling oil prices and economic dislocation battered even seaworthy governments, and Argentina was thrown repeatedly onto the rocks. Time and again throughout the 1970s and 1980s, Argentina promised a fresh start and often a new currency, and each time failed.

In rich countries, the 1970s generally presaged a move to more free-market administrations and policies, as faith in the ability of governments to guide the economy disappeared. In the US, this eventually meant appointing the tough-minded Paul Volcker as chairman of the Federal Reserve, the central bank. Volcker successfully squeezed inflation out of the economy even at the cost of rising unemployment. The advanced countries experienced strikes and demonstrations and gasoline shortages, but they survived and stabilized.

Argentina slid instead towards military dictatorship. Political stresses between the civilian and military rulers – and some more traditional conservatives who thought that Peronism looked too much like socialism for comfort – reached the stage where an army junta took over in an out-and-out coup in 1976, just as the White House was changing hands peacefully and constitutionally again. But after the disastrous misadventure of seizing the symbolic but economically worthless Falkland Islands from the British and humiliatingly being forced into retreat, the junta too collapsed. As the Buenos Aires saying went: first the generals showed they could not manage an economy; then they showed they could not run a country; finally they showed they could not even win a war.

Their successors were little better. A 'lost decade' of stagnation and strife followed. Economies contracted and hyperinflation wiped out the value of households' lifetime savings in a few months – not just in Argentina but in many Latin American nations that had borrowed like the US without the earnings to support their borrowing. The promise of a fresh start with a new currency, the austral, in Argentina in 1985 lasted only a few months before inflation was once again running at thousands of per cent a year. Osvaldo Soriano, an Argentine author, wrote an article in 1989 noting that during the time it took him to type the piece, the price of the cigarette he was smoking went from 11 to 14 australes.

Among the investors who subsequently spent years mired in negotiations with bankrupt governments south of the Rio Grande were the big American commercial banks like Citigroup, who had placed a large and losing bet on the southern half of their continent acting like the northern half. The banks, wanting never again to expose themselves to that much risk of failure, broke up their damaged loans into pieces and sold them to investment funds and individual investors.

Sadly, when the time came, these investors proved as liable to episodes of self-delusion and absurd optimism as the banks had been. They were soon given a good excuse. The demise of the Soviet Union reduced the ability of murderous and thieving right-wing dictatorships to keep power by proclaiming themselves a fortification against communism. The lost decade gave way to a golden one.

In the 1990s, many fragmented markets around the world once more dissolved into one. Like the Golden Age of the late nineteenth century, the lurch forward of globalization was helped by a shove from new technology, this time in information and tele-communications rather than ships and railways. As in the Golden Age, transport times fell: the internet compressed to zero the time taken to transmit anything that could be digitized. As in the Golden Age, the US and Argentina were both leaders of the charge. And as in the Golden Age, the US weathered the storms of volatility and change while Argentina, having promised a heroic rise, once again succumbed to a fatal flaw.

This time the hubris was embodied in the government of Carlos Menem. In manner and populist appeal he was not altogether unlike an Argentine version of the US president for most of the 1990s, Bill Clinton. Both were governors of impoverished backwater states whose charm and charisma propelled them into the presidency. Menem chose a cabinet of talented technocrats, many of them educated at the same American universities as their counterparts in the US administration and the International Monetary Fund. Although from a Peronist background, Menem edged away from economic isolationism, deciding there was one useful thing Argentina could import from America: credibility. He linked the Argentine peso irrevocably, or so the intention was, to the US dollar. This meant adopting US interest rates and fixing the amount of pesos circulating in the country to the amount of dollars held in the government's foreign exchange reserves. Argentina could only borrow like America when it acted more like it.

This was a high-risk course. Argentina had got used to printing as much domestic currency as it liked. It now had to earn dollars with an economy that had for decades forgotten how to export. It also required public spending to be controlled: a government persistently spending more than it earned would increase the need for dollars to fund it. It required Argentina to do two things at which it had been bad. It required, in fact, Argentina to stop acting like Argentina.

For a while, it seemed to work. Inflation dropped and the economy stabilized. A widescale privatization programme followed. The IMF, desperate to find a model globalizer to parade to the rest of the developing world, unwisely began touting Argentina as an exemplar. Menem was invited to address the 1998 IMF annual meeting in Washington, the only head of government thus honoured apart from Bill Clinton, the host. But once again Argentina proved a delinquent, better at borrowing than earning. It was cheap to borrow in hard currencies like the dollar for much of the 1990s, as money poured into emerging market countries. After 1998, though, when a succession of Asian countries and Russia were hit by a financial crisis, it became harder for any emerging market country to roll over its debt. The drying up of capital markets after 1998 did not in any sense compare with the credit drought of the First World War, but the melancholy withdrawing roar of the tide was enough to leave some overloaded boats stranded.

Investors started pulling dollars out of the country. Argentina had borrowed too much when it was easy for it to survive when it became hard. As dollars flowed out so the supply of pesos had to fall too. In countries that controlled their own currencies, like the US, the severity of the worldwide economic slowdown in 2001 could be minimized by rapid cuts in interest rates, the price of money. The US Federal Reserve slashed the cost of borrowing in 2001, ensuring that the American economy would go through only a brief and shallow recession despite huge falls in the inflated share prices of technology companies.

In Argentina, whose currency was tied to another, a shortage of dollars in its reserves drove up interest rates to punishingly high levels as demand for the limited supply of hard currency rocketed. Argentina was caught in a death spiral. Higher interest rates crushed businesses and bankrupted families. In desperation, Buenos Aires doubled up its bets, borrowing billions of dollars from the IMF in the hope that the economy would pull out of its dive. It failed to convince the investors on whom Argentina depended, and in December 2001 the IMF pulled the plug. Argentina was forced into the largest government bankruptcy in history.

Income per head dropped by nearly a quarter in three years. The central government had no money to bail out the provinces, as Washington had rescued New York City in 1975. Instead some promptly started printing their own currency, a faint echo of the monetary chaos of pre-independence America. Five presidents came and went within two weeks. The country became a laughing stock. Rudi Dornbusch, a respected, if outspoken, economist at the Massachusetts Institute of Technology, in all seriousness suggested that international committees of experts take over and run the finances of Argentina. Bank accounts were frozen and unfrozen, some accounts forcibly changed from dollars into devalued pesos. The rich, as usual, did well, holding assets in dollars. The bars and restaurants of central Buenos Aires could have been in Manhattan: they were as packed as ever.

Even the machinations of clever ministers had not enabled Argentina to escape its familiar problems: inability to control the finances of the provinces, a small and stunted export sector, an economy too dependent on volatile agricultural earnings; and, perhaps above all, a sense of entitlement hugely out of line with its historic achievements.

The Argentines themselves were not the only ones to believe that their country was, fundamentally, a solid, stable European nation incongruously tacked on to the edge of a dysfunctional subcontinent. The suckers of the 1990s included, with a twist of vicious historical irony, thousands of not particularly well-off Italian investors, whose view of the country to which their forebears had emigrated a century earlier was sadly misplaced. The investors who filed case after case against the government of Argentina in the law courts of New York were furious and bewildered that a country that boasted so strongly of its credentials as a first-world nation should renege so spectacularly on its debts.

At dozens of different points of departure over the previous two centuries it could have gone the other way round. It could have ended up as British investors suing the US in the courts of Buenos Aires as America after Washington had frantically borrowed in sterling, the euro, the peso – anything to keep from another bankruptcy.

In fact, it still could. During the second Golden Age of globalization, the US too was not immune from the deception that everything was fine as long as it could keep borrowing. Throughout the 1990s and 2000s the American economy as a whole ran an ever-larger trade deficit, financed by borrowing from abroad. The vendor finance arrangement of the First World War was reversed: the rest of the world, particularly Asia, was now lending the US the money to buy imports, though in this case iPods and LCD TVs rather than machine-guns and military uniforms. This was not entirely the US's own doing. It was driven by the rest of the world, particularly Asian governments, shovelling money at the US by intervening to sell their own currencies and buy dollars. But the administration of George W. Bush compounded the problem by perpetually pointing at the current account deficit as a source of strength, not of weakness. It was evidence, it said, of the willingness of the rest of the world to lend to America, not of the US's own reluctance to save.

What sparked the financial crisis in the US was the way that borrowing was being financed domestically. Decades of deregulation had produced ways of borrowing and new financial assets so complex that not even the banks that produced and sold them really understood what they were doing. Similar overconfidence to that which has carried Buenos Aires into disaster after disaster took hold. Critics were dismissed as doom-mongers. The short-term interests of banks and other financial institutions were allowed to prevail over the rest of the economy. A property bubble was allowed to inflate absurdly. Mortgages were extended to people with bad credit histories – the Argentinas of the US housing market. Those loans begat yet more borrowing, as the mortgages were turned into new financial assets and sold on to investors who allowed themselves to believe they were far safer than they were. Hubris met nemesis, and the bubble burst.

The crisis has presented the US with the biggest threat to its financial systems and ecomomy since the Great Depression, a challenge that will take years to meet. If it fails to recognize the flaws and correct them, as it slowly and painfully learned to do on that earlier occasion, the trajectory of its future wealth and power will be lowered. There is a great deal of ruin in a nation, particularly one as resilient and flexible as America. But its rise was not preordained, and neither is its continued pre-eminence.

Argentina, meanwhile, remained true to form in its own response to the crisis. Having initially announced with familiar hubris that the country would be unaffected, its government decided that a good way to deal with the loss of investor confidence would to appropriate the country's private pensions. Thus came another novel twist in the century-long story of the Argentine government seizing its people's savings whenever it got in trouble.

All in all, it would be wise to keep betting on the US eventually finding the right way out of the financial crisis and Argentina continuing to harm itself. Out of the two great hopes of the western hemisphere in the late nineteenth century, one succeeded and the other stalled in the twentieth. It was history and choice, not fate, which determined which became which. It is history and choice which will determine which is which in a century's time.

2. Cities

Why didn't Washington DC get the vote?

Countries pushing off from the same starting blocks can go in very different directions. For another study in similarities and differences, take two cities that look a lot like each other. Each is a proud capital of a republic with a mission to spread its civilization abroad, dominated by gleaming white marble buildings with columns, domes and friezes, home to a self-regarding bunch of pompous 'senators' and the very centre of a mighty sphere of imperial influence backed by crushing military power. Yet one, by far the biggest settlement the world has ever seen, is full of fractious, impatient inhabitants continually bought off with handouts by nervous city bosses. The other is a small, quiet town, the only one in the country whose citizens are denied a voting representative in the national legislature.

The first is ancient Rome: the second, modern Washington DC. The architecture of the second is even modelled on the first. Yet because Washington DC is the capital of a stable democracy rather than a volatile imperial oligarchy it has turned out entirely different from its prototype. Like countries, cities are shaped not just by impersonal economic forces and geography, though these have a big influence, but by choices made by governments and their people.

The earth has become a predominantly urban planet. Each day about 180,000 people around the world leave the countryside to move to a city. For the first time in history, as of some unknown date in 2007 or 2008, a majority of the world's population live in towns and cities. And *Homo sapiens sapiens* is becoming an urban species at an astonishing and accelerating speed. Cities have absorbed nearly two thirds of global population growth since 1950. London's population took 130 years to grow from one to 8 million. Bangkok in Thailand took 45 years, Dhaka in Bangladesh 37 and Seoul in

South Korea just 25. London in 1910 was seven times bigger than in 1800, but Dhaka now is forty times bigger than it was in 1950.

Barring a cataclysmic and unprecedented change in the flow of history, cities are the future. But not all towns and cities, and not all urbanizations, have looked the same. Countries have urbanized well and badly, some for mainly the right reasons and some for largely the wrong reasons. Cities have steadily become bigger, and taken a larger share of human habitation. But many have grown too big while others were kept too small, sometimes both in the same country. The trend towards bigger settlements came from the endless pressing of time and technology. But not only do technologies change – what cities look like and how they work depend on the choices taken by them and the countries in which they lodge.

Rome was the centre of what was then the most powerful civilization in history. But, as a city, it revealed all too clearly the flaws in the realm that it ran. The Roman empire was essentially a system of military conquest which supported itself by extorting tax from the vanquished. It turned into a vast armed rent-collecting machine vulnerable to overstretch, greed, decadence and collapse.

During 130–50 BCE, as the Roman republic moved towards becoming an empire, it extended into Gaul and further into eastern Asia, and even did a trial run of invading Britain. Rome was becoming bigger and richer through ruthless organization rather than superior economic or trade technology. It was not its role as a trading centre that was chiefly responsible for the expansion of the imperial city. All conquered land became the property of the city of Rome: all roads led there. Essentially, a single city could extract rent from half the civilized world.

And that is precisely what Rome became – a parasitic city of rentiers, bureaucrats and hangers-on as much as a centre of commerce and industry. Between 130 and 50 BCE Rome's population expanded at a truly astonishing rate, from 375,000 to around a million. It became twice as large as any city before in human history. No city would again reach one million inhabitants until London during the Industrial Revolution, eighteen centuries later.

Any imperial capital was bound to grow, but not at the speed and to the extent that Rome did. Its growth owed much to political expedience. At this stage of history, the most credible threats to the authority of Roman rule came from close to the city. It was less vulnerable around the far-flung fringes of its possessions than it was in the middle. Near home its authority was repeatedly challenged by Italian rebels, who forced it to extend Roman citizenship to all Italians.

A tradition of giving grain direct to the inhabitants of Rome was thus extended to a large number of nominally Roman citizens. Given that warfare made the Italian hinterland increasingly unsafe, and that the city government in Rome was not about to set up an elaborate series of soup kitchens throughout Italy, the grain was distributed only to those who came to Rome to receive it.

Any Reaganite economist from a Washington think-tank would have predicted precisely the result: hordes of idle Romans hanging around the city demanding welfare. By 46 BCE some 320,000 people, nearly a third of Rome's population, were receiving grain. Unemployment and underemployment were rife, and the city became horrendously overcrowded. Thousands of citizens loafing round with nothing to do also became restless and peevish. To keep them from causing trouble, the Roman authorities built vastly expensive stadia and staged gladiator and animal fights. At their height they were running more than one set of games a week: imagine a city today volunteering to stage a continuous and indefinite Olympics.

From this comes the common expression for the bribes paid to placate a fretful populace, 'bread and circuses'. The largesse was paid for by the conquered provinces, which had no such ability to threaten the rulers, and from whom tax was extorted by the occupying Roman armies. (The provinces also provided most of the gladiators and the animals.) The hinterland was taxed to subsidize the city; the periphery was exploited to pay for the centre. There was no mileage in anyone hanging around Londinium expecting free bread for life and a season ticket for lion-versus-rhino fights on Saturdays.

When the political imperatives diminished and the policies changed, so did the imbalances. Julius Caesar, who came to power in 49 BCE, managed to restore order in the Italian hinterland and apply means-testing to grain handouts. The growth of the city slowed in response. But the weaknesses of letting an avaricious city determine the running of an empire would eventually help to doom it.

Interestingly, some of the successors to Rome were also in Italy: the city-states of the medieval period like Venice and Florence. But they exhibited the opposite characteristics. They lived mainly by their wits and their skills rather than by conquest. Along with similar cities in early modern northern Europe – Antwerp, Amsterdam – the likes of Venice were settlements that acted as the trading entrepôts for an entire region.

Venice, which in 1330 was the third-largest city in Europe, thrived on providing finance and commercial services to the peoples around the Mediterranean. Venice and other Italian city-states featured and sometimes pioneered many of the instruments of modern financial capitalism: bills of exchange to finance contracts, trade credit to insure sellers against non-payment, forward-selling markets to fix prices months ahead of delivery, private individuals lending to public authorities. Florence became the banker for much of Europe, its coin – the gold florin – becoming the standard currency for international trade. Such cities relied on their ability to conduct business for any economy within trading or communicating reach. They traded goods, services and money on behalf of others. To earn a living this way they had to sell their own ability to sell.

But what is the point of cities, in the end? For centuries the trend all over the world towards concentrating people in towns has been driven by an unrelenting economic logic that followed the basic human hierarchy of wants. First came food, shelter and basic clothing, which could be produced in the countryside – first hunted and gathered and then farmed. Then, as agriculture became efficient enough to move beyond hand-to-mouth subsistence cultivation, came better clothing and material possessions made by non-farmers, or farmers with spare time on their hands.

They did not absolutely have to live in bigger settlements, at least not at basic, personal-scale levels of production like hand-weaving and wood-carving. The origin of the expression 'cottage industry', after all, was that rural dwellers could move beyond farming without moving house. But quite often they did. (Humans are social beings: they like living next to each other.) And even without specialist craftspeople moving to the city, an economy where food and goods are traded meant having centres of trade, so towns emerged and enlarged through markets, commerce and transport if not by manufacture. The size of urban populations, certainly in medieval Europe in the first half of the second millennium, was a good indicator of general prosperity.

Once in train, this process rarely went into permanent reverse, and in fact accelerated once economies moved into industrial production. Crudely put, the profits needed to drive industrialization came from more productive agriculture. More productive marketized agriculture almost always meant bigger, more efficient farms and fewer farmers on the land. As the industrial revolution took hold, factories required workforces both large and concentrated, and trade between them in turn increased demand for transport hubs. Thus were rural economies urbanized. People were both pushed from the countryside by the increasing mechanization of agriculture and pulled towards the city by the growth in better jobs with a future.

Being urban, or urbane, is inescapably bound up with the modern, in politics, philosophy, language and culture as much as in economics. As the philosopher René Descartes said of Amsterdam in 1631, cities are an 'inventory of the possible'. In the old German proverb, 'Stadtluft macht frei' – the city air makes you free. Though the goods they were trading may have been made by enslaved colonies or bonded serfs, the essence of the commercial self-regulating city was freedom within – freedom of belief, of travel, of action. Liberties attained in the city often presaged liberties that would one day come for all. It was in Renaissance

Florence that the dangerous ideas of 'humanism' began to circulate – that people could seek truth and morality within themselves, not merely have them handed down by a supreme being or his appointed representatives on earth. When the count of the northern province of Flanders tried to reclaim a runaway serf he found in the market in Bruges, one of the Low Country cities that flourished alongside Amsterdam, the middle-class merchants who ran the municipality drove him out of town.

It is not all quite so positive. Both good and bad sides of modernity are inescapably bound up with urbanization. Cities are tougher, faster and richer than the countryside, but also often dirtier, more violent and more brutal. The economic powerhouse of modern Italy is neither Rome nor Venice but the northern Italian city of Milan, which became first an industrial and then a business capital. And in a painting of Milan from 1910, *The City Rises*, by Umberto Boccioni of the Italian Futurist school of art, the shock of becoming urban is elevated into the violent turmoil of creation itself.

The technique of the painting mirrors its theme: it is the pivot point of Boccioni's transition from the softer, pointilliste landscape aesthetics of Impressionism to a harder-edged, Cubist-influenced style of dynamism and drama. In an industrial Milan of scaffolded buildings and smoking factory chimneys, manpower and horse-power – rendered literally in a chaotic swirl of straining draught horses and their struggling handlers – drag the city towards its future.

As ever, the balance of good and bad can be tilted by peoples and governments. History provides instances of cities succeeding and failing; of the urban goose being killed for its golden eggs and of it being force-fed so violently that it ceases to lay.

It was the first of these that eventually weakened Venice. Unlike Rome, Venice avoided getting itself too clogged up with a hinter-land of scroungers. But it too succumbed to imperial avarice – in this case, coming from without rather than within. The republic declined as it was targeted by a variety of assailants, principally the Spanish and French and the Ottoman empire.

Similar fates befell the prosperous southern European cities that grew between the fall of Rome and the rise of Venice. These were trading centres that emerged under the Saracens and the Moors – Islamic Arabs from north Africa and the Middle East. In the eleventh century, the biggest city in Europe was Córdoba, in what is now southern Spain, with a population estimated by some at 450,000. The second biggest was Palermo in Sicily, estimated at 350,000. London at the time was a tiny 25,000 people and Paris 20,000.

The Moors and Saracens ran open and largely peaceful trading empires. But in the first few centuries of the second millennium, the Arabs were pushed back into north Africa and the Middle East and the powerful, centralized European monarchies that took over were interested mainly in what they could squeeze out of the cities, not how they could nurture them.

At this stage of history it was much easier to tax urban commerce, which was physically concentrated and generally ran on a cash economy, than rural trade, which was dispersed and frequently involved barter. But cities were central to economic growth, providing the trading centres that allowed specialization and development to occur. So areas passing from nurturing to acquisitive rule tended to go backwards.

The d'Hauteville brothers from the Norman kingdom, for example, invaded and established a principality in southern Italy in the eleventh century. After a decade-long battle for Sicily, they took Palermo from the Saracens in 1071. The d'Hautevilles ran what by eleventh-century standards was a tightly centralized kingdom that wrung tax revenue out of their possessions to fund further military adventure. By 1200, the population of Palermo had shrunk by nearly two thirds.

Similarly, Córdoba, a great trading centre of the Moors, reached a population in the eleventh century that, according to some estimates, no other European city would match until the seventeenth. Weakening itself by breaking into a series of internal struggles, the Moorish civilization was subject to Christian invasion and 'reconquest' from the north, whereupon its cities shrank. The job was completed when the Habsburg empire took over southern Spain and taxed its cities to fund wars against the French and others. Córdoba shrank to a seventh of its former size.

Such urban reversal, certainly in absolute numbers, is unusual. More typically, government and public reaction helps to shape how quickly and in which fashion cities get larger and populations as a whole urbanize. And even those countries adopting policies that discourage rural flight are generally trying to smooth the transition, not to stand in the way of history.

Conveniently enough for the comparative historian, the British Isles, among the pioneers of modern urbanization, have displayed three markedly different models of managing the move: the careful, the reckless and the brutal.

In England, the change was gradual and relatively painless. Like much of western Europe, England had started generating significant surpluses in agriculture by the eleventh or twelfth century and the process of consolidating small-scale agriculture into larger and more-efficient farms could begin. But the 'enclosure' by landowners of open ground or of strip farms, where individual peasants tilled sections of collectively held land, took several centuries. Responding to popular protests and occasionally outright rebellion, and after warnings from the Church, the monarchs of the Tudor family in the fifteenth and sixteenth centuries slowed the process down with a series of 'enclosure acts' to placate protesting villagers. Later, country-dwellers often voluntarily moved to towns when industrialization created better jobs and better prospects in textile mills and the like.

In Scotland, however, both the Crown and the landowners paid less heed to their small farmers. In 1745, the king's armies crushed the 'Jacobite' rebellion that tried to install a Scottish Catholic, Charles Edward Stuart (variously known as Bonnie Prince Charlie and the Young Pretender), on the English throne. The Crown subsequently viciously suppressed any sign of dissent from Scotland, leading landowners to care relatively more about London and themselves and less about their tenants. When the gains in profitability from turning over scattered small plots to large sheep and cattle farms became apparent, the change was abrupt. The result was the Lowland and Highland Clearances, the forced removal of tenant farmers to make way for bigger and more-productive farms which began in the eighteenth century with no powerful monarchs standing in the way. It inundated Scotland's big cities, Glasgow and Edinburgh, with indigent refugees.

And in Ireland, there was an even greater indifference on the part of the government and their local satraps. Many of the landlords were absentee English Protestants who were physically, religiously and socially distant from their Catholic tenants. The change, accordingly, took place in a way that in practice if not intent resembled genocide. Famines followed a disastrous potato harvest and mass land evictions in the middle of the nineteenth century. Two million of the Irish peasants who survived, out of a pre-famine population of about 9 million, rapidly emigrated, many further afield to the cities of Liverpool, Boston and New York.

Evidently urbanization works better, and the creation of cities is more peaceful and constructive, if there is a high ratio of urban pull to rural push. These lessons in how to urbanize are currently being tested not over decades and centuries but over years and, sometimes, months. The growth that took a century in cities like London is taking a quarter of that in the fast-rising cities of Asia, and the time continues to shrink.

Mistakes are becoming rapidly, almost immediately, obvious. The timescale of urbanization is being telescoped by the pre-existence of production technology. The cities of China do not have to wait, as did London, for the invention of the steam engine and better ways of smelting iron. Two centuries of industrial and post-industrial technology, not to mention billions of dollars of foreign investors' money, are waiting for any country that can pull away from subsistence farming and start to grow.

There are evident modern-day equivalents of the divergent experiences of England, Scotland and Ireland. Shanghai is doing noticeably better than Mumbai or Lagos. The rural Chinese migrants desperate to move to the cities, knowing that even a job in a sweatshop beats life on the farm, are slowed down and regulated.

Internal migration controls limit rural depopulation. And new urbanites are somewhat anticipated in the expansion of cities and the planning of new centres to which they can be diverted. But in India, an uncontrolled flood of refugees fleeing drought and crop failure in the villages of Maharashtra and Gujarat turn up in badly run cities like Mumbai. Half of Mumbai's population lives in shanty towns or slums, with little access to water or electricity, no title to their land and no security over their homes.

Even worse than allowing a great surge of rural refugees to turn up in a city unplanned is giving them even more incentives to do so. Yet over the last century, in many of the world's poor countries, that is precisely the pattern that has created some of the worst urban imbalances on the planet. It comes not so much from entirely ignoring the wishes of the people as from listening only to those who shout the loudest or are the most threatening.

Argentina's industrializing fetish was not an anomaly. Throughout the twentieth century, developing countries kicking off the colonial harness wanted immediately to do what the imperial trade system had often deliberately prevented them from doing – build up their own industry rather than importing manufactures from the colonizing Europeans. As with Argentina, doing so often meant trying to tilt the playing field towards manufacturers. They were subsidized directly through tax advantages and handouts, and imported goods were made more expensive by imposing import tariffs on them.

But the main effect of policies that skew prices towards industry is not just – or not mainly – to redress imbalances in competitiveness between newly born home-grown manufacturers and the established beasts prowling the international economy. It also changes the prices between city and countryside. Industry historically needed agriculture to get it going by providing the profit surplus to fund investment. But once it was up and running it frequently found its interests at odds with those of farmers. A defining moment of British industrial history came when the Corn Laws, which had protected landowners and raised the price of food, were repealed. As we will see later, this helped not just working-class consumers, for whom food was a huge part of the weekly household budget but manufacturers, who could thus hold down wages without affecting the real incomes of their employees.

In many cases, developing countries went one further, not just removing the floor beneath agricultural incomes but actively trying to put a ceiling on them. Food price controls became a very frequently used weapon in the battle to encourage economies to shift from farm to factory. The problem with artificial induce- ments, as in Argentina's sorry history, is that it often creates the appearance without the reality. Shifting relative prices created push, sure enough, but it turned out to be less good at creating sustained pull.

An hour's flight north from Lusaka, the capital of the impover- ished southern African nation of Zambia, is the country's 'copper- belt', where the world's second-largest deposit of the metal is mined. As we will see later in discussing the distinctly mixed blessing of being endowed with oil or other minerals, the presence of deposits of commodities like copper always posed a risk to the balance of the economy.

Kenneth Kaunda, Zambia's first president after independence from Britain in 1964, made things worse. He subscribed to the standard African view that Zambia needed to build an industrial base, and that taxes and import tariffs should be used to encourage it. In Zambia's case, as in the cases of so many other African countries, this meant that the natural risks from possessing natural resources were compounded by a bad policy decision. In effect, the countryside was taxed to pay for the towns. Food prices were strictly controlled and subsidies were handed out to industry. Because the copper miners and their industry were politically powerful, they too got favoured treatment. The copper mines, having been nationalized from the private company Anglo- American, were given hefty subsidies and their miners well paid.

Give people a big incentive and they will generally react to it. As food prices were held down, hurting farmers selling their surplus produce, a mass decampment ensued from the Zambian country- side to the towns. Shanty towns (or, as the latest iteration of international development jargon has it, 'peri-urban settlements') are a familiar feature of African cities, where this policy error has been repeated many times. But with the exception of South Africa, where the contrast between the hard pavements of central Johannesburg and the vast sprawl of Soweto reflects a particular history of racial separation, there are few towns that beat the dramatic gap between formal and informal urbanity in the Zambian copper-belt.

Ndola, the biggest settlement on the copper-belt, is today a small neat colonial-era company town of perhaps a dozen blocks square, low bungalows set back in tidy if faded lawns. Around the centre sprawl shanty towns of mud, thatch and occasionally brick comprising a million and a half desperately poor Zambians. The slum-dwellers spend their lives trying to make a living off the miners, mainly by hawking to them food, cheap soap, clothes and trashy plastic toys – and, in the case of a distressing number of teenage girls, selling them sex. Drive a couple of hours into the countryside – during which time the roads rapidly give out into deep gullies of dust and mud – and it is largely empty.

It was not as if the country, or Kaunda himself, was unaware of how his policies were distorting the economy. Kaunda was by no means a visionary statesman, but he was a long way from the worst of the post-independence African leaders. Nor was he unaware of the dangers of breakneck urbanization. He mentioned the issue time and again in the early 1970s as the high metals prices and the industrialization campaign were bringing thousands every month out of the countryside, and launched a 'Go Back To The Land' campaign to control the flood. But rhetorical exhortation was not enough to undo the effect of hard economic incentives. And when it came to actually changing policy, the ideology and political exigency of urban industrial development always won out.

It has become a familiar pattern in Africa: mass urbanization without mass industrialization. By and large, Africa does not do cities well. The farmers left the countryside, but without the increased agricultural productivity that was a feature of European and North American rural depopulation. So there were no increased surpluses to invest in industrialization, and nor did extensive borrowing from abroad create sustainable development. There were, therefore, not enough jobs in factories for them to go to. Those industries that did exist generally did not survive the rapid removal, in the 1980s and 1990s, of the tariff walls that had earlier protected them from more-efficient foreign competition. Moreover, controls on food prices too often simply meant not enough food.

When the bankruptcy of African economies drove them into the arms of the International Monetary Fund and the World Bank, the Washington-based institutions that lend to poor countries, the twin sisters attempted to reverse the pro-urban bias. A common sign of an IMF lending programme being adopted in a developing country was an ensuing urban riot, as city-dwellers objected angrily to the removal of their privileges and the consequent rise in food prices.

The process of artificial urbanization is hard to reverse. Even attempting to do so in countries in Africa often required the intervention of an outside body with an unusual amount of influence such as the IMF. (In any case, in practice the process had often gone so far by then that attempts to level the playing field between city and country had little effect.) Even when it is obvious to any reasonably well-informed observer with an eye in his or her head that cities have been privileged way beyond the economic justification for them, they have by then often created a self-reinforcing political imperative. In the kind of countries where errors like this are often made, where governments are unstable, nervous and subject to direct action, it is often easy for a city – and, critically, the capital city – to punch well above its political weight.

There is a particular risk in ignoring the mood of the capital that a trio of monarchs – Charles I of England, Louis XVI of France and Tsar Nicholas II of Russia – learned to their cost and paid for with their heads. When it comes to exerting political power, those within rioting distance of the royal palace have a better means of making their grievances known than do equally disgruntled peasantry muttering into their gruel as they go about their miserable rural lives hundreds of miles from the capital.

In a strong democracy like modern-day France – and, to a lesser extent, in a strong autocracy like China – it makes little difference where any malcontents live. Everyone has the same vote, or the same impotence in the face of the overweening state. By contrast, in regimes liable to violent overthrow or susceptible to direct political pressure, it can make a great deal of difference. In countries with a history of stable democracy, an average of 23 per cent of the urban population lives in the central city; in unstable dictatorships with a history of coups and revolutions, it is 37 per cent. And once cities manage to exact disproportionate tribute from the rest of the country, the trend can become self-reinforcing. The incentive for rural flight towards the city increases, and so does the political imperative to keep the urbanites happy.

It was through anticipating these problems that the founding fathers of the United States made Washington DC what it is. When the US was created, the states were suspicious of each other and wary of handing over power to a federal government, and feared that placing the capital city within one of their number would give that state undue influence. So Washington was deliberately created to be a small and deracinated capital in a 'federal district', not a state. This became a familiar tactic in the modern world, as the dullness and remoteness of Canberra, Wellington and Ottawa testify.

Political inertia, and entrenched reluctance to changing the US constitution without an extremely good reason, has kept it that way ever since. In modern Washington, there is plenty of blatantly open political favouritism going on, particularly the ludicrous federal spending commitments that go under the pleasing local name of 'pork'. But the pork is not distributed to Washingtonians. The citizens of the District of Columbia have no senators, and only a non-voting member of the House of Representatives. Remarkably, the Republican Party sometimes does not bother even standing a candidate for mayor of Washington, on the grounds it is such a solidly Democratic city that they would be wasting their time and money, and it is so small it hardly matters who runs it. (Most local Republicans in any case live in suburbs in the surrounding states, Maryland and Virginia.)

The American War of Independence began on the principle of 'no taxation without representation'. Pointedly, many Washington DC car licence plates now bear the protesting slogan 'Taxation Without Representation', since the US continues to ignore the precept in its own capital city. Like ancient Rome, the town has plenty of hangers-on, in the form of the political consultants and lobbyists who find it expedient to be near the political action. But Congress pays them attention and buys them lunch because of their ability to influence campaign contributions and votes back in Texas or Iowa, not because they will one day besiege Capitol Hill or burn down the White House until their own taxes are cut in half.

None of the three unfortunate European monarchs managed to make his capital city anywhere near as quiescent. While none of the cities became quite as bloated as imperial Rome, the politics of the capital played a disproportionately large role in the governance of the country.

London's influence was well established by 1603 when James I, father of Charles I and first in the line of Stuart monarchs who succeeded the Tudors, came to the throne. It had more balance between politics and commerce than did Rome, the influence of each reinforcing the need for the other also to be present. The twin roles were neatly encapsulated in the city's geography. London was in fact two cities, the political centre of Westminster to the west and the commercial, consumer and entertainment nucleus of the City of London to the east. (The lawyers, typically, inserted themselves between the two and have been there ever since. They were temporarily joined in the twentieth century by journalists, another, less privileged, class of hangers-on.) Westminster and the City were umbilically connected by the Strand, which today has been subsumed into densely urbanized central London but which was then a thoroughfare more than a high street, with open fields close by its northern side.

In 1606, the London bookshops carried a newly translated English edition of the *Treatise Concerning the Causes of the Magnificence and Greatness of Cities* by the Florentine diplomat Giovanni Botero. In it, he explained that the growth of a city was helped enormously by the 'residency of the Prince therein', attracting 'all such as aspire and thirst after offices and honours'. In London's case, he was half right. Commerce often depended on the Crown, the term given to the constitutional executive power of the monarchy. But the Crown needed the support of commerce.

By Stuart times, Parliament, which had previously met in a number of different cities, had settled almost exclusively on London. It exerted increasing control over the ability of the Crown to raise taxes. James I and Charles I, who chafed against this constraint, resorted more and more to borrowing from the financiers of the City and selling exclusive licences and monopolies to favourites. Almost anything that people really needed, and for which demand was hence unresponsive to price, or 'inelastic', could profitably be taxed: salt, wine, soap, even playing cards and dice. One favourite way was to allow only those holding a royal licence to sell such goods.

My own home city of Chester, in north-west England, has a folk song that reflects the power, and the danger, of holding such a monopoly:

> There was a jolly miller once lived on the River Dee
> He worked and sang from morn till night, no lark so
> blithe as he
> And this the burden of his song forever used to be
> I care for nobody, no, not I; and nobody cares for me.

With the prestigious and lucrative earldom of Chester – today's earl is Prince Charles, heir to the throne – came a grab-bag of rights to raise money in various ways, granted by the monarch. They included the right to compel all locally grown grain to be ground at the earl's mill. Evidently possessing a sound grasp of the microeconomics of monopoly pricing, the earl subcontracted to a single miller, who was able to charge farmers pretty much what he chose. The miller's lack of popularity among his customers and his utter unconcern about it, as recorded in the song, become easily explicable. So does the fact that when the Civil War between Parliament and the king broke out in 1642, Chester, dominated by its monopoly-holding aristocracy, took the royalist side.

Licence-holding was not exclusively a London phenomenon, nor even an urban one. But the richer merchants of London did benefit more than most from the sale of trade monopolies. This was risky both for them and for the king. For many, the use of taxes and licences by the Crown and its small cabal of aristocratic allies reflected the malign influence of Catholicism and its rigid, alien hierarchy. Following campaigns of religious persecution in the sixteenth century and the Catholic attempt to blow up Parliament in 1605, Papacy had become a shorthand for arbitrary exploitation and a general scapegoat for anything that went wrong. The prices charged by the Catholic-dominated Westminster Soap Company, which held the London soap licence, provoked street riots enlivened by the unlikely chanting of 'No more Popish soap!'

Milking monopolies was especially dangerous in London. Its population was divided by extremes of wealth and swollen through migration. It went from around 50,000 in 1500, making it the fifteenth-biggest city in Europe, to 350,000 in 1650, second only to Paris. Londoners were crammed together into a city of cramped, stinking medieval streets. Proximity bred contempt. A century later in 1746 Giacomo Casanova, on one of his libertinistic visits to London, recorded: 'A man in court dress cannot walk the streets of London without being pelted with mud by the mob ... the flower of the nobility mingling in confusion with the vilest populace ... the most wretched porter will dispute the wall with a Lord.' It was said at the time that it was a mistake to confuse the babble of a London coffee-house with the roar of the nation, but at a time when transport and communication were slow and expensive, the noise of the latter could often by drowned out by the former.

Rumour, anger and the radical ideas of anti-Papist Puritanism spread rapidly in this febrile, foetid atmosphere. One of Charles I's advisers said that Parliament's popularity among the London crowds 'is their anchor-hold and only interest'. The London mob – the word itself was invented in the seventeenth century – was regarded by many royalists with scorn and disdain, as much because of its propensity to carry disease as its predilection for violence. (Cheaper soap might have helped.)

Respect for its size and fear of its power might have been more appropriate than contempt for its sanitary standards. The London crowds did include unemployed, menial labourers and apprentices – the latter, in their own view underpaid and overworked, being a particularly volatile bunch. But there were also a lot of smaller merchants and tradesmen, excluded from the charmed coterie that encircled the Crown, and whose political motivation extended to more than cheaper soap. Samuel Pepys, the diarist of seventeenth-century England, himself heard a crowd 'bawling and calling in the street for a free parliament and money'. At second hand, he reported: 'It is said that they did in open streets yesterday, at Westminster, cry "A parliament! A parliament!" And I do believe it will cost blood.'

It did, indeed, cost blood. In elections in December 1641, Puritan radicals won control of the City Common Council, the local authority, and with it power over the City's militia. Together with the House of Commons, they set up a Committee of Safety (a term echoed a century and a half later during the French Revolution with Paris's Committee of Public Safety, an altogether bloodier body).

In January 1642, with conflict between Crown and Parliament rising, Charles attempted to arrest five Members of Parliament in person, only to find that, forewarned, they had escaped. The City militia protected the five the next day as they paraded triumphantly in central London. Charles was frightened out of the capital five days later, retreated to Nottingham to declare war and spent the next seven years trying unsuccessfully to fight his way back. His return to the royal palace in Whitehall in 1649 was less than triumphant: it was to be publicly executed by order of a Parliamentary leadership that had defeated and captured him. By protecting Parliament when it defied the king, London won the most important victory of the Civil War before the war had even begun.

If anything the Parisian mob played an even more defining role in the French Revolution. It helped to escalate what had started as an exercise in creating a constrained constitutional monarchy in place of the absolutist rule of Louis XVI into a murderous, drawn-out chaos that ended with the blood-stained birth of a republic.

Having gained a sense of their own power by storming the Bastille prison in Paris on 14 July 1789 (albeit finding only seven prisoners inside to release), Parisians created their own city government, the Paris Commune, and established the National Guard as its military force. The first governments of the revolution, the national assembly and legislative assembly, which wanted a limited monarchy somewhat like the English model, were swept aside. Louis XVI and his family were prevented from fleeing and in effect imprisoned inside the Tuileries palace in the centre of Paris by a mob dominated by *sans-culottes* – so called because they eschewed, or could not afford, the fashionable knee-breeches worn by richer Frenchmen.

With the help of the mob the radical leadership, particularly Georges Danton, head of the administrative *département* of Paris and commander of the district battalion of the National Guard, forced the legislative assembly to dissolve itself in 1792. A new national convention was elected which declared France a republic and executed the king. Struggles for control between the various power-bases in Paris started the mass killings of royalists, priests and, increasingly, anyone who was declared an enemy of the revolution, and not until 1795 did moderates take control and end the Reign of Terror.

In both Paris and London, the cities' violent past has left indelible marks on the architecture. Famously, when the French emperor Napoleon III commissioned Baron Georges-Eugène Haussmann to redesign Paris between 1852 and 1870, his new broad boulevards admired for their sweeping vistas had grimly practical as well as aesthetic purposes. Their width was designed to give cavalry and artillery wide thoroughfares down which to charge and a clear field of fire, the better to suppress any future popular uprising. Washington DC has similar avenues, named after the states, which cut diagonally across the perpendicular monotony of the familiar American street grid system. (On one of them, Pennsylvania Avenue, stands the White House.) In Washington's case, the avenues reflected the influence of French architects without having the same practical imperative in mind.

In London, the forbidding two-storey windowless 'curtain wall' that now surrounds the Bank of England in the heart of the City of London was added after the Bank (along with nearby prisons at Newgate and Fleet) was badly damaged in the 'Gordon riots' of June 1780. The riots, named after their leader, followed an anti-Catholic demonstration (sound familiar?) of more than 40,000 people that got out of hand. The Bank was thereafter guarded at night by a picket armed with muskets. The guard was ended only in 1973, by which time the threat of mass anti-Papist mob violence was thought to have diminished sufficiently to take the risk.

In Russia, control of the capital not only brought down the Romanov dynasty of Tsars but, even more dramatically, showed how a small, disciplined political movement focused on the capital could seize control of a country of 170 million people covering 6.5 million square miles.

Russian Tsarism was a vulnerable despotism which suppressed the rise of any alternative locus of power such as the country's feeble Duma (parliament), yet which itself held frail authority over a vast and sparsely populated country. Undermined by Russia's dismal military failure on the Eastern Front of the First World War, the Tsar abdicated in February 1917 after a massive rolling revolt grew in Petrograd (formerly St Petersburg, the name Russified a couple of years earlier to placate anti-German sentiment). Starting with industrial workers, the rebellion then progressed to thousands of mutinying soldiers. This was a popular uprising but not a communist revolution. The 'Bolshevik' political grouping led by Vladimir Lenin and Leon Trotsky, which would eight months later take control of the country and become the Communist Party of the Soviet Union, was taken by surprise. Many of its key members were not even in Russia at the time, giving rise to the faintly comic spectacle of a bunch of revolutionaries hurrying home to catch up with a revolution.

The real genius that led to the Bolsheviks' eventual triumph was their increasing control over Petrograd's 'soviet', or workers' organization, through the months that followed. They watched their rivals punch themselves out and exhaust local popular support by trying to run a provisional government for Russia after the February revolution. Amid mounting discontent with the war, which was still continuing, the Bolsheviks' October revolution (or 'October uprising' as it was more accurately initially called) was a special forces assassination of a tottering government, not a pitched battle against the commanding heights of a functioning state. The climactic 'storming' of the Winter Palace, the central seat of government, met almost no resistance. More people were accidentally killed in the making of the film director Sergei Eisenstein's subsequent classic movie on the episode than died in combat during the event itself.

Had the political identities of the country as a whole led the October revolution in 1917 and decided the political shape of the nation, post-Tsarist Russia would have been dominated by the Socialist Revolutionaries – a rural party whose priorities were to give peasants title to their land. In practice, with the city and the country desperate for stability and the Socialist Revolutionaries' supporters spread across Russia's vast interior, the Bolsheviks found it amazingly easy simply to dismiss the Constituent Assembly which was supposed to take power and in which the Socialist Revolutionaries had a clear majority, and take control themselves.

Unstable governments have learned the appropriate lesson about paying attention to their immediate surroundings, and the result is frequently a capital bloated beyond all economic logic. Some examples are striking. We saw in the first chapter how Argentina's misguided policies and attitudes warped its development – a landholding class that did not live on the land, an indulged hothouse

of industrial companies that could not survive being plan
in the fields of international competition and, like early
England, an economy distorted by a cronyish, corrupt governm.
that hedged it round with regulations, monopolies and licences. It
is not entirely surprising that more than 35 per cent of Argentines
– not 35 per cent of its urban population, the average for unstable
democracies, but 35 per cent of the entire nation – live in Buenos
Aires.

The pattern is common across Latin America. Mexico City, a
small capital of fewer than 3 million in 1950, whose dysfunctional
expansion created one of the modern world's first vast slums, now
has a population pushing 22 million. A well-practised routine in
the city's post-war growth involved a group of rural migrants
pitching up, squatting on vacant land on the outskirts and choosing
a leader who agitated against the ruling PRI party. The government would promptly give them title to the land and provide them
with some basic infrastructure, whereupon they would fall into
line behind the PRI. Another small chapter in the bloating of the
congested, polluted capital would be complete. Given the influence of the central government, even the governors of Mexico's
regions find it politically prudent to spend a lot of their time in
Mexico City.

Some of Asia does better, particularly where authorities are able
and willing to plan, and where rural emigrants actually have jobs
to go to. True, the metropolitan district of Bangkok, an impossibly
congested city, contains 9 million people, while the next-biggest
city in Thailand, the laid-back travellers' hang-out of Chiang Mai,
has a population of just 150,000. But a lot of the very rapid growth
in Asia is coming in second-tier cities. In China, a deliberate policy
of encouraging smaller cities to grow, to relieve the pressure on
the heavily populated coastal metropolises, has produced a prolifer-
ation of cities rather than just a swelling of the existing ones. The
officially designated number of cities has risen from 193 to 640
since 1978, and the share of the population living in the huge
conurbations like Shanghai, Beijing and Shenzhen has in fact
declined.

China has also experimented with making new cities more sustainable. Many cities are depleting their water tables – those in Manila, Shanghai and Bangkok have dropped sharply in the past few decades. China is conducting an intriguing experiment with the Dongtan EcoCity, built from scratch on an island off Shanghai, which is designed to create a city both environmentally and socially sustainable. The so-called 'ecological footprint', a measure of the land and water area needed to support each person, averages 5 hectares in cities in rich countries; for Shanghai it is 8; for sprawling car-dependent Houston 14. For Dongtan it is less than 3. Construction, though, has lagged behind schedule, and whether it will prove a replicable model remains to be seen.

There is another challenge with which cities, and not just the catch-up cities of the developing world, have recently had to deal. So far we have seen how cities were created by the industrial demand for concentrated workforces and the need for hubs of distribution and trade. But in the world's rich countries, as manufacturing has become more capital-intensive and made up a smaller share of the economy, the demand for large agglomerations of industrial workers has ebbed. The empty ghostly hulks of Michigan car towns show that cities that have outlived their original purpose will not necessarily find a new reason to exist.

With the rise of services in the economy, and particularly with better telecommunications and most recently the internet, has the entire point of traditional cities in fact disappeared? Could urbanization go into reverse? In the 1970s, there were genuine concerns that this was so. Several cities, including the world's defining metropolis of New York, seemed on the verge of collapse. With crime soaring and businesses fleeing, New York City very nearly went bankrupt. The initial refusal of Gerald Ford, then president, to bail it out with federal cash produced one of the great newspaper headlines of all time, in the *New York Post*: 'Ford to city: drop dead'.

Any city with a large manufacturing or transport function, and particularly if it had both, was vulnerable. Liverpool, the port in north-west England that handled much of Britain's transatlantic trade, had been one of the country's richest cities in the nineteenth century. At its height it was the centre of global commerce in salt and cotton, and hosted a commercial exchange (if not a physical market) for slaves. The decline of its port and of British manufacturing almost halved Liverpool's population from 867,000 in 1937 to 442,000 in 2001.

The demand for transport hubs has been declining for a century. Of the twenty largest cities in America in 1900, seven were ports where a river met the ocean (Boston, Providence, New York, Jersey City, Newark, Baltimore and San Francisco), five were ports where rivers met the Great Lakes (Chicago, Milwaukee, Detroit, Cleveland and Buffalo), three were on the Mississippi (Minneapolis, St Louis and New Orleans), three on the Ohio river (Louisville, Cincinnati and Pittsburgh) and two on east coast rivers close to the ocean (Philadelphia and Washington). But the cost of transporting manufactures dropped by 90 per cent in real terms in the twentieth century, removing the need for each region to have its own manufacturing and distribution hub.

A century of cheap internal combustion engines meant people could propel themselves and their goods over long distances at ever lower cost. Cheap transport pushed Americans away from Cleveland and Detroit and towards the cheap land and warm weather in sprawling low-density sunbelt cities like Phoenix, Arizona, which has grown by a third to 1.5 million people in the last fifteen years. Most of those twenty cities named above are bywords for industrial decline. Only six make today's top twenty. And of America's sixteen biggest cities in 1950, only four have a larger population today than then, even though the national population has doubled since.

On the face of it the twenty-first-century revolution of information technology (IT) and digitization ought, perhaps, to have completed the job. Teleworking can remove the need to transport people to the workplace or even have a physical workplace at all. And yet several of the cities that seemed to be dying in the 1970s

– New York, Chicago and London – have since had remarkable revivals.

In a sense, what they have done is to re-create the spirit that inspired the city-states of medieval and early modern Europe. Globalization, and particularly the digitization of information, means that cities have again begun to owe more to their ability to convene international markets than to their direct links with local economies.

For the elites in many highly specialized industries like advertising, it would appear that face-to-face contact with clients and with each other remains essential. The most digitized and computerized industries – media, software, financial services – huddle in expensive urban or suburban enclaves like Silicon Valley and Wall Street. In central London's Soho, a small and highly specialized industry of post-production movie companies continues to cluster. If you don't drink with other producers in the pubs in Soho, you miss out on the best work. New York is the only one out of the sixteen largest cities in the north-eastern or Midwestern states whose population is larger than fifty years ago.

Similarly there is no particular reason that anyone at all, apart from government officials, should live in Madrid. The city sits forlornly in the middle of a high plateau – remarkably, it is the highest capital in Europe – which is brutally hot in summer and chilly in winter. Yet by retaining a critical mass of corporate headquarters and financial services it has fought off the challenges of more superficially glamorous second-tier cities like Barcelona.

Agglomeration is replacing the location of natural resources and physical trade as a main reason for living in cities. Even entirely new industries generally create an urban cluster rather than spreading themselves around evenly. The southern Indian city of Hyderabad went from one million to 7 million inhabitants in a couple of decades when the IT industry appeared out of the ether. The immigrants who work in many growing industries, also, move to where similar immigrants already live, creating a self-reinforcing dynamic.

But because clustering could take place anywhere, the competition between cities has become more acute and the difference between successes and failures more evident. When Chicago was the only big port on the southern west coast of Lake Michigan, it had a local natural monopoly. When the importance of physical trade declined, it became merely one of the many cities – Detroit, Cleveland, Milwaukee – that could have been the commercial and finance hub of the Midwest. Chicago had not just to coexist with the competition but to beat it – in particular expanding its commodity trading business and holding it in the face of competition from the likes of New York.

In the same way that modern technologies often mean winner-take-all companies or products (such as Microsoft Windows), a limited number of cities will specialize in one industry. Tokyo, Hong Kong and Singapore share Asia's financial market trading, and have held it with tenacity in the face of competition. Many predicted, for example, that Shanghai would take Hong Kong's role as the entrepôt for China when the territory was returned to the Chinese in 1997. Singapore offered 40,000 visas to professionals from Hong Kong that year, particularly in finance, hoping to consolidate its own position. It never filled the quota. They stayed in Hong Kong, where the concentration of expertise and experience in the city won out.

Once a city gets a dominant position in a growing and highly skilled industry like international financial services, it is hard to shift. Highly skilled workers move to cities that already have a preponderance of people like them. A little like medieval city-states, places like London and New York already look at least semi-detached from their surrounding economies. They are more international, more ethnically mixed and more liberal about social and sexual mores. Try to imagine the mayor of an American city other than New York living for a while, as did Rudy Giuliani, with a gay couple, and moving a girlfriend, not his wife, into the mayoral residence.

Becoming a cluster is a keenly sought achievement, but there are few examples of one successfully being built deliberately, straight from scratch. An interesting experiment (which Singapore, among others, started watching anxiously) was undertaken in Dubai, which poured billions of dollars of the Emirates' oil money into the city to try to create clusters like biotechnology research. But such artificial attempts, requiring massive injections of money, always run the risk of creating distortions and bubbles, and the Dubai experiment ran into some trouble after the Emirates' state-backed companies racked up more debt than they could handle.

Another, related, reason for the revival of cities is as places to live. People like to hang out with similar people for play as well as work. It is not just the financial but also the dating markets of London and New York that are much deeper and more liquid than in the provinces. Cities are not just good places to produce services but the best places to consume them. The marginal income of consumers in rich economies is spent mainly not on more stuff – computers, TVs, even clothes, all of whose prices are in any case dropping – but on personal services: eating out, gyms, facials, movies and theatres. This gives a natural advantage to cities, because the more other people there are, the more likely it is that such services will be provided.

And this is particularly true as demand becomes ever more specialized and exclusive. Consumers want not just to see the same movies that everyone can see in provincial towns but world-class theatre and music, to eat food not just from chain restaurants but from world-class kitchens. Selfridges, the long-established London department store, ran an advertising campaign a few years ago designed, it would appear, to infuriate visitors from the provinces. 'It's Worth Living in London' the strapline ran, above a series of photographs of rural tedium. The iconic screen representation of New York in the 1970s was *Taxi Driver*, which depicted the city as a violent, amoral dystopia; that of the latest decade – *Sex and the City* – shows it as a safe, indulgent adult playground.

In America, the ratio of housing costs to real wages in cities has risen sharply in recent decades. People, it appears, are choosing to live in cities for reasons other than employment. Cities like New York and London – and even Washington DC, never high on anyone's list of buzzing metropolises – have managed to rehabilitate no-go areas close to the city centre. Often this has more to do with leisure than with work. The south bank of the Thames, for example, a vibrant if seedy area back when Parliament was in revolt against the king, has recently been revitalized by the opening of the Tate Modern art gallery and the enormous success of Borough Market, now one of London's hippest food markets. Back in the 1970s, at the nadir of its existence, New York's Times Square was a derelict, crime-ridden wasteland; it has since been reborn. Even if the populations of these cities are stagnant, as they sometimes are, it does not necessarily reflect failure. City living increasingly means single people living alone, and a continual churning whereby new urban dwellers replace those who burn out, or start reproducing, and head for the suburbs.

If current trends continue, there will be many more cities but also, quite likely, a bigger contrast between relative winners and losers. Just as globalization subjects companies to fiercer competition, increasing further the returns to successful businesses and reducing those to failing ones, so the gaps between the cities that are winning and those that are losing will become increasingly obvious.

All of this speaks not just to cities continuing to play a central role in the future of human well-being but to the way those cities are run becoming ever more important. The golden eggs are getting bigger, and the geese more fractious. Single-industry cities are also susceptible to declines in that industry. Given the substantial damage being inflicted on the financial services industry by the economic crisis that spread so rapidly in 2008, cities like London and New York where the bankers gathered are likely to have to work harder to continue to thrive. Tolerance for pollution, congestion, high taxes and poor transport will diminish along with pay bonuses. Clusters can disperse as well as gather. Florence, Venice, Antwerp, Bruges, even Amsterdam – all, over the past millennium, have at one time or another been city-state entrepôts of huge international significance. All are now relative backwaters.

A successful city is a hard thing to build, and a world-class one even harder. But incompetent or wrong-headed governments have stunted and even destroyed so many in the past that complacency and fatalism in the face of urbanization are profoundly misplaced.

That said, I would suggest that the disenfranchisement of America's capital city has pretty much done its job. With the tradition of stable democracy now so deeply sunk into US society, we can probably risk extending its benefits to all. Perhaps it is time after all these years to draw a deep breath, take a chance and give Washington DC the vote.

3. Trade

Why does Egypt import half its staple food?

If ever there was a place where the wheat of the world should be grown, it is Egypt. The Nile, the longest river in the world, each year floods its valley and a huge, spreading delta, thoroughly soaking the rich alluvial soil that the current has itself carried across Africa and deposited over thousands of years. The river and its delta have been compared to a lotus – a long, apparently fragile stem holding up a heavy blossom of intense vitality.

So fertile are the soils after the floods that farmers do not even have to plough or hoe. Eyewitnesses report them sowing grain once the floodwaters have receded and letting loose herds of pigs on the fields to tread the seed into the rich, damp earth. The pigs are brought out again for the harvest, threshing the reaped corn by trampling on it. The country is a granary for the region. The great cities of the Mediterranean depend on its barley and wheat exports to feed themselves.

Then again, why would anyone grow wheat in Egypt? A country with a large and swelling population, with very little rainfall of its own, its limited farmlands are watered by a river of highly variable flow. It is situated in one of the driest inhabited regions on earth, where water for drinking, let alone for agriculture, is preciously guarded. Wheat is a thirsty and not particularly valuable crop, and pouring away billions of litres of water on growing it would surely be a serious misallocation of resources. The country, along with almost all the rest of the Middle East, is one of the biggest grain importers in the world.

The country and the river are the same, and the rationales for exporting or importing wheat are in both cases absolutely sound. The difference between the two scenarios has been wrought by the effects of time and, crucially, trade. The first description was of Egypt during ancient times, when it was first ruled by the pharaohs and then subsumed into the Greek and Roman civilizations. The story of the pigs trampling in the seed was from Herodotus, a Greek historian of the fifth century BCE. Egypt supplied much of the grain that, as we have seen, was handed out to the citizens of ancient Rome. For it to be one of the great grain-producing regions of the ancient world made perfect sense. Egypt was one of the most fertile countries within the trading area of the Mediterranean and Black Sea, a region then circumscribed by the existing technology of transport as the longest feasible range of bulk commerce in grain.

In the second, contemporary scenario, the market for wheat has expanded to encompass the world. If Herodotus pitched up in today's Egypt he would still recognize the country's staple food – the flatbread that has been eaten since before pharaonic times. But standing at the Alexandria docks, he would be surprised to see not ships full of grain departing for Rome but ocean-going vessels arriving laden with wheat from Odessa, Montreal, Louisiana and South Australia. One of the Mediterranean's wetter countries is one of the world's drier ones. An economy with a natural advantage in a limited market may turn out to be rather a poor performer in a larger one. There is little point throwing away its precious water on growing food that can be bought from abroad much more efficiently. Much like ancient Rome, modern Egypt imports half its staple food.

Egypt has allowed its new relative scarcity of water to determine – if only partially, as we shall see later – what it does with its own resources and what it imports. When economies specialize in a particular kind of product, it is often determined by the relative abundance of land, water, other natural resources and labour. This is particularly so for agricultural crops, whose connection with the local geography and climate is so immediate. By trading with each other, countries can benefit from a resource owned by their trading partners while sharing the benefits of their own.

Thus modern-day Egypt is importing more than grain. It is importing water. There may be no ships laden with forty-foot containers full of fresh water lining up outside the ports of Alexandria and Cairo. But by buying in wheat, Egypt is, invisibly and implicitly, importing millions of tons of the water that is used to grow it. This commerce in 'virtual' or 'embedded' water, like many of the most remarkable achievements of the world trading system, happens on its own without intelligent, or at least manifest, design. No grand plan; no treaties; no teams of international bureaucrats. Just the market.

In fact, it is remarkable not how much embedded water, labour and land is shipped around the world economy but how little. Powerful constraints of transport costs, inertia and political resistance stop economies becoming dependent on produce from abroad. The political constriction became much more prominent in recent years when sharp hikes in food prices sparked panic buying and riots across the world. The desire for self-sufficiency intensifies for something as visceral and as bound up with senses of identity and nationhood as our daily bread.

For trade to be worthwhile, transport costs – shipping charges, time, the risk of spoil or loss, and the uncertainty of price and demand – have to be outweighed by the extra profit to be gained by taking goods from a place of plenty to one of scarcity. Unsurprisingly, the history of trade is one of the small, light, durable and reliably expensive being the first to establish regular trade routes. The heavy, bulky, perishable and cheap follow on slowly behind. As the cost of transport declines and its speed increases so the range of tradeable goods widens. But this process can take centuries.

Though his intent was to contrast the beauty of ancient and medieval trade with the ugliness of the modern, John Masefield, Poet Laureate for nearly forty years, described this in a poem of elegant simplicity, 'Cargoes':

> Quinquireme of Nineveh from distant Ophir,
> Rowing home to haven in sunny Palestine,
> With a cargo of ivory,
> And apes and peacocks,
> Sandalwood, cedarwood, and sweet white wine.

> Stately Spanish galleon coming from the Isthmus,
> Dipping through the Tropics by the palm-green shores,
> With a cargo of diamonds,
> Emeralds, amethysts,
> Topazes, and cinnamon, and gold moidores.
>
> Dirty British coaster with a salt-caked smoke stack,
> Butting through the Channel in the mad March days,
> With a cargo of Tyne coal,
> Road-rails, pig-lead,
> Firewood, iron-ware, and cheap tin trays.

Small, light, durable, expensive: silks and spices formed some of the world's first global supply chains. The cinnamon mentioned by Masefield was being brought home to Spain, which extended its trading empire in the fifteenth and sixteenth centuries across Asia and to South America. But the same spice – particularly valued as a food preservative – was traded overland between south and south-east Asia and the Middle East at least as early as the second millennium BCE. The trade, controlled for many centuries by Arab and Persian traders, was significant enough to have been mentioned in the Old Testament.

Water comes a long way down the list of obvious goods to trade. True, there is a lot more of it in some parts of the world than others, and the potential gains in efficiency in moving it from wet to dry would be considerable. But it is exceedingly heavy and bulky. And despite the rising cost of water in the dry nations of the world, water is rarely worth the cost of shipping direct.

There was, it is true, at one point a thriving water trade between North America and India in frozen form. In *Walden*, the nineteenth-century writer Henry David Thoreau described thousands of tons of ice being cut from the lake by which he lived in Massachusetts. The blocks were shipped to Bengal to find their way into underground ice houses to furnish sweating British colonial officials with cool water and ice cream. In the 1870s, New England was exporting 12,000 tons of ice a year to India, Latin America and east Asia. Even on a six-month sea voyage, the chunks were big enough for much to arrive unmelted.

But it was in truth not the water but the cold that was being exported. When steam-powered ice-making machinery was invented and installed in India at the end of the nineteenth century, the ice trade with North America evaporated. Still, there are intriguing parallels between the ice trade of the nineteenth century and the virtual water trade of the ancient Mediterranean and today. India was in effect importing the bitter New England winter embedded in the blocks of ice. Rome and other urban centres in ancient times, and Egypt and other dry countries in the twenty-first century, implicitly buy water from wetter nations embedded in the crops they import.

A simple look at a trade map for a water-intensive product like wheat betrays a clear geographical pattern. The water, in general, goes from wet countries to dry. It is cheaper, other things being equal, to grow crops in countries where water is abundant, so they will tend to displace crops grown in dry nations.

Governments across the world are drawing up plans to manage their water stocks, working out how to allocate them between farmers and urban dwellers, how much they can take out of the river systems without causing serious environmental damage, and so forth. Their task is eased by the market, which has dealt with vast discrepancies between countries by sucking water around the world trading system. Yet the growth of Egypt as the granary of the ancient world owed a great deal to forcible government transfers, as well as to the silent operation of the invisible hand of market forces.

The potential for growing grain in the Nile valley and delta was obvious from very early on. Along with the similar but smaller basin of the Tigris and Euphrates in Mesopotamia, modern-day Iraq, it was one of the original wellsprings of irrigated agriculture. It was in the Tigris–Euphrates and the Nile valleys that humans coalesced into communities of settled farmers rather than roaming bands of hunter-gatherers. The most heavily inhabited areas of the modern Middle East are still the Nile and Euphrates riverbanks.

By the time of Herodotus, Egypt had been united as one realm under the rule of the pharaohs for more than two and half millennia. But the growing of barley and a primitive form of wheat had been established well before that, as had early versions of artificial irrigation to capture the potential of the river.

Wheat and barley are both highly dependent on water, and the elemental importance of the river soaked into the politics, culture and religion of those who lived around it. The lives and identities of several deities took inspiration from the waterway: Hapi, a god in the shape of a frog, represented the delta or its annual floods. The Egyptians oriented their compass towards the south, the source of the Nile, and the Egyptian calendar was built around the seasons of the river, the new year starting with the mid-summer flood.

The natural irrigation of the annual Nile inundations, between what is now July and October, would probably have allowed a single crop season over about two thirds of the area covered by the flooding river. During the two millennia before the pharaonic era began around 3000 BCE, farmers extended the reach of the river. They built terraced fields along the valley, dredged the natural overflow channels that held floodwater in ponds' after the level of the water had receded, dug ditches to breach the low points of natural levees and lifted water directly from ponds or channels into fields by bucket.

One of the more important artefacts of pre-pharaonic Egypt is the romantically named 'mace-head of the Scorpion King', a fragment of limestone sceptre which shows a warrior monarch digging an irrigation ditch with a ceremonial hoe. (The scene is pleasingly reminiscent of a modern-day photo-opportunity politician turning the first spadeful of earth on the foundation of a new highway.) The swampy and forested delta itself, as opposed to the upper valley, was harder to cultivate. But it began to dominate economic life around 1400 BCE onwards.

The importance of the river and its flow was evident from the political and social turmoil that accompanied its fluctuations. Low floods meant trouble. Though the Nile was more reliable than other rivers, it was still erratic. In the third millennium BCE, a series of low floods caused widespread rioting, looting of grain stores, cannibalism and starvation. Hundreds of bodies were left rotting in the perfidious river.

During the reigns of the pharaohs Ramses III and Ramses VIII in the twelfth century BCE, water shortages drove up the price of wheat by twenty-four times relative to the price of other goods. The fear of low waters that haunted Egypt's rulers made it into the Old Testament in the form of the pharaoh's nightmare about seven fat and seven thin cattle, and seven good and seven stunted ears of grain, interpreted by Joseph to mean seven years of plenty followed by seven years of famine. Such erratic harvests and their devastating impact are lasting evidence of the inconsistency of the Nile floods.

Nonetheless, monuments to the success of the Egyptian civilization in overcoming them still stand in the desert. Egypt had a precociously centralized and well-ordered society, and as early as the third millennium BCE had developed relatively sophisticated systems of irrigation and grain storage. The temples and pyramids left by ancient Egypt are testament to its skilful management of food supply, which enabled sufficient labour to be spared from farming the land to carve columns and haul blocks of stone.

Egypt, along with Sicily and the wheat-growing regions around the Black Sea, also developed into the main grain exporter for the Mediterranean. The fifty days after the summer equinox were regarded throughout the Mediterranean as the prime days for trading. This was as much because they followed the Egyptian harvest – wheat was planted after the flood receded in the autumn and then reaped in the spring – as because of the weather's mildness and suitability for sailing. As irrigation became more sophisticated so the population and the productivity of the Nile valley and delta increased. Grain exports paid for imports of items in short supply in Egypt itself, including silver, iron and wood, and for the hire of foreign mercenaries.

Apart from the extraordinary advantage of irrigated agriculture, two things helped to make longer-range Egyptian grain trade economic. One was the massive urban concentration in Rome, as we saw in the chapter about cities. Rome's size created a demand for food that any surrounding agricultural breadbasket would be hard pressed to meet. The second was the Mediterranean itself as a supply network.

Transport by water was much faster and cheaper than over land. In ancient Egyptian script, symbols of ships were used to denote travel. One modern estimate has it that in the Roman empire, transporting a load a mile by land in an ox cart would cost the same as shifting it 5.7 miles by river or 57 miles by sea, meaning that it was more cost-effective to ship grain from a port at one end of the Mediterranean to a port at the other than to drag it by road up the Italian mainland.

To begin with, river transport helped Egypt itself become closer to a single market, bringing grain from the inland provinces more than 400 miles away to the ancient capital of Memphis, near modern-day Cairo. And then it was grain shipped by sea from Egypt and Sicily that enabled ancient Greece and Rome to free themselves from reliance on their own agricultural hinterlands and, particularly in the Greek case, highly unreliable rains. As the philosopher Aristotle said: 'Food comes to the rulers of the seas.'

This trade was greatly enhanced when Rome conquered Egypt in 30 BCE. Henceforth it could exact grain as taxes in kind rather than going to the bother of having to find its own exports to pay for them. Indeed, much of the Egyptian trade in grain, within the country as well as without, had more to do with forced transfers by a rigid hierarchical society than with the free exchange of goods in an open market. The very peak appears to have been reached in the first century CE, in response to a drive to supply Rome with grain. In other words, the height of Egyptian grain production came not in response to prosperity and freedom for its citizens but colonial exploitation by a controlling foreign power. This is a pattern that recurs.

The Romans expended a great deal of effort to reduce the risks to grain shipments. They more or less stamped out piracy throughout the Mediterranean, and at one point the emperor

Claudius indemnified merchants against losses caused by storms. Panic sometimes set in when the grain shipments from north Africa to Rome were delayed, and the Bible records St Paul travelling on an Alexandria grain ship that was wrecked en route off Malta. But in practice ancient Rome suffered remarkably little from food crises, thanks to its supplies from abroad.

Despite the limited ship-building technologies of the time, a reasonably large chunk of the Roman empire's total grain consumption was traded around the Mediterranean. One estimate suggests the empire's output was about 18 million tonnes of grain. Perhaps half a million tonnes was traded freely over medium or long distances and more than twice that in shorter journeys. Another 1.8 million tonnes travelled long-distance after being exacted in taxes in kind. If we count taxes in kind as trade – and even without taking it by force, Rome would still have had to get the grain somehow – that is a substantial amount. In truth, it was remarkable how much was traded at all. Relative luxuries such as olive oil and wine, which could not be produced in all parts of the Greek or Roman empires, were fairly obvious contenders for trade. Grain, being bulkier, heavier, cheaper and more likely to spoil or be eaten by rats, was another matter.

The infrastructure of long-distance commerce was increasingly impressive. In 301 CE, the emperor Diocletian declared an edict of costs for transport journeys, which was set up in stone inscriptions throughout the empire and included more than 1000 prices for trips of varying lengths. The fidelity of the listed charges to actual prices has been disputed. But there is a clear pattern of big per-mile discounts for long voyages, and particularly voyages by sea.

The regional marketing of goods and particularly food became more sophisticated as metallic currencies were adopted through the empire and hence trade became easier. Local markets were held throughout the empire, often once every eight days – the length of the Roman week.

When the Roman empire collapsed in the fifth century CE, the trading system was damaged with it. As the infrastructure of trade including sea lanes, roads and markets eroded, so did the commerce that had flowed through them. Slowly, over several centuries, the trading networks were rebuilt, first by Islamic empires centred around the Mediterranean and the Middle East and then by the city-states of Europe such as Venice and Genoa. By 1300, the coastal regions of the Mediterranean, benefiting from the same advantages of sea trade as a millennium earlier, had rebuilt a trading network to supply the cities of Italy, southern France and Spain.

As before, the building of an intra-European trading system and then longer trade routes started with the small, light and expensive and moved on to the big, heavy and cheap. In the thirteenth century, the Mongols swept across the steppes of Asia and established an empire that stretched from China to the Mediterranean. Henceforth the extraordinarily difficult overland route that had brought silk from east Asia to ancient Rome at enormous expense became much safer and cheaper. Say what you like about the Mongols – and we will encounter their injurious influence on some of the civilizations they subdued in later chapters – but they certainly helped trade by enforcing the peace. It was partly uncertainty about the overland silk route after the collapse of the Mongol empire, together with the desire of the Portuguese to outflank the Islamic merchants who dominated the spice trade, which led to Columbus accidentally stumbling across the Americas in 1492.

Within Europe, the same pattern of trade also slowly emerged. The first goods to be exported in significant quantities were of high value and often produced by a skilled industry that could not be easily replicated elsewhere even if the raw materials could. It was they that first bridged the gap between what were generally two discrete European trading zones, one concentrated on the coasts of the north-west and another round the Mediterranean.

Woollen cloth from north-west Europe started to gain a large market from the eleventh and twelfth centuries onwards. It formed such a vital part of the English economy that the Lord Chancellor, traditionally the head of the English judicial system, still sits on a sack stuffed with wool in the House of Lords. Cotton cloth came from the Italian republics from the thirteenth century and olive oil and cork from Spain and Portugal.

The European wine industry, though supplying a fairly exclusive elite, had concentrated itself into areas of specialization from the twelfth century in parts of France, the Rhine, Portugal and Spain, with the former wine makers in England and the Low Countries collapsing. In 1300, the south-western French region of Gascony was exporting 100,000 tonnes of wine to London each year. When grain prices fell in Europe after the Black Death in the middle of the fourteenth century reduced the demand for basic food, peasants in Aix-en-Provence petitioned their landlords to let them switch to vines, pleading: 'It profits us nothing to grow grain.'

Regions close to the sea and navigable rivers and with large urban areas, which reduced the average transport costs, saw faster growth in trade than elsewhere: Flanders, northern Italy, Paris and London, and the valleys of the Po, Rhine, Seine, Garonne, Thames, Elbe, Oder and Vistula.

Areas that established trade routes selling small-volume, high-cost items were later able to expand their export basket. The heavily forested northern European Baltics, for example, were originally drawn into the trading system as a source of furs. But their damp, temperate climate later made them ideal to supply timber and grain to the drier and hotter parts of Europe. The Black Sea region also started off with furs, along with delivering the luxury goods coming along the overland routes from Asia, before re-creating its Roman role as a grain supplier.

But trade in bulk items grew only slowly. Heavy and consistent demand was often not enough to overcome problems in supply. The need was certainly there: in medieval Europe, people spent about half their income on food, and around half of that was on bread. Bread had a low price elasticity of demand – the amount consumed changed little with the cost, with the result that a shortfall in supply in one place drove up prices rapidly and hence the incentive for others to come in and make up the shortfall. Writing at the end of the seventeenth century in England, Gregory

King, a civil servant with a preternaturally good grasp of statistical economics, formulated a law that a 10 per cent fall in supply pushed prices up by 30 per cent.

The inelastic demand should have encouraged the growth of international trade in grain in the same way that oil, another commodity with few close substitutes, is heavily traded in the twenty-first-century economy. Yet under the 'tyranny of distance' – transport costs and the uncertainty of trade – international commerce in grain was slow to develop. As late as the sixteenth century, even the sea-going Mediterranean zone probably traded only about 10 per cent of its grain output.

During a food crisis in the sixteenth century, the Italian republic of Venice sent a representative to the grain-growing Baltic states to investigate the possibility of securing supplies. He reported back that carrying grain overland across Europe would have been prohibitively expensive, quadrupling its price en route. (As a comparison, silks traded across the world from China to Italy only trebled in price, at least while the Mongols were protecting the trade route.) Even food from Sicily, where there was a long tradition of exporting grain, more than doubled in price on the relatively short journey to Spain. A load of grain that cost 10 Spanish reales at the Sicilian farmgate ended up costing 22.5 reales on arrival, with overland transport adding 3 reales, an export licence 5 reales, the sea-freight to Spain 3.5 reales and insurance another reale. The competitive advantage of the exporter had to be considerable to overcome such a cost disadvantage.

Only for very large concentrations of consumers, generally cities like London with excellent transport access, was there a particularly big and efficient commerce in basic foods. Even then, as with ancient Rome, this owed something to governments intervening in the market rather than letting it run freely. The London authorities lobbied hard for commerce in food to be skewed towards their interests. When London outgrew the ability of the surrounding area to supply it with grain, its population having been swollen by rural migrants, it started a vocal political campaign. As early as 1516 the Lord Mayor of London began to send out agents to English ports to monitor whether grain was being sent abroad that might otherwise be destined for the capital. Later that century the London authorities somewhat ambitiously proposed that no laden grain ship putting in at an English port for any reason be allowed to carry its cargo away again.

Such suspicion of open commerce may have created some trade routes. But it also helped to retard the development of more sustainable trading patterns. Active and influential groups of merchants were often important in assembling a critical mass of trading infrastructure that brought down costs. Dutch traders, for example, helped to pioneer commerce in perishable goods like fruit, vegetables and flowers for which the country remains famous. But food shortages have a particular way of putting the messenger out in public to be shot at. The merchants and middlemen that helped bring markets into existence were frequently blamed when market prices rose. (In fact, they still are: every time petrol prices rise there is public disapprobation of 'price-gouging' oil companies and petrol stations, and 'market speculation' has been blamed for rapid rises in food prices in recent years.)

Medieval England had laws against 'forestalling', or buying large amounts of food on the open market while prices were low with the intent of reselling when they had recovered. Adam Smith later likened this prejudice to the fear of witchcraft. The example of the Sicilian grain trade above shows that the single biggest cost was the *tratta* or export licence, also a requirement for grain traders in early modern England. Much of the barrier to open trade was artificial, not natural. As in ancient Rome, the power of a centralized state may have been instrumental in getting a trade route into existence. But when the natural barriers of transport costs fell, the influence of governments was frequently to retard trade rather than to advance it.

When significant international trade in bulk goods – particularly with economies outside Europe – did open up, it owed much to two things. One, Europe was bumping up against limits to production at home. Two, the dramatic 'differentness' of the New World with which it began to trade generated huge efficiency gains. It was one thing benefiting from the relative dampness and empty land of the Baltics versus the Mediterranean. Exploiting the water and vast expanses of terrain of the New World was an advantage of an entirely different magnitude.

By the eighteenth century, population growth had put increasing pressure on the natural and human resources of the advanced countries of western Europe. The same was true of the richer and more densely populated regions within Japan and China at the same time. At this stage, as the historian Greg Clark has shown in a remarkable study, higher population growth across the world had succeeded only in depressing living standards, as the greater number of people put pressure on the limited amount of productive land and other resources. On average, remarkably, it appears that people were no better off than they had been centuries or millennia before.

There has been a long and inconclusive argument about why it was northern Europe and particularly Britain, rather than Asia, that in the nineteenth century managed to break out of this pattern, industrializing first and fastest and seeing sustained increases in income per head. One intriguing explanation (though not one to which Clark adheres) is that the benefits of trade with the Americas relieved northern Europe of the constraint of not having enough land, allowing it to raise productivity.

By 1800, the core areas of Europe (most of western Europe, especially England and the Netherlands), the Pearl and Yangzi river deltas in China, and the Kinai and Kanto regions of Japan were facing similar problems. They had experienced a large rise in population and output. In Europe, the population doubled between 1750 and 1850. Increasingly European, Chinese and Japanese economies were trading with geographically more peripheral regions for land-intensive commodities, particularly timber for building and firewood. Western Europe bought trees from the Baltic; the Chinese Yangzi delta got its timber from the upstream Yangzi region and from Manchuria. But the environmental stresses they were placing even on the wider trading areas were evident. In China, the production of food and fibre, including extensive cotton farming, kept up with a rising population, but only at the cost of serious deforestation.

In England, one of the most advanced and densely populated parts of Europe, the price of wheat relative to that of other goods increased by 40 per cent between 1760 and 1790. And that was before the Napoleonic wars made food yet more scarce and supply even more of a problem. Already importing grains from Germany, Poland, Russia and elsewhere, England turned to food imports from Ireland, which by 1824 was supplying an amount equivalent to about 10 per cent of Britain's entire output in agriculture, forestry and fishing. Britain also had considerable difficulty increasing production of crops like flax and hemp, used for clothing.

Timber for construction and firewood became in particularly short supply. It was even harder quickly to step up the supply of slow-growing trees than it was of grain and other crops, and in any case forest was being cleared for arable land as well as for building and burning. Masefield's firewood-laden ships 'butting through the Channel' were responding to what by the eighteenth century had become an acute shortage. British firewood costs increased sevenfold between 1500 and 1630; Denmark, another heavily populated region, lost around 80 per cent of its forest cover between 1500 and 1800.

With a rising population, many Europeans shivered in the dark. One estimate suggests that the continent produced fuel equivalent to just half a tonne of coal per person per year in the eighteenth century. That was higher than was consumed in China and Japan, but then northern Europeans had to contend with bitter winters and had a particularly energy-intensive style of cooking.

The discovery and exploitation of the coal reserves of Europe, and particularly Britain, helped a good deal. But even with that supply of fuel, there was a pressing imperative to import timber, food and fibre, and implicitly the land and water used to grow them. Britain's overseas possessions and colonies were, wherever possible, stripped of the resources on which the small and crowded mother country was running low. British colonialists went searching in heavily forested colonies from Quebec to Madras for wood, particularly the high-quality timber used to build ships. By the time of the American revolution in the late eighteenth century, a third of the British merchant fleet was built in the North American colonies.

In one valiant but spectacularly inept piece of forward planning, Britain even went to the considerable effort of establishing one of its Australian penal colonies on Norfolk Island, a remote speck in the ocean a thousand miles away from Sydney. (The island's second claim to fame was later being settled by descendants of the mutineers of the HMS *Bounty*.) When the first attempt was made to settle a colony there in 1788, the hope was that the trunks of the tall trees with which the isles were liberally forested would make masts and spars for Royal Navy ships, and that flax could be grown there to manufacture linen. In the event, the so-called 'Norfolk Pine' tree, not technically a member of the pine family as such, made a less than heroic contribution to the service of the British empire. It turned out to be so brittle that masts made of its timber would have snapped in the first big gale.

The trade with the Americas, and particularly the plantation colonies of north-eastern Brazil, the Caribbean and later the Southern states of the US, was a great deal more fruitful. They had plenty of land and water. Though there were no huge technological breakthroughs during that time – the advent of iron-built steam ships was not until the nineteenth century – the British navy replicated the Roman success in suppressing piracy, this time throughout the Atlantic rather than the Mediterranean, allowing cargo to travel on unarmed unescorted ships with smaller crews.

Just as Argentine agriculture was later in effect set up as a supply base for Europe, so the export monoculture of the plantation colonies, sending abroad a few products in bulk, was also well suited to the economies of scale needed to get Britain what it wanted cheaply and quickly. Along with timber, the Americas sent sugar and cotton to Britain, helping Britons cope with their resource crisis by increasing their caloric intake and allowing them to retain energy through warm cheap clothing.

Sugar, as we will see in a later chapter, became one of the main fuels for the workers of the Industrial Revolution. Sugar made up perhaps 4 per cent of total British calories in 1800: a century later it was 18–22 per cent. To grow the same amount of calories by farming wheat or potatoes in England would have required an extra 1.9–2.6 million acres of farmland. To replace the timber imported from North America in 1825 would have needed something like another 1.6 million acres of European forest. Given that the total arable land in Britain was about 17 million acres, trade in just those two crops meant adding perhaps a quarter more 'ghost acres' on to Britain's available land resources. Add in cotton, and the effect of the New World becomes truly dramatic. To replace cotton imports in 1830 with wool, Britain's traditional homegrown fibre, would have required an additional 23 million acres given over to sheep farming – more than the country's entire crop and pasture land combined.

Of course, Britain and Europe more generally had to pay for these imports, but they could do so with the labour and capital-intensive products, particularly manufactures like clothes and shoes, in which they had begun to specialize. Since the colonies were based on slavery – and American cotton was produced by slaves even after the institution was abolished throughout the British empire in 1834 – Britain did not have the problem that other countries encountered. China and Japan found that the farm-workers who produced the cash-crops in which they traded would get distracted into subsistence farming or cottage industries and have to be lured back with higher wages.

The fruitfulness of the transatlantic trade was aided by the fact that Britain was increasingly comfortable with letting the compara-tive advantages of its economy vis-à-vis those in the New World play out. The repeal of the Corn Laws in the middle of the nineteenth century was a sign that the British political establish-ment was prepared to regard importing agricultural produce and exporting manufactures as a consistent pattern in its economic future. It preferred buying in food and fibre from around the world to aiming for self-sufficiency. Gradually, though it took longer for some countries than others, most of Europe took the same view.

Wheat from the US, Canada, Australia and Argentina – and the Ukraine, once a railway had been built to the Crimea to carry grain – completely changed the pattern of European agriculture. The opening up of the pampas and the prairie also drove millions of now uncompetitive European farmers off their land, and in very many cases caused them to emigrate to their competitor countries in the Americas, where there was an abundance of land and a shortage of labour. A series of bad harvests hit Europe in the 1880s, but rather than a disaster for European consumers it was a business opportunity for New World producers. Unlike the spike in prices that might have been expected from the experience in earlier centuries, the real price of wheat (adjusted for movements in general inflation) in Europe fell by 15 per cent between 1873 and 1896.

So much for importing embedded or virtual land in the eighteenth and nineteenth centuries. When it comes to the virtual water trade of the twentieth century, though the pattern of competitiveness is clear, there remains considerable scope for natural advantages to be given much freer rein.

Only recently have many people come to see that water is rather like oil. It is essential to the running of a modern economy, demand for it is unresponsive to price in the short run, though it may be more flexible in the medium term, and its owners have a disturbing tendency to mismanage it in spectacularly silly ways. The second of these characteristics often gives rise to the third. Patterns of water use built up over time, even if circumstances have now changed substantially, are not easy to shift. In particular, the physical and social infrastructure of farming is often reliant on water being used the way it has always been used, which often means given away free or sold well below its real cost. Farmers are reluctant to abandon a way of life because of the scarcity of something that they frequently regard as a right. And like oil, water often comes out of the ground cheaply until it runs out. Countries can continue misusing it for a remarkably long time with no apparent consequences before the party comes to a sudden stop.

The control of water, particularly through dams, was one of the great symbols of progress and nationhood of the twentieth century. It is not hard to see why. In a century of rising and increasingly urbanized populations being supported by a smaller number of farmers, the ability to control the water supply became more important.

Dams also provide power, another essential input to the modern economy. The Hoover dam on the Nevada–Arizona border and the series of hydroelectric and irrigation projects of the Tennessee Valley Authority were among the most potent and enduring symbols of Franklin D. Roosevelt's New Deal, the programme of public works and government intervention designed to combat the Great Depression and modernize America. The Aswan dam, built in 1959–70, was the pride of modern Egyptian nationalism under Colonel Nasser. Jawaharlal Nehru, first prime minister of an independent India, said that dams were the temples of his modern country. The great dams of the twentieth century held back floods, powered cities and made deserts bloom.

There is, in fact, no generalized water shortage in the world: the planet has enough to feed and wash its inhabitants. Nor is there likely to be one as long as the global population, following current projections, stabilizes below 10 billion, and water-saving technologies continue to be developed in farming and industrial production. But localized water shortages do exist, thanks to a hefty degree of misallocation. Much water is given away free when, as with any scarce resource being parcelled out, it should instead be given a price. As a United Nations report put it a couple of years ago, there is a shortage of water in the world in the same way that there would be a shortage of Porsches if they were priced at $3000 each. Sell something too cheap, and too much of it will be used.

One of the reasons for the persistent underpricing is the clear trade-off between the conservation of water and other aims frequently regarded as desirable, particularly the elusive concept of 'food security'. Like the 'energy security' that is so exercising politicians today, particularly in the US, food security is frequently confused with food self-sufficiency. The first means ensuring there will always be enough to eat; the second means growing it yourself.

Self-sufficiency protects a country from certain risks, such as a disruption of trade through war, economic blockade, blackmail or other unusual events. But it makes the nation's food supply dependent on the reliability of the domestic economy's own farming. As the Irish discovered during the nineteenth-century famines when the potato harvest failed, that can be dangerous.

These questions of food security are particularly acute in the Middle East and north Africa – Egypt, Algeria, Libya, Tunisia and Morocco – because of the shortage and variability of water supplies and the size and rapid growth of populations. Managing water supply is critical to life. A map of the region shows an almost perfect fit between annual rainfall and population density, with people crowded along the relatively rainy coasts of Morocco and Tunisia. The exceptions are the even more heavily peopled Nile and Euphrates valleys where the water arrives horizontally rather than vertically and in larger amounts.

Humans use water mainly for agriculture. Each individual needs about a cubic metre of water per year to drink, and somewhere between 50 and 100 cubic metres for washing and so forth. But the overall 'water footprint' – the total water used to support each individual and by extension each country – mainly reflects food production. The food each individual consumes takes at least a thousand cubic metres of water to produce or, in the terminology we introduced before, has a thousand cubic metres of water embedded in it. Within international trade in goods, 80 per cent of the flows of virtual or embedded water are in agricultural products, around three quarters of which is in crops and a quarter in animal products.

In the Middle East and north Africa, the agricultural use of water has a much higher political and environmental profile than elsewhere. Crop production in temperate zones like western Europe is largely based on rainfall. The water is contained in the soil and replenished naturally rather than pulled out of rivers or streams. But in the Middle East most soils are arid and farmers make widespread use of irrigation. Globally, only around 11–12 per cent of surface freshwater (water in rivers, lakes and streams) is stored in reservoirs. For the Middle East and north Africa, the figure is 85 per cent. The result is widespread use of irrigation. Iran, for example, has the fifth-largest irrigated area of farmland of any country in the world and holds enough water in reservoirs to irrigate a lot more.

Thousands of years after the pharaohs, irrigation remains vital to Egyptian agriculture. Traditional water-holding methods based on capturing the annual floods were radically updated in the twentieth century when the Aswan dam was built, and year-round irrigation provided to Egyptian agriculture. Big dams have acquired a bad reputation in recent decades: their economic benefits have been systematically oversold and the environmental and social costs of blocking large rivers and resettling villages often ignored. But Aswan appears to have been one of the considerable successes. Its direct benefits from irrigation and electricity production are worth about 2 per cent of the country's national income. It has also protected farmers against poor harvests and the residents of the Nile valley against floods, a form of insurance reckoned to be worth another 0.4–1.7 per cent of gross domestic product.

Yet limited water resources, no matter how well managed, cannot always keep pace with a rising population. In terms of the water needed to support its consumption of food and goods, and for drinking and washing, the Middle East as a whole started running short in the mid-1970s.

Politicians in the region, concerned at the accusation that they have left their countries high and dry, fiercely deny that they have run out of water. But by this they generally mean that they have enough water for domestic washing and cooking and to maintain the industrial and agricultural jobs currently in existence. That may be true. But it is a much different concept from the 'water footprint', as well as being a far narrower one, which takes account of how much water each nation consumes, not how much it uses in its own economy. The difference is made up by the net amount of embedded water in imports – how much is sent out of the country minus how much is bought in. Tony Allan, the academic who invented the concept of virtual or embedded water, reckons that with their populations growing and water use rising, Israel and the Palestinian territories ceased to have enough water for self-sufficiency as early as the 1950s, Jordan in the 1960s and Egypt in the 1970s.

Stark warnings that the wars of the future will be fought over water, not oil, have become a commonplace. The dry Middle East, a cockpit of ethnic, religious and political tensions, is the obvious place for them to start. Yet the big rise in population and water use in recent decades has manifestly failed so far to spark widespread conflict.

There has been tension over water in the region for millennia. Gideon, delivering the Israelites from the hands of the Midianites in the Book of Judges in the Old Testament, instructs them to seize the river when overthrowing their oppressors: 'And Gideon sent messengers throughout all mount Ephraim, saying, Come down against the Midianites, and take before them the waters unto Bethbarah and Jordan.' The ancient Egyptians were perennially concerned with preventing the Nile from being diverted or blocked and mulled over the idea of invading Sudan, upstream from Egypt, to secure it. When Britain took over control of Egypt at the end of the nineteenth century, colonial officials had to strike an agreement with Ethiopia to secure their promise not to divert the waters.

The tension between the modern state of Israel and its Arab neighbours has always been liable to flare into conflict, and water seems like a good candidate to act as a recurrent *casus belli*. In the 1950s, not long after its creation, Israel started to build a canal system known as the National Water Carrier. The plan was to transport water from the Jordan river and the Sea of Galilee, the freshwater lake that lies upon it, to the Negev desert. The Arab reaction was less than welcoming: Syrian artillery opened fire on the Israeli construction teams in 1955 and King Hussein of Jordan denounced 'the theft of Arab waters'. After years of attempts at mediation by the US came to nothing, the Arab League devised a plan to divert tributaries of the Jordan inside Syria's borders to foil the Israelis. The proposal prompted air and artillery bombardments by Israel to prevent the waterworks being completed.

Yet since then, despite rising populations and water use and the completion of the National Water Carrier, no water war has broken out. Israel's peace treaty with Jordan in 1994 did include a water-sharing deal. But well before then, the water constraint was eased by the tendency of both countries to start importing water embedded in food. In the three decades after 1970, the value of the food import bill for the Middle East and north Africa increased seventeen-fold. Much of this growth came along with the massive rise in global oil prices in the 1970s, since it gave the oil-producing nations of the region higher export earnings with which to buy their imported food. Between 1970 and 1982, the value of per capita agricultural imports for the region increased tenfold – a big increase even at a time of high inflation. (The need for export earnings to import virtual water is an important one: dry countries in sub-Saharan Africa are actually quite small buyers of virtual water because they have so few exports with which to pay for them.)

The situation for Jordan, a small country with a population of 6 million – a tenfold growth over the past half-century – is particularly dramatic. Eighty per cent of its water needs are met by the import of virtual water, far more even than other dry countries in the region. Each year, more water is now imported into the Middle East and north Africa in virtual form than physically flows into Egypt via the Nile. This, as Tony Allan says, is the kind of water redistribution that engineers could only dream of. Middle Eastern politicians and farmers may regard reliance on imports as evidence of the failure of their agricultural skills, but it makes more sense to see it as a resounding success for trade. Egypt, with a population of about 80 million, is now the world's second-biggest wheat importer, buying about half its grain from abroad. For the country to revert to growing all its own cereals would take about a sixth of the entire water stocks held in the Aswan dam reservoir.

But this does not mean that the Middle East keeps all its own water at home. Jordan and Israel have a thriving export trade selling vegetables, herbs and other high-value agricultural produce to Europe. On the face of it, it seems perverse to import water with one set of crops while sending it abroad with another. In reality, it can be perfectly logical. The weight or value of what can be grown with the same amount of water varies considerably from crop to crop. It takes about a thousand cubic metres of water to grow a ton of vegetables, for example, compared to 1450 cubic metres for a ton of wheat, while a ton of beef uses a striking 42,500 cubic metres of water via the feedstock used to raise cattle. Beef is the biggest single contributor to the flow of virtual water for precisely this reason. It makes up 13 per cent of global virtual water trade compared with 11 per cent for soya beans and 9 per cent for wheat.

And even though beef fetches a higher price per ton than do vegetables, the financial returns on water for farmers in the Middle East are still dramatically different. Vegetables generate 50 US cents per cubic metre of water, wheat 8 cents and beef 5 cents. In countries where the market has been allowed to operate, it has responded. European supermarkets regularly stock herbs from Israel and Jordan. Crops like herbs and vegetables are relatively light on the use of water, and indeed of land, but they use labour quite intensively. They are therefore suitable for dry, densely populated countries with little fertile soil.

China is in a similar situation. Its huge population has placed considerable strain on the country's limited water. Often, the giant Yellow River, in whose valley settled agriculture first started in China, now runs dry before it reaches the sea. But though China's demand for water has gone up rapidly as its people have started eating much more meat, a sign of their rising income, the country has relieved some of the pressure by importing water- and land-intensive crops like soya beans which are used to feed pigs. In return, it exports labour-intensive produce like mushrooms and garlic, not to mention its colossal and profitable sales of manufactured goods, which use relatively little water in their production.

But the pattern of resources flowing from places of abundance to places of shortage is very often violated by the artificial constraints of policy. The world's largest net exporter of virtual water is, bizarrely, Australia, which is the second-driest continent on earth after Antarctica. We will see later just why it is so common for small groups of producers – frequently farmers – to be able to capture government policy and turn it to their own ends. Often it is easier to do this with water than with other resources, since water is frequently either given away free or priced in a peculiar way.

The logic of trade being determined by resources involves the price of that resource reflecting its true value. Countries with a lot of fertile land and not many people, for example, will tend to export land-intensive agricultural produce because land will be relatively cheap. But when resources like water are handed out free, or for different prices to different groups of producers and consumers, those decisions can become distorted.

Australia is a country with a lot of land. But it is also very dry, and has a fragile ecosystem. Nonetheless its export-oriented farmers help to send a net 64 billion tonnes of virtual water out of the country each year. The amount of water for irrigation being taken out of the huge 'Murray–Darling basin', a river system that starts up in tropical Queensland and the high New South Wales mountains and empties into the sea by the southern Australian city of Adelaide, is causing marked environmental damage.

Australia has a relatively sophisticated water trading system. But though it allows farmers to sell water rights among themselves, it severely restricts their ability to sell them to industry and the cities. As a result, Australia continues to export low-value but thirsty crops like rice and cotton while its cities suffer from severe water restrictions. In practice, by giving away its scarce water radically below cost to farmers, Australia is depriving its own cities while subsidizing consumers in the rest of the world.

Except when there is a drought, water rights trade among Australian farmers at about A\$100 per million litres or thousand tonnes. Water rights in the cities trade at ten times that. If there were a free trade in water, many farmers would sell their allocation to the cities rather than, for example, keeping rice fields under water for five months of the year. The country would cease to export net virtual water in such huge quantities. But the political imperative to keep the farming industry alive has so far prevented the market logic of scarcity and abundance being allowed to function. True, Australia's government has announced a plan to buy out some farmers' water rights and leave the water in the river systems instead, but environmental scientists say that it needs to go much further.

Despite the rise in imported virtual water, the same remains true in many parts of the Middle East and north Africa, thanks to governments failing to price water sensibly. The all-time record for spectacular defiance of common sense must go to the government of Saudi Arabia, which elected to use a large underground water aquifer to become, in the early 1990s, the world's sixth-biggest wheat exporter. It pumped up vast amounts of water from the aquifer, which does not refill itself, to create irrigated wheat fields literally out of the desert. Fortunately, relative sanity has since prevailed, and the country has become a big net importer of embedded water.

But the undervaluation of water persists. Many Middle Eastern countries implicitly subsidize the overuse of water by their farmers by maintaining high government support prices for crops while keeping out cheap imports with steep tariffs. They also subsidize credit and energy for farmers. In countries like Iran and Syria, which still have strong limits on trade and retain government control of water rights, the value of exports of water-saving crops like fruit and vegetables barely rose in the twenty years after 1980 while other countries were rapidly expanding theirs. In Morocco, low-value sugar beet and fodder crops have traditionally received special water allocations, together with tariffs protecting them from lower-priced imports. It has been estimated that taking away their tariff protection would cut their net profits by 40 per cent. But those farmers could entirely make up for that loss if they were allowed to sell their water rights to other growers producing higher-value crops. In December 2005, farmers in Tadla in

Morocco, echoing the fourteenth-century peasants of Aix-en-Provence, called a demonstration to argue just that.

Globally, imported virtual water contributes about 16 per cent to the average national water footprint, not a great deal when one considers the huge differences between countries in endowments of water. Without such trade, global cropwater use in growing cereals would be 6 per cent higher – not a negligible saving, but not a dramatic one. Part of this is because of other natural influences like the availability of land and labour, but a good deal is to do with artificial restrictions on letting the market work.

Even in Egypt itself, embedded water imports provide only around a quarter of the country's water footprint. Food security – defined as food self-sufficiency – is a god to which Egyptian politicians are obliged repeatedly to pay homage. The country retains import restrictions and subsidies that prevent it becoming too dependent on the rest of the world for food, even at the cost of using some of its limited water in a highly inefficient fashion.

Around the world, the global food price crisis that began in 2007 has only encouraged this tendency. Rather than governments recognizing the importance of allowing the most efficient producers in the world to exploit their advantages, they have retreated towards growing everything themselves. The Philippines, a crowded and populous country which grows rice expensively and inefficiently on mountain terraces, nonetheless announced its intention to become self-sufficient.

It is easy to understand the political imperative that pushes each country towards doing so. No-one wants to rely on a fickle international market in which prices can rise very suddenly and risk being left without food. Such retreats into self-sufficiency will prevent the specialization that turned Egypt from the granary of the Roman empire to the world's biggest importer of wheat, and in both situations managed to feed huge urban populations with reasonable efficiency and calm.

Like much of the trade that makes up the global economy, embedded water is a market perpetually struggling to break free from impediments both natural and artificial – the cost of transport, the attachment to national self-sufficiency, the inertia that comes from custom and practice and customs and excise. The real question is not why does Egypt import so much of its staple food, but why doesn't it import more?

4. Natural resources

Why are oil and diamonds more trouble than they are worth?

There is a haunting story by John Steinbeck called *The Pearl*, in which Kino, a poor Mexican fisherman, discovers to his terrible cost the destructive power of natural wealth. He finds a giant pearl – not a once-in-a-lifetime but a once-in-a-century gem. 'It is the Pearl of the World,' he declares. His horizons lengthen. He can buy a rifle; he can send his son to school.

But his treasure brings nothing but evil. 'All manner of people grew interested in Kino – people with things to sell and people with favours to ask,' the narrator writes. 'Every man suddenly became related to Kino's pearl, and Kino's pearl went into the dreams, the speculations, the schemes, the plans, the futures, the wishes, the needs, the lusts, the hungers, of everyone, and only one person stood in the way and that was Kino, so that he became curiously every man's enemy. The news stirred up something infinitely black and evil in the town; the black distillate was like the scorpion, or like hunger in the smell of food, or like loneliness when love is withheld.'

The local pearl buyers collude to try to cheat him, pretending that it is of little value. Kino is attacked by unknown figures in the night. He flees with his family to the big city to sell the pearl himself. On the way, thieves follow him and kill his son while hunting for the prize.

Kino's treasure is unique and irreplaceable and becomes more important than life. In the end, it is worth less than nothing. Many countries, being apparently blessed with lucky gifts of rare and precious minerals, also find themselves worse off for having found them. Like the pearl, the discovery of oil or diamonds induces envy and greed, turns traders into thieves and business people into bounty-hunters, encourages rivalry over cooperation and in the end often causes more harm than good to the finder.

The destructive power of gems is particularly perverse. In the final analysis, many of them are valuable only because they are valuable. There is nothing irreplaceable about diamonds. Cubic zirconia jewellery can be made indistinguishable from diamonds to all but an expert eye; gems for industrial use can be created artificially far more cheaply than by mining the natural stone. And the price of diamonds was kept high for decades as they were bought and kept in vaults by a global cartel. When the human race is put on trial, this will be one of the strangest and strongest charges against it: that it valued men's lives less than a gem whose price hung upon nothing but itself, and which was hauled up from the dark recesses of the earth, cut and polished into a jewel of white fire and then returned, unseen, deep underground.

Oil, a central ingredient in modern industrial production, is at least a more sensible mineral over which to fight. Indeed, the resource curse has become a far more important phenomenon in the twentieth and twenty-first centuries as the petroleum-fuelled internal-combustion engine has taken over as the main source of power for transport and manufacture from the coal-fired steam piston and the oat-driven horse.

Until fairly recently the idea of minerals being more trouble than they were worth might have struck many as odd. Few outside a coterie of development economists would have been familiar with the body of work on the 'resource curse' – a blight with an agreeably piratical sound, like the Curse of the Black Pearl that dogged Captain Jack Sparrow in *Pirates of the Caribbean*. Now the pendulum of opinion has begun to swing. The corrupting power of mineral wealth has been graphically shown in movies like *Blood Diamond*, set in the civil war that raged in Sierra Leone in the 1990s and turned it into one of the most deprived nations on earth. When the Saddam Hussein regime fell in Baghdad, one of the first lines of public questioning was how the newly liberated Iraq could avoid the mismanagement of its oil that had characterized so many other Middle Eastern countries.

There is, perhaps, a danger of excessive optimism giving way to unthinking pessimism. Oil and diamonds have indeed often proved to be worth less than nothing for most of the inhabitants of the countries in which they are mined. But some countries have successfully managed them, and not just those that were already rich, peaceful and well-governed before the mineral wealth arrived. 'Extractive industries', as oil, gas and mining are rather prosaically called, have frequently been handled very badly. But they can be managed well.

It seems bizarre that discovering something that is greatly prized should impoverish its finder. But economies, by and large, become rich because they can make and provide goods and services, not because they own a source of basic commodities. And it does not take a gigantic degree of unearned wealth to imperil a country's desire to earn an income even when that income would be greater than its inheritance. The layabout offspring of rich families often end up poorer than the industrious progeny of more modest parents.

Even at times of soaring oil prices, the amount of income generated by mineral resources in a modern, advanced economy remains low. Even for an oil producer like the UK, mineral extraction is only just over 2 per cent of its national income. Norway is often held up as the example of an economy enriched by oil (and, as we shall see, one of the few that has managed it well). It is the world's tenth-biggest oil exporter (outranking Nigeria and Kuwait) and regularly ranks as one of the two or three richest economies on the planet per head of population. Yet Norwegian oil only became of great value as recently as the 1970s, at which point Norway was already a rich economy. And though it is richer than its less fortunate Nordic counterparts such as Sweden, Denmark and Finland, the difference is not dramatic, in the range of 10–20 per cent per head.

Now, the contribution of natural resources is not measured purely in the jobs and income that come from extracting them. If they can provide the first link in an extensive economic supply chain, where more and more value is added as the initial product is processed or used as a single input in a larger process, their discovery can have an impact way beyond their apparent economic contribution. They may in fact do little more than kickstart a process in which they then play a relatively minor role. Peat, a solid, compacted moss that grows slowly in the bogs of Ireland and Scotland, has traditionally been used as a low-value fuel on smoky home fires. Cutting peat has made no-one rich, and never will. But treating barley malt with peat fires and water that has filtered through peat bogs to make Scotch whisky has created a multibillion-pound industry out of a few dozen remote, soggy valleys on the Celtic fringe of Europe.

Conversely, diamonds exported from the mines of west Africa have for centuries been cut not in Africa but in Antwerp or Amsterdam, where the combination of technical skill and reliability outweighed the higher costs. India, and particularly Mumbai, has more recently been taking over as the centre for cutting and polishing gems, but western Africa has yet to become a centre of significant value-added in the diamond industry. As too often, as a later chapter on supply chains demonstrates, the continent has for a variety of reasons struggled to capture anything but the most basic stages of production.

So why are minerals not more useful? First of all, it is in the nature of oil, gas and mining to benefit only a few workers. Most of the countries that have very rapidly reduced poverty did so with labour-intensive mass-production industries providing a large number of low- or medium-paying jobs. The most obvious cases are the east Asian 'tiger economies', starting with Hong Kong, Taiwan and Korea and moving on to Malaysia and now China and Vietnam, and the traditional first step on the ladder of development is to make clothes.

The only capital equipment required for a garment factory is a building and some sewing machines. Most of the rest is down to the skill, time and effort of the workers. But in extractive industries the process tends to be very capital-intensive, employing many more machines than people. Oil and gas extraction generally requires giant, high-technology drills, offshore platforms and vast systems of pipelines operated by a relatively small number of employees.

For countries sufficiently advanced to manufacture their own extractive machinery, this may not matter too much to the economy as a whole. The jobs can be created at one remove in the factories that make the drills, even if the drills themselves require few workers to operate them. But for countries that import much of their machinery, a significant part of the returns on mining disappear abroad with the purchase of capital goods. In countries like these, the benefits accrue to the owners of the equipment and the business and to a relatively small number of workers.

Not only that, but the operation of a big commodity-exporting industry can actually prevent jobs being created in the rest of the economy, a phenomenon known as the Dutch disease. Though it sounds like a blight on elm trees, the malady in fact refers to the fate of the Netherlands in the mid-1970s. The soaring price of oil and gas made the country's gas deposits – unusually easy to get at, being onshore – into a valuable export. Money to buy the gas flooded into the country from all over, and as the dollars, francs, Deutschmarks and yen were changed into guilders, the Dutch national currency, the exchange rate rose. This made other Dutch exports uncompetitive. A thousand guilders' worth of tulips would have cost a London wholesaler £665 in January 1970, but by December 1979 she would have had to shell out £1168.

Essentially, resources devoted to growing tulips, or whatever the rest of the Dutch economy produced, shifted towards gas extraction. And because the gas industry employed many fewer people than tulip-growing did, overall unemployment in the Netherlands actually rose. The effect of higher economic output on employment was more than offset by a shift from labour-intensive to capital-intensive industries.

Finding natural resources is rather like winning a big cash prize on a lottery. Thereafter it hardly seems worth working, given how much you have earned by sitting there. But in the longer run, you may in fact be better off by continuing to work, particularly if it means that income and skills continue to rise. And almost certainly you would be happier than sitting around in a cloud of cannabis smoke and self-loathing like the disaffected unemployed youth of the late 1970s Netherlands, gripped by the ennui of those for whom, in this case quite literally, nothing they can do is worth doing. (Or, at any rate, no-one will pay them for it.)

The pattern repeated itself with much worse effects in developing countries, like Zambia. In country after country, the discovery of minerals or a surge in their price led to a collapse in agriculture, as farm products – which compete on tough international markets – became unprofitable. Farmers moved to the cities to look for manufacturing jobs. But since industry was also displaced or discouraged by a high exchange rate and inflated costs, those jobs did not exist.

Moreover, the effect of a job-light development model has worrying implications in some countries for reasons beyond the purely economic. The oil-rich Middle East, for example, is full of young men living in economies that appear fairly successful. Saudi Arabia, for example, has a per capita income of nearly $15,000, in the top third of global rankings. Yet its true unemployment rate is estimated at up to 25 per cent and is concentrated among the young. And since its demographic profile is weighted towards youth – half of Saudi males are 22 or under – the country has a large and fractious constituency of the type that has proved vulnerable to the appeal of radical Islamism.

Big increases in oil-producing countries' income rarely translate into sustained catch-up. The first great oil shocks in the 1970s involved a large shift of income away from oil-importing countries like Japan and most of Europe and towards oil exporters, notably the Middle East. The Arabs had the rest of the world over a barrel. It was inevitable that oil importers would take a hit on their real incomes. Some, such as Germany, where unions and management agreed to share the burden by holding down wages and prices, coped with it better than others, like Britain, where a destructive round of leapfrog wage claims took hold. But the oil exporters did not use the shift in prices to catch up the incomes of the importers. By 2000, Saudi national income per head was still below that of countries like the Czech and Slovak republics, which had been communist command economies a mere fifteen years before, and less than half that of the western European average. A lottery bonanza is not a substitute for a dynamic, innovative economy.

As part of Libya's rehabilitation in the eyes of Western countries after the September 11 attacks, Colonel Mu'ammer Gaddafi, its ex-pariah leader, called in outside consultants. They included Michael Porter, a Harvard academic specializing in the 'competitiveness' of economies, to advise him on what he could do to diversify the Libyan economy. One consultant reportedly described Libya as 'a mess'. With price and wage levels too high, because of the oil, to be competitive in manufacturing, Libya's economy has struggled to find something else it can do.

Appropriately enough, one of the few oil states that seems to have diversified successfully is one without much oil of its own. Dubai, one of the United Arab Emirates, has generally been much less dependent on oil than other Gulf states. Having long developed a role as a trading post, with a good deal of smuggling of gold and other contraband to India on the side, Dubai managed to expand this into becoming a banking and finance hub. It has added tourism and even a cluster of biotechnology research from scratch. The emirate has dealt with the uncompetitiveness problem by bringing in cheap temporary workers from India, Pakistan and Bangladesh who have an income and living conditions way below those of the pampered Dubai citizens.

But the resource curse can trip up even economies that are making valiant attempts to diversify. The Dutch tulip kings are not the only flower-growers to have suffered from the Dutch disease. Perhaps one of the most extreme examples happened a few years ago in Zambia. The republic of Zambia was built on copper – 'born with a copper spoon in its mouth' as the saying went. Travellers arriving at the national airport in Lusaka are greeted by a fountain made out of a huge chunk of copper ore, and a giant map of Africa made out of burnished copper hangs on the wall of the arrivals hall just to make the point absolutely clear.

Like many African countries, Zambia's management of its copper resources after independence was a sad history of inept resource nationalism. By 1970 it had taken control of the copper mines from Anglo-American, the mining company that, fulfilling at least half its name, is listed jointly on the stock exchanges in London and Johannesburg. Zambia then proceeded to squander much of the proceeds from rising commodity prices in the 1970s and seriously to mismanage the mines themselves. Konkola Deep, a mine which extracts copper from the second-biggest deposit in the world, drops a kilometre and a half underground through strata of sodden rock. Hundreds of thousands of cubic metres of water have to be pumped out of the mine each day to keep it functioning. But under state ownership, maintenance and investment were neglected. By the 1990s, when Kenneth Kaunda, the first president, had finally been ousted from office, copper prices were low and it could only attract bids at a knock-down price with a promise of a sixty-year tax holiday. The buyer? Anglo-American.

By the time the global copper price soared again in 2006, buoyed by demand from China, Anglo had sold the mines on to a variety of foreign owners, including companies from China, Canada and India. The riches lying deep in the Zambian earth are staggering. At the prices prevailing in mid-2006, the copper deposits under Konkola Deep were worth $1.4 trillion. Had it been free and straightforward rather than expensive and complex to extract, that would have been enough to pay off a third of America's national debt. But Zambia itself got a rather small slice of the benefit. As the mines were foreign-owned, the profits from the mining operations left Zambia to be distributed to shareholders in London, India and Beijing, in the latter case the Chinese government. Because of the strikingly generous deals needed to attract investors when the copper price was low, the companies paid little tax on profits and very low mineral royalties on the value of what they mined.

Moreover, they used largely imported machinery and equipment. The Chinese owners even brought in their own Chinese miners, much of whose wages were saved to send home. In other words, the majority of the value of copper mining in Zambia was most likely leaving the country. Nonetheless, perhaps because of speculative pressures in a fairly small and thin foreign exchange market, the national currency, the kwacha, rose by 70 per cent against other currencies.

Zambians had rightly been urged by rich-nation aid donors, development economists and all and sundry to diversify their exports and rely less on copper. They had responded with an industry growing flowers, fruit and vegetables to fly to European supermarkets, a model similar to the east African country of Kenya. Suddenly, travellers' initial impressions of the Zambian economy changed. Before they even landed to see the copper ore fountain at the airport, passengers arriving at Lusaka could see vast circles of bright green scattered over the brown landscape around the capital where mangetout, roses and green beans were being grown for shoppers in London and Madrid. The Zambezi river that marks Zambia's southern border also provided the base for a growing tourist industry. Robert Mugabe's disastrous rule in neighbouring Zimbabwe had at least one good side-effect for Zambia: European tourists increasingly preferred to see the thundering splendour of the Victoria Falls from the Zambian side.

Suddenly, these hard-won gains were under threat from a soaring currency. The value of export earnings, being in dollars, fell. The costs of domestic farm-workers and hotel staff, being in kwacha, stayed the same, and the result was a big hit on profit margins. In other words, the rise in the copper price and hence the currency meant that a collection of brand-new high-value labour-intensive export businesses whose benefits were mainly paid to Zambians in kwacha were being threatened by the long-established presence of dangerous, dirty mines where profits, capital investments and some wages left the country to be handed over to foreigners in dollars, pounds, rupees and yuan. A more poignant example of the Dutch disease would be hard to invent.

The Dutch disease is a purely economic manifestation of the resource curse, where a mineral resource crowds out potentially more profitable activity in the economy. But there is a political dimension to the overbearing dominance of a single limited commodity as well. And if anything, the politics has the potential to be even more inimical to development than the economics. We noted earlier in the chapter that a country does not, by and large, get rich having a mineral resource and nothing else. So it is highly counterproductive if oil or diamonds do not just make other activities unprofitable but change the entire mindset of the country and the motives that spur people and businesses to engage in the economy. Oil and diamonds frequently lead to bad government and war.

The great paradox of capitalism is that destruction brings creation. Companies trying to put each other out of business in fact bring many more businesses into existence and people into jobs as they strive for better technology, for more efficient ways of operating, for a smarter way of pricing their product – for anything that will win them more customers and give them an edge over the competition. But this only works if certain rules of the game are observed. Competition has to be based on agreed norms and within set boundaries, rather than aiming to win at all costs. Football, as the philosopher Bertrand Russell once observed, would not be a desirable sport if defeated teams were put to death or left to starve. (Admittedly, though, there would be fewer accusations of a lack of 110 per cent effort as the teacups flew at half-time, and it would surely rake in millions on pay-per-view.)

Nor would it produce great football if teams could use any means necessary against the opposition to score a goal – gouging, maiming, knives, cudgels, assault vehicles, calling in airstrikes. Similarly, business creates benefits when there is fair competition over products and pricing within the law such that the most efficient business wins. Consumers do not benefit when companies are free to do whatever they want to get a competitive edge, including cheating, stealing, bribing, intimidating and assaulting.

One of the problems with a limited natural resource is that, once possession has been gained by whatever means, it is hard to challenge. Unless another deposit of the same mineral can be found within the same economy, it is often insulated from competition. Mineral resources often give a return far above what it costs to produce them. This is because, unlike conventional economic activity, supply is limited by nature and hence excess profits cannot be competed away. The state oil company – and many oil companies in developing countries are nationalized – may be making gigantic profits from its refinery, extracting oil at a cost of $1 a barrel and selling it on the world market at $100 a barrel. But no private operator can open a rival oilfield in the same country and undercut the incumbent unless there is a new oilfield to find. High oil prices will induce companies to go searching for new fields, of course, or make it economically viable to extract oil from existing but inaccessible deposits, but the process of discovery and extraction is slow and expensive.

In economics terminology, the oil companies are earning 'economic rent', which refers not to a slum landlord putting the frighteners on his tenants but to a producer being paid much more than they actually need to continue production because other companies are not allowed to compete away the profit. Controlling a resource for which there is a permanent ready market and little or no competition and which requires nothing more than keeping the drills going should produce one of the greatest benefits that all monopolists crave – a quiet life. But when a government gets involved, to keep it that way requires spending enough on armies and presidential guards to prevent anyone else seizing control. This kind of competition does not benefit the country as a whole. The economy becomes a fight, and frequently an illegal and violent one, over the control and benefits from a given resource, not an open competition to build a better mousetrap.

Extractive industries are notorious for their corruption. They hang out, as it were, with the wrong kind of company. There is a theory about currency known as Gresham's law, which states that the circulation of counterfeit money eventually results in the legitimate notes and coins being hoarded. If you know your gold sovereign is genuine, you will not want to use it as currency in a transaction where you might end up with fake coins in change. The bad drives out the good. The same can be true with companies. It is not the best companies for the job that get oil contracts, necessarily, but those willing to bribe, particularly since they are so hard to challenge once they have the contract. And so honest and decent companies find it hard to compete. Oil companies – including those of Western democracies – have, over the decades, done some pretty repellent things to keep the stuff flowing, and to the lasting shame of their governments they have often had official backing.

Even in rich, stable democracies where the revenue is collected honestly, the distribution of oil revenue can cause tension. Alaska, for example, is sufficiently rich in oil and gas that it has no income tax and in fact hands out a dividend to each citizen, which over the past decade averaged around 1500 dollars a year. Periodic arguments have broken out, one of which went all the way to the Supreme Court of the United States, about whether recent arrivals in Alaska were entitled to as much of a bonus as long-term residents. It is perhaps fortunate that to get the hand-out you have to move to a cold, remote state where it is dark for more than twenty hours a day in winter, which presumably deters a large number of bounty-hunters. If oil was discovered in sunny southern California and the petroleum pay-outs started, the western seaboard might start to crumble into the Pacific from the weight of Americans flooding into San Diego with their hands out for free dollars.

And in countries where the weakness of democracy and government makes it easy arbitrarily to raise taxes and steal the money or use it to buy favours, or simply to cream off revenue outright, the struggles become extraordinarily destructive and all-pervading. There is nothing so dangerous to a nervous government as the rapid rise of a potential new power-base funded by a dependable stream of money outside state control.

When the Organization of the Petroleum Exporting Countries (Opec) was formed in the 1970s, it aimed to extend the monopoly of oil over the whole world – to create a global cartel. But even at the time there were some who foresaw the result. Juan Pablo Pérez Alfonso, the Venezuelan who was Opec's first head, predicted, sadly, unexpectedly and all too accurately: 'Ten years from now, twenty years from now, oil will bring us ruin. It is the devil's excrement. We are drowning in the devil's excrement.'

As we will see at more length in a later chapter, the dominance of oil and gas in the Russian economy has helped to weaken democracy in the country, and seems likely to keep things that way. And it is no coincidence that the four longest-serving rulers in Africa, all autocrats, are from oil zones. Their governments do little more than keep themselves in power, being frequently embroiled in armed conflict, and certainly deliver very little to their citizens. They are what the academic Ricardo Soares de Oliveira calls 'successful failed states'.

Mineral resources can also provoke various other kinds of destructive competition: from rebels within, from states without and between owners and workers. Many civil wars founder on the inability of one side or another to keep supplying itself, even if it controls part of the country. The South lost the American Civil War partly because the supply lines of food and armaments to its military were so stretched. Both sides in the English Civil War in the seventeenth century encountered rioting opposition from locals tired of being continually shaken down for food and money. But civil wars funded by natural resources that can be sold outside the country can continue pretty much indefinitely.

Historically, resource-rich countries, particularly those that have other characteristics that are associated with conflict, such as poverty and low growth, are much more likely to break out in civil war. Jonas Savimbi, the leader of the rebel movement UNITA in Angola, ran what was in effect an alternative state in the jungle for nearly twenty years. He fought a civil war that began as soon as Angola gained independence from Portugal in 1975. He continued fighting, with occasional breaks for botched elections and failed peace accords, until his death in 2002. It was a remarkable achievement of organization and leadership. In a different life Savimbi might have made an excellent corporate chief executive, though probably not one well known for harmonious relations with his workforce. He did receive large amounts of aid from abroad, being skilled at playing the Soviet Union and the US off against each other and receiving funding from both. But the mainstay of his operation, which explains why it outlasted the money from Cold War paymasters, was his control over the diamonds of rural Angola.

Diamonds, in particular, are a near-perfect mineral with which to fund freelance rebel movements or alternative governments. They act almost like a global currency, being small and light and holding their value well. Despite the attempts of an international campaign, the Kimberley Process, to register their source, they are also very hard to trace. The Sierra Leone civil war dragged on for a decade from 1991 after the Revolutionary United Front, the main rebel movement, gained control of diamond mines and used the wealth to fund their operations. Gold is heavier but also useful. Oil is bulkier and harder to extract but, like Visa or Mastercard, also widely accepted.

Minerals do not just help prolong civil wars: they also attract unwelcome attention from outside. One of the misfortunes of the beleaguered Democratic Republic of Congo (formerly part of Zaire, which was a byword for African corruption and mismanagement) is to have deposits of coltan, a mineral used in the manufacture of mobile phones. It also has diamonds, copper and gold. Several countries, including Uganda, were widely reported as having sent troops over the border to plunder the resources during the DRC's civil war between 1997 and 2003. Uganda's protestations of innocence were not helped by the fact that it started exporting minerals not actually found in nature in Uganda.

Another useful and hence disastrous aspect of minerals is that governments with them find it easier to borrow. It is hard to seize the assets of a state that defaults on payment, though some 'vulture funds' suing Latin American and African nations for defaulted sovereign debt have had a go. So lenders to governments in effect usually have to extend credit without collateral. They are much keener to lend to those they know will have minerals that can be sold for hard currency. In fact, in some cases borrowing has been collateralized directly on the oil revenues themselves, meaning that the foreign lender can seize the proceeds to ensure repayment.

Many developing countries have built up spectacular debt burdens from borrowing recklessly from reckless lenders, but it is hard to top the oil producers. By the time Saddam Hussein's regime fell in 2003, Iraq had accumulated and defaulted on debt somewhere between two and four times as big as the entire economy, estimated to equal around $6000 for each Iraqi. Getting the government financially back on to its feet involved the biggest debt relief in history. Similarly, while dozens of African countries had their debts to other governments and official institutions like the World Bank written off as part of an international scheme, oil-rich Nigeria's debt was by far the largest. It needed an $18 billion write-down to give the government financial room to move.

Those working in the mines, at least if they have the right to organize collectively, also often spend a lot of time trying to divert a higher proportion of the revenue towards themselves. If the workers know that the company is making money hand over fist, the incentive for them to try and grab some of it for themselves becomes much higher. Trade unions that can halt production, particularly while mineral prices are high, are in a similar position to bandits blocking a mountain pass. This applies in spades if the mineral produced, such as oil or coal, is essential to the running of the wider domestic economy.

It is not surprising that across history and the world, mining frequently produces the most militant trade unions. Harold Macmillan, the Conservative prime minister of Britain in the first half of the 1960s, used to say there were three organizations he made it a rule never to antagonize: the Roman Catholic Church, the Brigade of Guards and the National Union of Mineworkers. Not until 1984 did Margaret Thatcher risk taking on the coal miners. By that time the British trade union movement was much weakened by the hollowing out of manufacturing and there was a bigger supply of foreign coal to replace domestic output. Even then, the miners' strike, which dragged on for a year between 1984 and 1985 and turned into one of the decisive political victories of Thatcher's decade as prime minister, was a close-run thing.

The US trade union movement, though much smaller, was similarly built around the foundations of coal, copper and silver miners. Their closest modern equivalents are in Chile. Not even a quarter-century of trade union suppression under the dictatorship of Augusto Pinochet could eliminate the ability of the country's copper miners to scoop up a big chunk of the increased income that comes from a rise in global copper prices. Every big rise in the price brings a ritualized confrontation when the unions threaten to down tools, and sometimes do so, in a game of chicken with the government. Neither side wants mining to come to a halt, but each knows there is a lot of revenue to be bargained over by threatening to stop it.

Even at a much more removed level, tanker drivers for oil companies in the UK have traditionally been paid much more than comparable drivers in other industries, though the degree of skill and danger involved is identical. Indeed, the cost to the country and the employer that oil tanker drivers could inflict became evident in the fuel protests of 2000. A handful of drivers nearly brought the economy to a halt by going on a wildcat strike. The great baggage train of the economy was held up by a few dozen bandits at a mountain pass.

Digging and drilling also often go together with sex and drugs, and not in a good way. Mining and prostitution have long been mutually reinforcing bedfellows. Miners are usually relatively well-paid men isolated from wives and families, and hence given to concurrent sexual relationships, including with prostitutes. In developing countries in particular, this increasingly means they are vulnerable to HIV–Aids. Areas like the Zambian copper-belt are suffused with prostitution and infection. The bars are full of girls as young as twelve selling their bodies for a few dollars, generally with a dollar or two premium for not using a condom.

And the epidemic of crystal methamphetamine use in the US has been particularly acute among oil and gas rig workers. Crystal meth, it appears, provides a release from the boredom of being stuck out on platforms in the Gulf of Mexico for weeks on end.

Sometimes, accidents of history and geography provide neat little tests of just how corrupting minerals can be. São Tomé and Principe, a tiny two-island nation off the west coast of Africa, discovered oil in 1997–9. Even more than for the US and Argentina, there was a near-perfect control group for a natural experiment in the form of the nearby country of Cape Verde. It had many similarities to São Tomé and Principe: it had been a Portuguese colony, had also been made independent in the same year (1975), had experienced a similar first government after independence and had also achieved its first free democratic elections sixteen years after independence in 1991. Migration and other links between the two maintained cultural similarity.

The results of the oil discovery in São Tomé and Principe were enough to make a development economist hug herself with joy. They conformed precisely to the predictions of the resource curse. A series of surveys of the public showed that, after announcements were made about the discovery of oil between 1997 and 1999, the perception of corruption compared to that in oil-less Cape Verde increased by between 21 and 38 per cent depending on the subject covered (the allocation of education and state jobs, buying votes in elections and so forth). The highest increases were in those areas most closely connected with being in power and thus being able to gain control of the oil and secure future economic rent.

Like Zambia, São Tomé and Principe also received only a small fraction of the value of its find. In this case, it was not because the government had tried to pump the oil itself, since it was only discovered by American oil companies prospecting off its coast, but because it naively signed generous deals with those companies without realizing its own bargaining power.

The possession of natural resources sounds like an unremitting tale of woe. But some countries have successfully overcome the paradox of plenty and remained immune to both the political and the economic Dutch disease. To do this, two things need to happen. One, the revenue deriving from the resource needs to be managed in a way that does not distort the rest of the economy. Two, the revenue needs to be sufficiently ring-fenced from acquisitive interests and the threat of political expropriation.

Neither of these is easy. Countries that achieve them tend to be already rich from other means, so the revenue is not the only prize on offer and other industries are sufficiently profitable and flexible to adapt. In Norway, oil revenue above a certain level is kept in a national oil stabilization fund, a giant state savings account. The money is held in dollars to prevent sudden surges of upward pressure on the Norwegian krone and released for spending according to projections of Norway's future wealth and future needs. Chile, which is the world's largest copper producer, has a similar system.

These funds need be treated like endowments, not windfalls. Spending should flow at a rate that could be maintained into the long term. To return to our lottery analogy, this would be a bit like putting a big win in the bank and spending the interest.

The money should where possible be spent on making the rest of the economy more competitive. Rather than handing out permanent subsidies to offset the effect on the exchange rate from the mineral exports, a more sensible route is to improve infrastructure, education and overall productive capacity. In developing countries, where such things tend to be in short supply and are often a severe constraint on further economic development, such spending could mean that, by making other markets work better, the mineral resource is actually a positive for the rest of the economy. Higher value-added industries, because they compete on quality as well as price, are also less susceptible to movements in the exchange rate, at least in the short term.

Some middle-income countries, such as Malaysia and Indonesia, both of which have substantial oil and gas deposits, have managed to limit the distortion of national politics and the economy by natural resources. In their cases, autocratic but relatively stable governments saw their personal interests as vaguely coterminous with the wealth of their citizens. They therefore didn't make the mistake of regarding their economies as zero-sum games. Malaysia has managed to spend its oil revenue according to a national development plan rather than spraying it around at random or to buy political favours – a policy that a more desperate or unstable government might be prepared to renege on. They were also relatively successful economies before oil arrived.

Far more remarkable are the few countries that started off with little but a single natural resource and made a success out of it. The most dramatic is Botswana, whose purpose in life appears to be to act as an exception to most rules in Africa and indeed elsewhere. Its remarkable achievement is to have used diamond wealth in a sensible, constructive fashion, allowing it neither to stop the economy growing nor to poison national politics.

Botswana became independent from Britain in 1966 during the great clattering-down of empire in Africa. While most of the rest of the continent succumbed to civil war, inflation, corruption, disease, crippling debt and economic disaster, Botswana, astonishingly, went on to be the fastest-growing economy in the world over the next thirty years. It grew faster than the US or Japan, faster than South Korea, faster than Hong Kong or Taiwan or China.

At the heart of Botswana's successful management of its diamond wealth is a revenue-sharing agreement with De Beers, the company that for a long while ran the world's diamond market. De Beers digs up the diamonds and Botswana keeps a portion of the revenue. The way the arrangement is structured gives De Beers sufficient confidence that it will be honoured for them to keep ploughing investment into the mines to keep them functioning. For Botswana it provides the security of a given amount of income, and the knowledge that it will share in the windfall gain from any rise in the global diamond price while being insulated against falls.

One of the things working in Botswana's favour, ironically enough, is that the diamonds are hard to get at. As in South Africa, they are buried a long way underground. By contrast, the diamonds in troubled west African countries like Sierra Leone are alluvial gems that can be picked up by panning the beds of rivers. The process of collecting alluvial diamonds may be labour-intensive rather than the capital-intensive business of drilling down for diamonds buried deep, but the workforce is rarely happy as a result. Harvesting alluvial diamonds is all too easy an operation for any gang of armed thugs capable of defending a few miles of riverbank and capturing enough prisoners to do the panning at gunpoint. A much more stable authority is needed to run an extraction operation for diamonds from mines as challenging as Botswana's. In practical terms, only a highly skilled privately owned foreign company like De Beers had the expertise actually to dig the diamonds out.

But while the deep-down diamonds helped, geology by itself is not destiny. There are a number of oil regimes (Nigeria, Angola, Sudan) which relied and indeed still rely on foreign oil companies to extract the devil's excrement. They still spectacularly mismanaged the proceeds.

The peculiarity of Botswana has attracted a lot of attention from political scientists and economists wondering why it is such a success and why its success is such an anomaly. Looking over the array of rationalizations that has been produced, it appears to be a struggle to keep such explanations from slipping towards tautology. Botswana is a success because it followed the right policies; Botswana is a success because it had better politicians or political institutions than other African nations; Botswana is a success because it was successful.

What seems very clear is that Botswana's success did not come principally because it was spectacularly lucky in the political, legal and social institutions it inherited from colonial history. Some highly successful economies such as Hong Kong had few natural resources but had colonial inheritances that turned out to be far more precious: the rule of law, fairly good infrastructure and a relatively well-educated population. In Hong Kong's case, that was partly because a business class formerly based in Shanghai ended up there after fleeing communism.

Botswana had none of those things. When it gained independence from the British empire in 1966 it had 12 kilometres of paved road, twenty-two university graduates and 100 people who had been educated to secondary school level. Indeed, because the British were unaware of the presence of diamonds, they devoted very little time or resources to the country, regarding it as a buffer between their other African colonial possessions in the region and the German and Portuguese colonies that flanked them.

Nor was it free of potential ethnic rivalry. Contrary to popular belief that it only has one tribe, Botswana in fact has several – though some academics claim they have given the country a comparatively benign inheritance through a helpful tradition of questioning and criticizing their traditional chiefs.

Hopes for the new country, which was landlocked and bordered apartheid South Africa and white-ruled Rhodesia, were not high. A British government report on Botswana's future in 1960 stated that it had 'dismal economic prospects . . . based on vague hopes of agriculture, salt and coal'.

Nonetheless it made a whole string of good decisions where other countries made bad ones. Sound political institutions, including the rule of law, if not multiparty democracy, managed to develop alongside the exploitation of diamond wealth rather than existing before it.

Seretse Khama, Botswana's first president, and his associates made a series of textbook moves. They created a national fund for the diamond wealth rather than fostering ethnic divisions by allowing tribes to appropriate the proceeds for themselves. They mined the diamonds slowly in order to match the capacity of the country to spend the proceeds wisely. (De Beers actually wanted to dig them out faster.) They chose projects for the fund in strict order of what economic return they were likely to produce. Khama even turned down an offer to prioritize the construction of the street that would pass by the presidential residence, saying that roads should be built in order of national priority. One of the few truly great leaders of post-independence Africa, Khama nearly didn't make it to the presidency at all: shamefully, the British had removed him from his previous post as tribal chief, fearing that his interracial marriage to a white Londoner would antagonize apartheid South Africa.

Rather than turn diamonds into a zero-sum game where De Beers' gain is Botswana's loss, the revenue-sharing plan has ensured that both benefit. De Beers gets predictability of income and the confidence that political interference will not interrupt its revenues. Botswana gets the diamonds mined honestly and skilfully and can plan on the basis of the diamond wealth it will receive.

De Beers is not bankrupted by having to buy expensive 'political risk insurance' against a sudden change of policy. Botswana does not fear that De Beers will one day without warning pack up and go.

By binding itself into a tough agreement with De Beers, Botswana showed that it was serious about the way it would manage its resources. It made what economists would call a 'credible pre-commitment'. It bound itself to the mast. In Homer's epic poem, Odysseus had himself tied to the mast of his ship before passing the island of the Sirens so he could hear them singing without being tempted to divert his ship onto the rocks of the island and suffer destruction and death. He knew from stories of the Sirens' bewitching songs that, while he had no wish to succumb to temptation, the only way he could avoid it was forcibly to prevent himself doing so in advance.

Botswana has now become rich and powerful enough in the relationship to start influencing more of its terms without fear of driving De Beers or other foreign investors away. In recent years, it has pulled more of the supply chain into the country by negotiating for De Beers to set up local operations sorting, cutting and polishing rough stones in return for being able to continue mining in Botswana.

By contrast, neighbouring Zambia, which first pushed out foreign investors and then mismanaged its mines, is in a much weaker bargaining position. Rather than being able to dictate terms as can Botswana, it was only after much deliberation that it has gingerly made a modest increase to its minuscule mineral royalties, taking back some of the gains from the foreign private investors who have been receiving so much of the income from its copper. The Zambian nationalization of copper after independence was politically attractive and appealed to a sense of redistributive justice. But over time it turned out to be unwise. Zambia went for short-term gain, found it could not sustain it and ended up harming itself. If you are going to push out international mining or oil companies when the mood takes you, you had better be sure that they will always need you more than you need them.

Botswana is not an economic paradise, and not just because of its stratospheric HIV rate. While it has avoided the political Dutch disease and developed some degree of supply chain integration for diamonds, the rest of the economy remains unimpressive. Unemployment and inequality are both high. It has not developed much else other than diamonds – it has just exploited diamonds very well. Still, that is enough to give the average Botswanan an income more than six times higher than that of the nearby Zambians. Not every country can emulate Botswana, because not every country has diamonds. But if every African country with a mineral resource exploited it as well as has Botswana, the continent would be vastly better off.

Two problems arise with trying to replicate Botswana's success. One, most governments simply refuse to bind themselves to the mast. Two, particularly in a continent like Africa with recent memories of domination by colonial powers, it is close to impossible for an outsider to come in and force them to.

Knowing what the right policies are does not mean it is straightforward to ensure they are implemented. During the 1990s and into the new millennium, a new consensus and a new campaign grew rapidly to try to obviate the resource curse in developing countries. It focused both on payers and on payees of mineral royalties, taxes and extraction fees.

The first step was transparency – trying to work out what size the pie was and prevent slices of it being handed out secretly in bribes. On the payer side, a campaign run by non-governmental organizations (NGOs) called Publish What You Pay was aimed at making oil and mining companies disclose their royalty and fee payments to governments. On the recipient side there was a new drive led by official aid donors such as the UK, known as the Extractive Industries Transparency Initiative, to encourage governments to act less like Angola and more like Botswana.

The second was to institute a broad framework governing how mineral resources should be spent, preferably involving a national fund based on the principles described above. An important part of the process was that the fund should be carefully monitored by local NGOs and, where necessary, outsiders like the World Bank.

But many countries simply refused to accept the principles. They are, after all, sovereign countries that can determine their own fates. And of course, mineral wealth gives them more power to do so, which is how we got here in the first place. Even for countries over whom the outside world had more leverage, the problem arose, as it often does, that trying to buy or force reform from abroad often fails. In one flagship project partly financed by the World Bank, an oil pipeline was built hundreds of miles across the remote deserts of the west African country of Chad to an oil terminal on the coast in neighbouring Cameroon. A certain portion of revenue from the oil sales was to be put into a transparently administered 'future generations' fund and most of the rest earmarked for health and education spending.

But Chad has shown few signs of emulating Botswana. Well-meaning World Bank officials are often no match for a determined government, particularly one unconstrained by the presence of much political opposition or scrutiny from domestic NGOs. After the pipeline opened, Chad's government repeatedly bypassed the provisions of the revenue agreement, shifting spending into military and security categories. The president declared a state of emergency that allowed him to spend the oil revenues as he wished. Eventually, in 2008, the World Bank threw up its hands and withdrew from the project.

It was to examine such tricky issues that the bank itself had hosted a protracted debate known as the Extractive Industries Review, which sought to assess the ability of developing countries to enrich themselves by exploiting oil, gas and mining. Sadly the review served as a clear display of the irreconcilable gulfs of opinion on the subject rather than a meeting of minds. Its review ran from 2000 to 2004 under the chairmanship of Emil Salim, an elderly Indonesian who had once been environment minister under the dictatorial President Suharto.

The review ended up recommending that the bank phase out funding coal and oil projects altogether. Given the influence of the US and EU over the World Bank, and the importance of

American and European oil companies, together with pressure from developing countries' governments for the bank to remain involved, that was never going to be adopted by the bank's management. But it reflected views expressed in a series of heated discussions at regional forums. Many development campaigners and academics argued that there could not be a sufficient guarantee that the resource curse could be overcome. There was simply no evidence whatsoever that extractives could systematically be relied upon to enrich the poor.

You can easily say what policies need to be followed. But unless you have the institutions to impose those policies and defend them, knowing what the right policies are is of limited use. And however it is that institutions evolve, it is not easy trying to force them from the outside. Almost by definition, resource-rich governments very often find themselves powerful enough to avoid such attempts to influence them.

Western oil and mining companies are easier for campaigners and Western governments to go after. Requirements can be imposed on them by legislation, and they care about the potential risk to their reputations from being involved in disastrous projects, as they have found from becoming embroiled in the violent politics of Nigeria's delta region. But Western companies are not the only buyers in town. A big new player, China, has emerged and shows few signs of playing by the same rules.

While no Western company would openly pump oil out of Sudan, given the massacre in Darfur and assorted human rights abuses, China has had no such scruples. Beijing makes the not unreasonable point that it is only doing what Western companies used to do before newfangled ideas like Publish What You Pay came along. In any case, Beijing says with some justification, it is forced into difficult countries because most of the existing oil sources have already been stitched up by the US and Europe.

In Steinbeck's *The Pearl*, after Kino and his wife have been attacked in the night but before their son has been killed, she pleads with him to throw it back in the sea. 'This thing is evil,' she cries. 'This pearl is like a sin! It will destroy us. Throw it away,

Kino. Let us break it between stones. Let us bury it and forget the place . . . It has brought evil.' He refuses. 'This is our one chance,' he says. 'Our son must go to school. He must break out of the pot that holds us in.'

Kino ought to have been right. But he was not. Neither, most of the time, are the countries that think they are blessed by resources: they find that a jewel which awakens envy, greed and hatred turns out to be not a jewel beyond price but a jewel worth less than nothing.

5. Religion

Why don't Islamic countries get rich?

The idea that Islamic countries fail to get rich became a staple concern of the international commentariat after the September 11 attacks on the US. The hijackers came from affluent families in a relatively well-off country, Saudi Arabia. But economic and state failure in Muslim Afghanistan had provided a headquarters for al-Qaeda, the fundamentalist organization that directed them. And the apparent lack of jobs and opportunities in the Islamic world, creating potential armies of angry young men, gave new resonance to an old concern.

But Afghanistan is at the least an extreme example – and in the recent past, it would appear, it is an exception. Over the past few decades, there has been no systematic tendency for the economies of Islamic countries to grow more slowly than those of countries dominated by other religions. So are there any questions to be answered here at all?

In fact, there are. Why is the performance of Islamic countries so uneven? Why, despite their relative success over the past fifty years, did they often arrive at the twentieth century poorer than those dominated by other religions? And even more intriguingly, why, during the thirteen centuries of Islam's existence, had the economies of its societies initially outperformed others before they fell behind?

And the issue of Islam and growth is part of a much broader line of enquiry about the effect of religious belief on economic performance. Are some faiths simply better than others for growth? Does Mammon lurk behind the mask of Christ, or Mohammed, or Buddha? Which prophets are most profitable?

A careful scrutiny of holy books and balance sheets down the centuries suggests the relationship is complex. The content of religious dogma or governing philosophies has not by itself proved to be a systematic impediment to economic success. Faith seems to exercise its influence on growth in a subtler, less deterministic way: rather than the theology itself, it has more to do with the actions of priests, politicians, monarchs and bureaucrats exploiting religious doctrine to pursue thoroughly temporal goals of wealth and power.

The argument about which gods are good for growth has built up a fairly lengthy pedigree of its own. The dynastic origin of this particular debate is *The Protestant Ethic and the Spirit of Capitalism*, a 1905 work by a German sociologist, Max Weber. Weber contended that the growth of a modern capitalist economy in early modern Europe, particularly in the sixteenth and seventeenth centuries, was associated with the low-church Calvinist Protestantism that emerged from the sixteenth-century Reformation and created such movements as English Puritanism. He went on to argue that the cultures of India, China and the Islamic world had proved inimical to capitalism. Weber's writings have spawned such an extended clan of contributions that it is worth examining the paterfamilias in some detail.

Weber is often misrepresented, which is not to say he was right. He kicked off with some analyses of the local Grand Duchy of Baden, which showed that Protestants were generally more successful than Catholics in business. (They were also rather better represented in the liberal professions and the higher perches of public life, so it is a bit suspicious from the start that he focused so intently on the private sector, but let that pass.) Going back and looking at the writings of Puritan thinkers after the Reformation, Weber claimed that Calvinist religious belief, while not causing capitalism in a simplistic way, helped inspire the mindset that encouraged it to flourish. This, he thought, explained the economic success of Protestant countries like the Netherlands and England.

Weber's account of the emergence of the Protestant ethic is almost impossible to disprove, as it would mean spending a large amount of time with seventeenth-century Puritans and a psychiatric diagnostic manual. Calvinism taught that entry into heaven was predestined. Those not chosen by God at the outset would never make it. Not for them the Catholic satisfaction of knowing that following the sacramental cycle of sin, repentance and atonement and dying with all sins forgiven would ensure entry to heaven. This, Weber reckoned, created an 'unprecedented inner loneliness' within the individual. The followers of Calvinism, he surmised, filled this void with hard work, perhaps with the subconscious belief that wealth and success would be a sign that they were among the saved, however contradictory that was to the actual idea of predestination. And because work was a 'calling' that glorified God, not a way of getting more money to spend on themselves, they eschewed conspicuous consumption. Puritans were not big on bling. From this rather demented and unhappy drive to fill their lives with order and material success, he thought, came a spirit that helped to inspire modern capitalism through a set of attitudes and behaviours: work as a good in itself; impatience with the traditional attitude that labour was a necessary evil and should be limited to earning enough to get by; saving rather than spending wealth.

As amateur psychology goes it is at least ingenious. It is, of course, next to impossible to prove what seventeenth-century Puritans were actually thinking. As the historian E. P. Thompson used to say, we cannot interview tombstones. But the circumstantial evidence of Puritan attitudes at the time – what people were writing and saying – is not particularly favourable to Weber.

A wider reading of the radical Protestant schools of thought of the sixteenth and seventeenth centuries – whose writings Weber himself cites – reveals a large number of sentiments which would struggle to make it into the curriculum of the Harvard Business School. While they did not glorify poverty in the way that Catholic social teaching often had, there were frequent echoes of the biblical warning that rich men rarely enter the kingdom of heaven. John Downame, a popular Puritan writer and preacher, argued: 'doth not common experience teach us that worldly prosperity is a step-mother to virtue, those being most destitute of it, who most abound in worldly things, and they most rich in spiritual grace who are most wanting therein?' Richard Baxter, one of the seventeenth-century writers Weber himself often cited as an example of the Protestant ethic, inveighed against the 'false rule of them that think their commodity is worth as much as anyone will give'.

This attitude travelled to North America with the Puritans. Whatever subsequently caused the United States to become one of the most successful capitalist economies in the world, it was not the theological intent of its Calvinist colonists. The fathers of the Plymouth colony railed against the 'notorious evil . . . whereby most men walked in all their commerce – to buy as cheap and sell as dear as they can'. The colony set maximum prices, wages and interest rates and said that the price of a cow was to be set by what the seller was deemed to need for a reasonable return, not what the buyer was prepared to pay.

William Bradford, one of the colony's early governors, said that an increase in material prosperity 'will be the ruin of New England, at least of the churches of God there'. That it was neither, and that Protestantism continued to flourish in North America alongside a highly successful economy, shows the malleability of theological doctrine when it meets the harsh reality of economic self-interest. Weber tells us that there were complaints about the 'greed for profit' of New Englanders as early as 1632, a mere twelve years after the *Mayflower* landed: if so, that was flatly contradictory to what their leaders were saying.

In practice, any association between radical Protestantism and gung-ho capitalism in England seems more likely to have involved the latter driving the former. We saw in the chapter on cities that the holders of licences and monopolies from the Crown under the monarchy were often Catholic, or at least the association was firmly embedded in the eyes of many of those excluded from the privileged elite. So it is not surprising that the smaller merchants and manufacturers would turn to the religion that also challenged the primacy of Rome.

English Puritanism was strong among small manufacturers of clothing and other goods and in the more economically advanced parts of the country, in and around London and in East Anglia –

the home of Oliver Cromwell, who became Lord Protector of England during its brief experiment with republicanism. But (as Weber himself accepted) Puritanism changed over time. The more worldly doctrine of the seventeenth-century writers, with their emphasis on hard work and wealth, was much more in line with the capitalist ideal than were the Reformation Puritans of a century earlier. Weber quotes from one seventeenth-century Protestant tract that appears to encourage capitalistic endeavour. But that in fact was the second edition of a work first published the previous century that had been silent on the matter. Perhaps it was the spirit of capitalism that inspired radical Protestantism in England rather than vice versa. Scotland, one of the most Calvinist countries in Europe, remained economically backward for centuries after the Reformation.

Protestant England and some districts of the Netherlands did indeed flourish from the sixteenth century onwards. But there were no large-scale banking, commercial or industrial activities in seventeenth-century England or the Netherlands that had not already been achieved in the medieval Catholic cities of Lyons and Augsburg or the northern Italian states like Venice and Florence. As we saw in the chapter on cities, during the Renaissance those Italian city-states developed sophisticated prototypes of the toolkit of modern capitalism.

Weber's analysis has not aged well in the century since it appeared. He claimed that at the time of writing (1905) Germans of the Lutheran rather than the Calvinist tradition of Protestantism exhibited 'easy-going congeniality' compared to British and Americans. 'Upon meeting Americans and English, Germans are normally inclined to perceive . . . a certain internal constraint, a narrowness of manifest emotional range, and a general in-hibitedness,' he opined. Today's Germans might be forgiven for finding those characteristics somewhat elusive in contemporary American tourists or visiting English football supporters.

For fans of the Protestant ethic, the last few decades of the twentieth century must have come as something of a disappoint-ment. Sociologists writing in the Weberian tradition in the 1960s regularly pointed out the underdevelopment of Catholic European countries. They were subsequently undermined by the rapid economic advance of Italy, Spain and the Republic of Ireland. With the exception of the relative failure of largely Catholic South America compared with the success of the largely Protestant North American countries, Protestant economic superiority over Catholicism is an increasingly hard thesis to make stand up.

So often are such analyses proved wrong that they struggle to rise above the status of ad hoc rationalizations of current events. Other familiar targets in the past were the religious and cultural traditions of Asia, particularly Hinduism and Confucianism. An Australian expert invited by the Japanese government in 1915 to assess the country's economic prospects concluded:

Japan commercially, I regret to say, does not bear the best reputation for executing business . . . My impression as to your cheap labour was soon disillusioned when I saw your people at work. No doubt they are lowly paid, but the return is equally so; to see your men at work made me feel that you are a very satisfied easy-going race who reckon time is no object. When I spoke to some managers they informed me that it was impossible to change the habits of national heritage.

Once again, psychology of dubious merit has been deployed to explain why a particular tradition is incompatible with economic growth. In the case of Asian religions, critics often draw on a distinction made by anthropologists. In 'guilt societies' governed by religions like Christianity, the norms governing social interaction are internalized within the individual. In 'shame societies' inspired by Eastern religions and philosophies like Confucianism, the disapproval of the wider community enforces good behaviour. By providing a monitoring mechanism embedded within the self, so the theory goes, guilt societies are better at giving their members the sense of drive and endeavour needed for a flourishing capitalist society.

It sounds vaguely plausible, but like the Protestant–Catholic distinction it has recently rather foundered on the rocky coast of

fact. Along with those idle easy-going Japanese, the alleged stagnation of the Oriental mind failed to prevent the swift self-
enrichment of a leading east Asian pack of Hong Kong, Taiwan,
Singapore and South Korea and latterly a second wave including
Thailand, Vietnam and China, not to mention the rapid growth
that India has achieved in the past fifteen years.

In fact, so ephemeral are intellectual fashions in this particular
field that there was a vogue during the 1980s for arguing the exact
opposite. Dozens of business books argued that capitalism actually
worked better when imbued with 'Asian values' – generally
defined as an attachment to social and economic solidarity rather
than destructive individualism and manifested in long-term
relationships between governments, investors and producers rather
than the promiscuous free-for-all of Western capitalism. Such
rationalizations died off somewhat in the aftermath of the 1997–8
Asian financial and economic crisis, in which it turned out that
some of those close relationships had also been distinctly dysfunctional.

Having lost rather a large number of bouts, the religions-
determine-growth thesis has nonetheless been hauled out of semi-
retirement for another shot at the title, this time taking a swing at
Muslim rather than Catholic beliefs. On the face of it, there is
much more promising material to work with in Islam than Papism.
Does the Koran not ban usury – the lending of money at interest,
an essential element of any modern market economy? Are Muslim
countries in the Middle East not a byword for economic stagnation,
living off oil earnings rather than producing goods and services? Is
the Islamic addiction to accepting fate rather than trying to make
something of yourself not so entrenched that the resigned shrug of
'Inshallah' ('God willing') routinely accompanies the making of
plans and promises in the Middle East?

In truth, while there are some ways in which the theology of
Islam seems unhelpful for growth, this has little to do with an
intrinsic anti-commercial bias, particularly not through the alleged
prohibition of usury. More likely, it happens that some societies
that adopted Islam proved to be resistant to change and reform,

largely for other reasons. And one or two aspects of Islamic religious dogma that were in fact initially helpful for economic growth failed to adapt and became a hindrance.

First, those facts about the recent past. There has been simply no tendency for Islamic societies to grow less quickly than others over the past half-century. This result was established by Marcus Noland of the Peterson Institute for International Economics, one of Washington's most respected think tanks, in a study published in 2003. His paper provoked a cacophony of yelps of surprise among fellow economists, but no convincing refutation. Indonesia and Malaysia, for example, have been relatively successful. And within countries with both Islamic and other religious communities, such as Ghana – a good way of isolating the specific influence of religion on growth – there was no evidence that Muslims were doing badly. If anything, Islam appears to be good for growth.

So why did Islamic societies not do better before the twentieth century? Historically, the underperformance of Islam started from the twelfth and thirteenth centuries onwards. The religion was founded in the seventh century CE, in some ways an attempt to purify and unite the 'religions of the book' – Christianity and Judaism. It spread and rose very rapidly, filling the space left by the implosion of the Roman empire.

In some respects, Islam was a more commerce-friendly religion, at least in its theology, than its main rival, Christianity. There is a widespread belief that the Koran imposes a blanket prohibition on usury – the lending of money at interest. But either in theory or in practice there is little to suggest that this had to be a major impediment to growth. The specific references in the Koran and other writings are to *riba*, which means 'increase' and appears to refer not to the charging of interest as such but the practice of applying penalty rates – doubling the amount owed in capital and interest if the borrower fails to pay back on time. This particular prohibition may have been motivated by self-preservation on the part of a new and cash-strapped religion. It accompanies passages about the preferability of paying *zakat*, a kind of tax then distributed as alms by the Prophet, rather than lending out money at interest.

Certainly the warnings against usury in the Koran are nothing like as strong as those in the Old Testament, and both Christians and Jews have had a long tradition of banking and finance.

There are other commercial restrictions in the Koran, but most refer to excesses of speculation and what might be regarded as profiteering rather than business itself. Apart from the obvious bans on trading in food and drink banned from consumption by Muslims, including wine and pork, the remaining rules on commerce read more like a guidebook on business ethics or a regulatory manual for the futures market than an injunction to monastic poverty. Speculation in essential goods like water is forbidden, for example. Also disallowed is entering into a contract for future delivery without knowing specific times and prices. But there is nothing in principle prohibiting such 'forward' or 'futures' markets, which reduce risk for both producers and buyers and have become an essential part of modern trade.

The general tone of the Koran and the Hadith – the associated teachings and deeds of the Prophet Mohammed – is that business should be conducted fairly and the proceeds used to support Islam, not hedging commercial life about with prohibitions and treating it with distrust. One reports Mohammed saying: 'If thou profit by doing what is permitted, thy deed is a *jihad* [holy act] and if thou usest it for thy family and kindred it will be a *sadaqa* [charitable deed] and truly a dirham lawfully gained from trade is worth more than ten dirhams gained in any other way.' This rather recalls the dictum of John Wesley, the founder of Methodist Christianity (and a favourite of that apostle of low-church capitalism Margaret Thatcher): 'Gain all you can; save all you can; give all you can.' Another cites Mohammed thus: 'The merchant who is sincere and trustworthy will [on Judgement Day] be among the prophets, the just and the martyrs.' The Prophet Mohammed was, after all, a trader before he became a preacher. And Islam is the only major religion to be founded by a trader.

An Arabic manual of commerce attributed to the eleventh century describes several kinds of perfectly legal merchant, including one who buys goods when they are cheap and sells them when prices have gone up. Another type arbitrages between two markets by knowing the difference in prices and the customs duties between them.

The Koran is capable of judicial interpretation in many different ways, not least because there are several schools within Islam, the main two being Sunni and Shia. But in the widely followed Hanafite tradition of Sunni law – which later provided the legal basis for the Islamic Ottoman empire – jurists provided many methods for getting around the theoretical prohibition on usury. Nothing induces theological malleability like a bit of self-interest, and according to one estimate three quarters of Islamic religious scholars in the ninth and tenth centuries were themselves active in business.

One familiar ruse was a sale and buy-back scheme: I sell my book to you for 120 dirhams with the money to be paid in a year's time. I buy it back for one hundred immediately. I keep my book: you have in effect borrowed a hundred dirhams from me for a year at 20 per cent interest. This trick was called a *mohatra* contract, and was so common that it became a standard commercial term used for centuries. Issuing a decree in 1679, the Holy Office of the Vatican condemned the idea that 'contractus "mohatra" licitus est', stating that such contracts violated the biblical prohibitions on usury. It doesn't say much for the thesis that Islam was an intrinsically anti-commercial religion that its standard lending contracts were too liberal for Christianity to tolerate. Even in the cases where Islamic jurists did come down hard on moneylending, Muslims frequently employed Christian or Jewish communities to do it for them. Where there was a will, there was usually a way round.

Certainly the first several centuries of Islam did not suggest it was inimical to economic development. While European societies were recovering from the collapse of the Roman empire and the trade routes that it had created, a succession of Islamic civilizations proved themselves to be politically, scientifically, economically, militarily and culturally advanced.

Islam linked the two trading regions of the Mediterranean and

the Indian Ocean and turned Arabic into the world's most important trading language. Swahili, a common tongue down much of
the east African coast, combines elements of Arabic with African
languages. It evolved to serve the extensive trade between the
ports of the Middle East and east Africa.

The Arab empire that expanded to control the Middle East
from the seventh century onwards was followed by the Moorish
civilization of north Africa that ruled much of Spain, hanging on
to the south until the fifteenth century. After the Mongols had
invaded and then converted to Islam in the thirteenth and fourteenth centuries, three great Islamic empires established themselves:
the Ottoman empire that took Constantinople from the Christian
Byzantine empire in 1453, renamed it Istanbul and expanded across
much of central Asia, north Africa and the Mediterranean Middle
East in the fifteenth and sixteenth centuries; the Saffavid dynasty,
based in what is now Iran, which controlled the Arabian peninsula;
and the Moghul dynasty in India. At their height, the Islamic
empires were far bigger and more powerful than anything in
Europe at the time.

Far from instituting a choking monolithic theocracy, some of
the most successful of these – particularly the Moors and the
Ottomans – generally allowed Christianity and Judaism to flourish.
The Ottoman empire, for example, although based on an Islamic
legal code, allowed Christians to be bound by their own laws in
cases not involving Muslims, and specifically forbade the enslaving
of Christians and Jews within the empire. The Ottoman empire
also had a lively exchange in ideas as well as goods, absorbing
new discoveries about geography and navigation from Europe and
developing its own expertise in engineering and astronomy.

Islamic economies were successful in increasing wealth by trade,
allowing each economy to specialize in what it did best. They
developed a sophisticated set of financial and trading institutions,
including forward markets: dates were sold at auction before they
were ripe, and wholesale batches of onions, garlic, carrots, radishes
and so on were also sold before being harvested. It seems likely
that Italian city-states like Venice imported forms of business

contract from the Islamic world, and the words 'tariff', 'risk', 'traffic' and 'douanes' (customs) have roots in eastern languages.

So why did the societies of the Islamic civilization stagnate, along with the Chinese, the other serious rival to European economic dominance in the first half of the second millennium? From the answer emerges a more subtle and less fatalist analysis of the role of religion in economic history. What matters, it seems, is less the precise doctrine than the uses to which the religion itself is put, and the willingness of societies to change or reinterpret laws grounded in religious belief.

Islamic economies struggled to increase productivity, or output per head of population. There was no great breakthrough in agricultural efficiency – the advance that would centuries later spur the development of Europe. Businesses and partnerships remained small. There were few examples of substantial private sectors operating genuinely independently of the state. Some did exist, including a medieval Egyptian textile industry. There were also some organized occupational guilds, such as pearl-fishing in the Persian Gulf, characteristic of later European capitalism. But they were closely controlled by bureaucrats.

Unlike those in Europe, Muslim cities were not allowed to develop into autonomous entities, nor to pioneer ideas of personal and commercial freedom. They remained centres of religious piety. The Islamic empires did not develop states that were primarily interested in technological progress or productivity. They spent more time fighting over what they already had or trying to seize more through invasion.

But this had a lot more to do with accidents of geography and history than with the theology or management structure of the prevailing religion. It was perhaps Islam's misfortune to have been born in the Middle East and maintain its centres of political power there, originally in Mecca and Baghdad. (It may well remain a misfortune today, given the deleterious effect of oil on economic growth discussed in an earlier chapter, but this bad luck somewhat predates the petroleum economy.)

Being in the Middle East meant bad luck on the resource

front: shortages of minerals and timber made the transition to a manufacturing market economy harder than it was in Europe. And, then as now, it was bad for peace. The Islamic world was plagued by destructive raids by marauders that frequently threatened to knock stable, sustained economic development off course. In particular, the growing threat of the Mongols in central Asia realized its destructive capacity under the rule of Genghis Khan in the thirteenth century. The Mongol invasion laid waste to cities across the Islamic world.

Baghdad, one of the great centres of Islamic rule and culture, fell after a single battle. The Mongols did not destroy Islam: though their east Asian heartlands tended towards Buddhism, they had no particular religious agenda to advance. In fact, by the beginning of the fourteenth century, the Mongols controlling central Asia and parts of the Middle East had converted to Islam. They rebuilt the cities and rejuvenated them as centres of learning and culture.

But they did demand complete obeisance to an absolutist monarch, and the result was that the empires were run literally with army discipline. The Mongol law code, attributed to the most famous of the Mongol autocrats, Genghis Khan himself, was a restricted military system. The state was run from the centre with the help of a large nomadic army that owed personal allegiance to the chieftain. The Mongol empires declined in the second half of the fourteenth century, but they left a legacy that combined a perpetual fear of invasion with attachment to military strength to repel or pre-empt it. As we will see later, this post-Mongol centralizing absolutist tendency also took hold in Christian Russia, with unfortunate results.

Those Muslim leaders who were able to stand up to the Mongols or take over once the Mongols began to retreat had to be tough military rulers. Characteristically, Islamic regimes extended themselves through military conquest, or had to fend off the threat of conquest by others. The 'Mamluk' sultanate that managed to hold back the Mongols from Egypt and Syria depended on soldiers who were bought as slaves, mainly from the Caucasus and round the Black Sea. The Mamluks, whose regime was dominated by a landowning military elite, taxed their cities heavily to raise money for the state.

The Islamic world, particularly the Mamluk regime, was hammered particularly hard in the fourteenth century by the plague that became known as the Black Death, which the Mongols had inadvertently helped to spread across the world by securing the overland trade route from the east. And each of the three great Islamic empires that arose after the Mongols – the Ottomans, the Saffavids and the Moghuls – was centralized and militarized. When necessary, those rulers used Islamic institutions as a means of shutting down debate, or at least they stopped discussion within Islam threatening the status quo.

By the fourteenth century Islam was becoming hardened, not opened up further for discussion as the Reformation would do for Christianity in Europe. In the sixteenth century, the Ottoman and Saffavid empires in particular regarded each other with intense rivalry. Each clung fiercely to its rival tradition of Islam, the Ottomans being Sunni and the Saffavids Shia. The liberal, questioning forms of Islam like the Sufi sect lost ground rapidly to the fixed certainties of existing Islamic law.

At the same time western Europe was, however slowly, edging its way towards restraining the absolute power of the monarch. Different groups – first landowners, then merchants and manufacturers – were creating alternative bases of power. These conflicts often took place through religious debates within Christianity, especially after the Reformation.

But if anything it was the failure of any one denomination to predominate, not the nature of Protestantism, which created a more open civilization with a variety of beliefs. The Reformation was not aimed at creating political and religious freedom. It wanted to maintain the unity of the Catholic church while reforming it. Its originator, the German theologian Martin Luther, was also rabidly anti-Semitic and repeatedly incited the persecution of Jews.

Nor was Puritanism as an organized creed originally intended to aim at political liberalism. After the monarchy was restored in England in 1660 and religious toleration began to spread, the

Massachusetts colonists were far more intolerant of other Christian sects than was the English society they had left behind. But Quakers and other such undesirables could go off and found their own homes in Rhode Island or Pennsylvania. It was because the Reformation only half succeeded in Europe and North America that it inadvertently led to a more pluralistic society. It is worth noting that the Catholic city-states like Florence that preceded Protestant England in capitalist development had also famously been centres of humanist freethinking.

By contrast the dominant culture in the operation of the Islamic empires tended towards military authority: top-down, unquestioning, with vast amounts of power vested in a centralized state. Like the Mamluks, the Ottoman empire was based on a corps of soldiers who started out as slaves. The lack of a well-organized merchant class meant that where Islamic practices might have proved unhelpful to economic growth there were not enough voices raised to lobby for change. One such example, ironically, may well have been the Islamic traditions of business partnership and inheritance. The irony comes from the fact that they were initially designed to help, not hinder, commerce.

Islamic rules governing business partnerships were created between the seventh and tenth centuries. They drew mainly from the customs and practices already established in the countries that came under Muslim rule: there is precious little in the Koran that determines how partnerships should be organized. The Islamic partnership generally involved an investor or investors, who bore the financial risk, and a merchant, who undertook trade on the investors' behalf. Unlike the equivalent contract under Jewish law, which required profits or risk to be split equally between investor and merchant, the profit shares under Islamic partnerships could be varied. In fact, this flexibility meant that Jewish traders in the Middle East well into the second millennium usually chose Islamic contract law in preference to their own.

But a combination of rules meant that, as time went on and economies became more complex, this form of partnership became increasingly restrictive. One rule was that all payments and principal had to be in cash in a single currency. The goods being traded could not be used to settle accounts. Another was that all partnerships were automatically dissolved on the death of a partner. These laws intersected unhelpfully with the Islamic rules on inheritance, which *were* laid out clearly in the Koran, and decreed that at least two thirds of the estate of the deceased was to be split between individual members of the extended family. While they may have made Islamic societies more equal, the inheritance rules also made it hard to create and sustain any large-scale business partnership. The death of a single partner meant the partnership was broken up and each of the many inheritors could demand their share in cash.

These rules prevented Islamic partnerships building up expertise and economies of scale. No-one was likely to commit money and time to a business that could collapse at any moment because of the death of one of many owners. As a result, enterprises tended to be small and short-lived, comprising usually just a handful of partners and covering only one trade mission at a time. As economies became more complex and the reach of trading areas increased, this put them at a disadvantage compared to European merchants. As we will see in later chapters, European countries started creating joint-stock companies where many partners could have transferable shares, and evolving the idea of the business corporation, a body recognized as being legally separate from its owners. No equivalent existed in Islamic law.

Many parts of medieval Christian Europe also had restrictive rules on inheritance that meant business enterprises were split between multiple inheritors. But, crucially, these were modified as time went on, with relatively little resistance from the religious authorities. By the seventeenth century, primogeniture – inheritance preference given to the oldest son – was the dominant practice in Britain and the Low Countries, which were then leading the continent in commercial sophistication, and spreading elsewhere. Primogeniture allowed business enterprises to grow with each generation and be passed on intact.

The crucial difference between Islamic societies in the Middle

East and Christian societies in Europe was not in the theology of the respective religions, or where the commercial law based on those religions had started. It was that European merchants were powerful enough to have inconvenient laws disposed of, even when that required changing the religious justification of those laws. Their counterparts in Islamic countries, for reasons largely unrelated to the nature of the religion itself, were not.

For a long while, the underlying weakness of this ossification of Islamic regimes was masked by a highly successful set of campaigns of imperial conquest. Like ancient Rome, the Islamic empires extended themselves enormously through excellent bureaucratic organization and military prowess.

The Ottoman empire reached the height of its power under Suleiman (known in Europe as Suleiman the Magnificent) in the sixteenth century, when it extended control across north Africa and became the most powerful political entity in the world. But it failed to extend itself further into Europe, having been turned back at the gates of Vienna in 1529. The empire did not cut itself off from external contacts with non-Muslims. But it did institute religious Islamic sharia law as the legal code for all Muslims, and the educational system became narrower and more doctrinaire.

It also remained a static society. Like the Roman empire before it, the Ottoman discovered there was a natural limit to the benefits to be gained merely from organizing the same technologies in a better way. First the lack of innovation began to constrain expansion and then it weakened the regimes against pressure from outside. Having failed to seize Vienna at the second attempt, in 1683, the Ottoman empire softened. Military discipline weakened and the battle over the tax revenue from the empire for the centre bred corruption and infighting, as it tends to do. Rebels tried, sometimes successfully, to set up breakaway regimes on the peripheries of the empire.

It became increasingly clear that Islamic empires could not compete with economic and military competition from Europe. Napoleon's Egyptian expedition at the end of the eighteenth century, in which he defeated Ottoman forces, was followed by increasing interference from the British throughout the nineteenth century, by the end of which they had in effect seized control of the country. The Moghuls, similarly, were weakened by revolts from the Hindus and by the rising British trading presence in the subcontinent in the eighteenth century.

Islamic nations reacted in the same way as they had to the Mongol invasions – maintaining a strong state to defend themselves against economic and political domination from abroad. Many have continued to respond in a similar way since. In modern times, this has manifested itself as a suspicion of foreign capital and foreign capitalism. The desire to retain power in the hands of a central authority has strengthened the hand of the state and those who control it.

In this context, Islam has sometimes provided a useful cover to governments wanting to maintain control over their economies and their people. It wraps the familiar economic nationalism of many developing nations in a cloak of religion. Frequently, as in modern-day Iran, the bureaucracy running the state itself, given its ownership and control of industry, has become an interest group struggling against the rise of alternative sources of wealth and power such as a strong private sector.

But such a role is not inevitable from the nature of Islam. The same defensiveness, interestingly, is also evident among those countries with Muslim populations that have deliberately distanced themselves from their Islamic identity. The secular modernizers of twentieth-century Turkey and Egypt, Kemal Atatürk and Abdul Nasser, also adopted a defiant economic statism as part of their defining political ideology. Nor is the present Iranian government's control over its economy unique to Islamic theocracies: there is a similar stifling stranglehold in secular Arab republics like Syria and (pre-war) Iraq.

And in otherwise fairly similar countries, the dominance of Islam rather than another religion rarely seems to predict why one government works and another does not. Malaysia, for example, despite retaining a strong Muslim identity, has been one of the most successful of the second wave of east Asian countries. In recent decades, it has embraced industrialization and used the state to encourage private enterprise and attract foreign direct investment. Indeed, it has done so more successfully than, say, the Christian Philippines or largely Buddhist Thailand.

So the part played by religion in economic development probably owes more to its political role than its theology. Perhaps, rather than its values becoming embedded in the psychology of its followers, religion affects growth mainly through its exploitation by the institutions of power. This should explain why Spain and Portugal underperformed in the first few decades after the Second World War. It wasn't that they were Catholic: it was that until the mid-1970s they were ruled by dictators who helped to keep them relatively poor and backward, and who closely aligned themselves with their Catholic church establishments further to enhance their own authority.

For an elegant exposition of how this might happen, we can turn to – well, intriguingly enough, we can turn to Max Weber, whose lesser-known works are, for my money, more interesting and convincing than his Protestant ethic blockbuster. Weber also compared Indian, Chinese and Islamic societies, all of which made it some way down the path of economic development and then seemed to stop. Weber's writings here relied less on amateur psychology and the power of internalized ideas and more on the operation of material interests. He awarded an important role to 'carriers' – particular groups in society who could find an affinity between certain important religious doctrines and their own interests. In China, Weber said, such beliefs were propagated by bureaucrats; in India they were transmitted by scholars and priests of the high Brahmin caste. And neither group had an interest in disruptive economic change that might have challenged their status in society. As simplifications go, this is not a bad one. As a motivating force it requires merely the human desire for wealth and power rather than a speculative psychology of personal desolation and fulfilment.

As with Islam, there is a temptation to read across from Hinduism, the predominant religion of India, to the country's social caste system, and conclude that it has held India back. As we will see in more detail in a later chapter, the caste system has indeed limited India's advance and continues to distort the country's economic development to this day. But it is hard to see the system, or the restrictions on economic activity that followed it, as the natural consequence of the beliefs of Hinduism. Rather they look like the operation of economic self-interest using a tendentious religious justification.

The evidence for Hindu theology inevitably inducing fatalism and economic stagnation is weak. For one, the doctrine itself is fuzzy. Unlike the monotheistic one-book creeds of Islam, Judaism and Christianity, Hinduism is an accretion of stories, poems and cults. It has a multiplicity of philosophies, gods (or the multiple representations of a single god) and sects, and has no central authority on doctrine and worship. There is no Hindu Vatican or Synod; there is little irreducible core of Hinduism.

The strand of belief that looks most antithetical to capitalism is that human souls, while part of an infinite reality, must go through a cycle of birth, death and rebirth to transcend their conception of themselves as individuals and become part of the greater truth. This, it is supposed, induces fatalism and apathy in the faithful. But in the sacred texts themselves, hard work – and, in some parts, actually gaining wealth – can be a means of achieving salvation. In the Mahabharata, one of the most venerated texts of Hinduism, appears the unequivocal statement: 'Wealth gives constant vigour, confidence and power. Poverty is a curse worse than death. Virtue without wealth is no consequence.'

The link between Hinduism and the caste system is also less straightforward than might initially appear. Distinctions between four different varnas, or classes of society – the priestly and scholarly Brahmin, the warrior Kshatriya, the merchant and artisan Vaishya, and the manual worker Sudra – are embedded in the traditional Hindu texts. But some ancient texts clearly show that movement between varnas is possible. That fluidity gave way to the exigencies of the struggle for economic dominance between different groups in Indian society. In other words, a religious justification was used to buttress a material advantage of one set of people over another. Thus the looser definitions of caste were tightened into a set of defined groups often based rigidly on occupation and from which members could not escape.

This owed more to the need to provide a docile agricultural labour force than it did to clear theological prescription. One theory of agricultural development, chiefly used to explain slavery, goes as follows. In agrarian societies with a scarcity of people and plentiful land, it is not possible for three things to coexist: free labour, free ownership of land and a non-working upper class. Where people are sparse on a large amount of ground, some way of tying the workers to the farm is needed if landowners are to live off their labour. Had it not been for slavery, for example, free labourers in land-rich North America could simply have wandered off and started their own farms rather than work for a subsistence income on the plantations. The ability of plantation owners to sit on their verandas drinking mint juleps and living off the profits would have been sharply reduced.

Various means have been used to tie workers to the land. Less drastic ones than slavery include indentured labour and limits on migration. But often they required a functioning bureaucratic state to enforce them. On the vast Indian plain, with a sparse and shifting population and a variety of local princely rulers, that state was missing. A hereditary caste system was a more efficient way to prevent labourers breaking out of the condition into which they were born. (It was notable that religions with objections to the caste system, Jainism and Buddhism, were strong in the Himalayan foothills, where a different, less labour-intensive form of agriculture prevailed.)

Those with a particular interest in propagating the system – the high-caste Brahmins – were much in demand by Indian princes as scholars and bureaucrats, because of their high levels of literacy. What better position to propagate a doctrine that entrenched them and their patrons in a leading role in society? 'Legitimation by religion has always been decisive for an alliance between politically and socially dominant classes and the priesthood,' Weber wrote.

In return for a dominant role running a prince's administration, the priests consecrated his position at the top of society according to what they said were the principles of Hinduism.

And over time, just as the Islamic partnership and inheritance system hardened and prevented economies adapting to changing circumstances, so did the ossification of social strata in India. It is hard for labour to find new ways of specializing when classes of workers are irredeemably bound in to a particular occupation. That is doubly true when those classifications are used to deny particular orders education or other ways to improve their condition.

And as we will see in a later chapter, after societies come to be ordered in a particular pattern, they can often become stuck that way. Once the caste system was established, it would have required vast amounts of courage and political energy to get out of it. To establish a new casteless community, a lower-caste leader would have had to persuade a higher-caste counterpart with the necessary complementary skills (such as a high level of literacy) also to break the code.

This fits the facts in India rather better than does the idea that Hinduism is intrinsically bad for growth. As far as we can tell, the Indian economy grew quite well very early on and then got stuck. It reached a relatively high per capita income in ancient times, which then remained about the same level from 300 BCE until the twentieth century. The economic and social system apparently delivered enough prosperity to avoid the kind of cataclysm that occurred in other societies, while not achieving growth in productivity.

Even with big changes in political rule, when the Muslim Moghul dynasty swept down from central Asia in the sixteenth century and eventually took over almost the whole of the subcontinent, the underlying system of economy and caste was left in place. As we will see, the British if anything tightened rather than loosened the social bindings, finding caste a useful device for dividing and ruling. The population of the Indian subcontinent increased from around 100 million in 300 BCE to 125 million in

1600 CE to 300 million by 1911 and the economy grew along with it, but per capita income was perhaps only 10 per cent or so higher in 1947 than it had been two centuries earlier.

Poor Indians are entrapped in poverty, but it is hard to argue that they choose it. Given a powerful economic incentive and the freedom to act on it, any objections raised by religion or culture are often trampled underfoot. In the 1960s, there were a series of scientific agricultural breakthroughs funded by Western institutions, the so-called 'Green Revolution'. Researchers developed new strains of wheat, rice and other crops with much higher yields than traditional varieties. They were rapidly adopted by growers in India, as in much of the developing world. There were few signs of farmers lounging around their fields pondering the mysteries of the cycle of rebirth rather than enriching themselves by responding promptly and substantially to a strong market signal.

In fact, when the Indian economy overall did break out of its feeble low-growth pattern in the 1990s, this was accompanied by the political rise of Hindu fundamentalism. A government led by the hardline Hinduist Bharatiya Janata Party took power in 1998. If anything it was rather better at achieving more economic liberalization than was the secular-led government that succeeded it. India's caste system and stifling bureaucracy are bad for growth and in particular bad for widespread reduction of poverty. But the connection of this to Hinduism is historical accident and political manipulation rather than direct theological cause and effect.

A similar process has been at work in China. Settled Chinese agricultural civilization began before that in India, several millennia before the birth of Christ. Just as agrarian societies coalesced around the Nile and Tigris–Euphrates river valleys, Chinese civilization began in the Yellow River valley with the planting of millet, later followed by rice.

China entered the second millennium not just ahead of Europe in wealth and knowledge but in a position to continue to dominate, and perhaps in an even more advantageous situation than India or the Islamic civilizations. Like Europe, China had a temperate climate, was relatively free of diseases and had good rainfall and large rivers. It had animals that could be domesticated, a long history of political organization and an established system of literacy.

By the twelfth or thirteenth century China was technologically far ahead of Europe. It had developed a water-powered spinning machine, and had worked out how to use coke rather than charcoal to smelt iron. One estimate has it that by the late eleventh century, China was making 125,000 tons of pig iron. Britain would not match this output until the eighteenth century. The list of Chinese technological breakthroughs is long and legendary, from the evidently revolutionary to the apparently mundane: gunpowder, printing, the compass, the wheelbarrow, the stirrup. Advances in one area were used to support those in another. Having developed techniques of irrigated paddy rice farming, far more productive than the prevailing rain-fed 'dryland' rice cultivation, the Chinese disseminated them throughout the country with how-to guides made with wood-block printing.

And then it decided that enough was enough. In one of the most remarkable pieces of self-inflicted damage, or at least deliberate self-restraint, in economic history, China gave up trading with the rest of the world. From the fourteenth century onwards the Ming dynasty that then ruled China started restricting foreign trade and contacts. The navy was disbanded, and transporting grain by sea abolished in 1415. Some forms of technological process simply ground to a halt: the machine used to spin hemp, for example, was never adapted to cotton. And while the population continued to expand and hence the economy to grow, China nonetheless gave up the lead in scientific discovery and geographical exploration to Europe.

The predominant religion in China is Buddhism, but the 'Buddha made me do it' explanation looks very weak. Unlike Islam or Christianity, Buddhism did not have a clerical authority that exercised much control over the state. And the moderate and meditative religious doctrine of Buddhism in any case tended to be associated with a generally more laissez-faire attitude to other religious beliefs and to the intrusion of religion into the economic sphere.

'Confucianism is the culprit' might get closer, not least because Buddhism was not officially introduced in China until the first millennium CE, whereupon it was synthesized into a distinct form known as Ch'an (also known as Zen) Buddhism. The influence of Confucius, the Chinese philosopher of the fifth and sixth centuries BCE, was already widespread.

The writings of Confucius do indeed contain paeans to stability and the maintenance of existing relationships of hierarchy within society. Those with a grudge against him might well argue that his views were inimical to the freewheeling creative destruction and social mobility of capitalist economies. Yet the modern experience of economies with a strong Confucian heritage, starting with Japan and Taiwan and now joined by China and Vietnam, suggests that there is nothing incompatible between that heritage and rapid economic growth.

However, certain aspects of Confucian thought proved helpful for one group in society in entrenching its power against another. In China, that group was the state bureaucracy. It is a commonplace worn to cliché that Chinese society is riddled with bureaucrats, something that the takeover of the country by state communism in the twentieth century did nothing to diminish. Perhaps less understood is just why the administrative culture is so pervasive. The modern concept of being Chinese is in itself an intrinsically bureaucratic creation.

The Han Chinese, who make up more than 90 per cent of the population of modern China, are that peculiar anomaly – an ethnically heterogeneous ethnicity. Their identity was created, or imposed, during the Han dynasty of 206 BCE to 220 CE, also the time when China officially became a Confucian state. Though there are different spoken versions of the Chinese language, the Chinese characters used are the same. Bureaucrats writing down people's names managed to assimilate a diverse group of ethnicities and tribes into a nationality which came to regard itself as a single people.

The role of state bureaucrats in recording and regulating the economy was already established by the time of the Han dynasty. The reference manuals of a low-level bureaucrat of the Qin Dynasty, which preceded the Han, suggest that the regime maintained almost field-by-field records for crops being grown throughout its empire, the details written on small strips of bamboo and carefully collated and stored. Some even suggest that the accumulated wisdom and practice of the bureaucrats in China play the role that religion does in other countries. Even if this is going too far, the influence handed to the bureaucracy by hardwiring their authority into the very nature of national identity gave them a great deal of power.

In the beginning, administrative skill may well have been good for China's economic development. As we saw with the spread of paddy rice farming, civil servants stored and disseminated useful information. Bureaucrats were chosen largely on grounds of competence rather than inheriting their influence. China's famous and gruelling system of civil service examinations, a system that began in the seventh century, was designed to ensure that the state was run by the best talent available.

But this class of bureaucrats (or 'mandarins') was not prepared to countenance threats to its own pre-eminence, and the unified system of examinations created a powerful drive towards consensus of purpose, philosophy and interest within the state. Bureaucrats were frequently the enemies of merchants and entrepreneurs, since they had the potential to create rival bases of power and wealth. In the case of China, the mandarins feared and despised both soldiers and merchants and did their best to control the two groups. The Chinese mandarinate found it easier to get away with this than others might have. The size and relative geographical isolation of China allowed it to be self-contained and self-sufficient in a way that European regimes were not.

The state's relationship with the creation of wealth was predatory. China's decision to curtail its trade was a deliberate one, taken by a relatively strong and centralized state. It came from those who were threatened by the disruption that growth and trade might bring. The precepts of Confucianism might have helped and legitimized them, but they were acting in their own, fairly brutal, self-interest.

It has often been in the interests of those running a state to limit economic growth in order to diminish threats to their own status. Religion is one of the tools they use. But in a different context, the very same religions can play a diametrically opposed role: that of drawing together a minority group and turning it into a thriving business community. The success of minority religious communities can stand as an interesting test of whether it is religion itself that hurts economic growth or its abuse by the state or a dominant interest group. Frequently you can take a religious or ethnic community out of a country where the state or an elite uses religion to squash entrepreneurship, transplant it into a different society and watch its alleged anti-commercial nature melt away.

The religious minority as a thriving business community is a phenomenon observed repeatedly throughout history. The Jews and French Huguenot Protestants of medieval Europe, the Indians in post-colonial east Africa, the Parsees in India itself, the Lebanese in west Africa and Latin America and the Chinese across south-east Asia: all have proved to be economically much more successful than the majority culture or religion in which they operate. One of the richest men in the world today, surpassing perhaps even Microsoft's Bill Gates, is reckoned to be Carlos Slim, a Mexican telecommunications magnate who is the son of Lebanese immigrants.

Their success endures despite resentment and envy. It is frequently the fate of such groups to be targeted by unscrupulous politicians. Appealing to the base instincts of the majority, demagogues say that the minority grouping is stealing from the rest of the country. The Asians of east Africa were scapegoated and driven out by thugs like Idi Amin, the murderous dictator of Uganda. Similarly there is perpetual growling resentment of the Chinese business families of south-east Asia. Usually subterranean, the prejudice surfaced in attacks on life and property during the Asian financial crisis of 1997–8. The business and finance role of the Jews has been one of the most reliable headsprings of anti-Semitism throughout their long history of being persecuted in Europe.

It would appear that the success of such communities owes more to the operation of group sociology than it does to the nature of their particular beliefs. Close-knit cultural and religious (and family) groups tend to dominate trade in poor countries because they provide a certainty and means of enforcing contracts that the wider economy may lack. Where commercial law does not work well and courts are too slow or too corrupt to enforce contracts, more informal forms of sanction can be very useful. The threat of exclusion from a charmed circle of business people and traders is one such. It is evidently easier to hold such a group together if all members have something like kinship or a religion in common. A collective identity also gives a signal to outsiders that a member of the circle is backed by the collective sanctions of all other members. Cross one trader and you cross them all; have one trader cross you and you can be confident that the other traders will punish her for it.

The operation of group sociology may, in fact, explain some of the traditional success of Jewish business communities within the Islamic and Christian worlds. It is perhaps not so much that they were Jewish as that they were minorities. Moreover, in many Christian countries they turned to banking and business because they were systematically excluded from other professions such as law or medicine.

All sorts of religions and cultures can provide group cohesion – even those generally considered a source of failure at home. There is not much sign of the alleged Confucian fatalism of China undermining economic growth among the wealthy Chinese traders of Malaysia or Singapore, or of fatalist Hindu stasis holding back the successful Indians in Nairobi or Kampala.

Indeed, there are enduringly successful minority Islamic business communities as well. Anyone wanting to change money for the best exchange rate in modern Nigeria in the mainly Christian areas in the south of the country will generally be rewarded by pulling up at a roadside mosque. One of many one-man bureaux de change will emerge out of the crowd. Proffered dollars are taken and the begowned agent disappears, clients displaying a remarkable degree of trust in a country better known for endemic corruption than successful business enterprise. The confidence is rewarded with the agent emerging in a few minutes with a wodge of well-thumbed naira. Entrepreneurial culture is deeply engrained in such operators: the rubber band holding together the fistful of currency generally has tucked in it a business card advertising a diverse range of other products and services. One given to me by a money-changer in Calabar in south-eastern Nigeria read 'Bureau de Change' below his name and then underneath that, in marginally smaller type, 'Peas, beans and hats'.

Nor are the money-changers an isolated example of Islamic business minorities. The Muslim Hausa ethnic minority have provided some of Nigeria's most successful traders both before and after independence from the British empire. They brought kola nuts grown in the forest areas in southern Nigeria to sell in the savannah regions of the north and sent grass-fed cattle the other way. As early as the 1880s, Hausa merchants pioneered the use of steamships to establish a sea trade route to Ghana.

Had Max Weber lived among the Hausa he might well have concluded that Muslims were good for growth and constructed his convoluted psychological theories around the tenets of Islam. Had he visited eastern Africa later in the twentieth century, he might well be scouring the Mahabharata for the secret of commercial success. Had he wandered all over modern-day south-east Asia, he might well be punting the works of Confucius as the world's first management book.

Moreover, Weber himself accepted that while the Protestant ethic had helped get modern capitalism going, it now had momentum of its own and could be adopted by any society. 'Victorious capitalism, in any case, ever since it came to rest on a mechanical foundation, no longer needs asceticism as a supporting pillar,' he wrote.

It is too easy to infer causality from a casual look at economies and dominant religions. The reality is much more complex and, happily, much more optimistic. Muslim societies can choose to succeed just as Christian or Jewish societies can without losing their beliefs. Religion does not determine economic fate. Islamic countries can get rich. In fact, some do.

6. Politics of development

Why does our asparagus come from Peru?

If you are a European, or less so an American, take a look at your supermarket or street food stall the next time you go shopping. If you live in an area where there is a consistent demand for fresh green asparagus, the chances are that – outside a short growing season in Europe and a slightly longer one in the US – the asparagus on display will have been flown from Peru.

Even allowing for the fact that fruit, vegetables and flowers are regularly flown from tropical countries to temperate ones, it may strike you as odd that, particularly in Europe, a cost-effective industry spontaneously emerged to airlift a perishable green vegetable thousands of miles around the world from the remote western coast of Latin America. You would not be wrong.

The development of the world economy may look like an onward march of impersonal market forces which lays all inefficiencies waste before it. In truth, as we saw in the chapter on water, some industries, and most particularly agriculture, are shaped as much by politics as economics. Their sustenance owes much to the fact that small groups of producers who will throw everything into protecting their livelihoods can often win out over much larger interests who care much less.

Sometimes the initial support may make economic sense, but protection continues well after the original rationale has gone. Eventually, the cabals of producers often lose. But by looking in this chapter at the various rises and falls of textile, sugar and banana producers, we will see that the process can take centuries.

And even when they are defeated, it is generally not because society as a whole has grown tired of the cost of cosseting them but because another, better-organized group of producers has come along to beat them in the lobbying game.

In the case of asparagus, the political imperative that first filled

European and American supermarkets with the products of Peru was the desire to get kids off drugs, or at least publicly be seen to be trying. Peru, along with other Andean countries, got a special trade deal in 1991 to give their farmers something other to do than grow coca to make cocaine. In the US, where geographical proximity to the Andean cocaine industry gives this particular resonance, the Peruvian asparagus industry not only benefited from lower tariffs (import taxes) to the US but from tens of millions of dollars a year in financial help from the US government. Asparagus is a high-value vegetable suitable for airfreighting, and Peru's farmers seized the opportunity. Exports to the US and to the EU, which granted similar access to its markets, rocketed.

In vain do the asparagus growers of California, Washington state and Michigan complain that they are being driven out of business by favoured imports from Peru – mainly produced, the farmers argue, in coastal areas well away from the mountainous coca-growing regions. There aren't enough of them; they have the misfortune to come from states whose farmers, for reasons we will see, punch below their weight when it comes to extracting favours from Congress; and no American politician ever wants to go into an election accused of being soft on drugs. In the meantime, Peru's vegetable industry, with the initial helping hand from trade perks, has become one of the country's most flourishing exporters.

Asparagus is not alone. The results of determined lobbying often hover somewhere between the richly comic and the surreal. An entire trade deal between the US and Singapore, for example, got stuck in a mass of chewing gum. The south-east Asian city-state had banned the tacky substance lest discarded gum disfigure any of its otherwise pristine pavements. But a US congressman from Illinois, where Wrigley is headquartered, threatened to hold up the deal unless the ban was rescinded. The upshot was a painfully constructed compromise. Some forms of chewing gum can now be bought in Singapore, though ostensibly for medicinal purposes, solely from pharmacies and generally requiring a doctor's prescription. To protect dairy farmers, it was illegal for many years to buy spreading margarine in Australia and Wisconsin. (A thriving community of margarine stores sprang up in Illinois just outside the Wisconsin state border.)

Meanwhile, at least according to some of the continent's more excitable newspapers, European women spent the summer of 2005 convulsed with fear that they would have to go braless. The European Commission imposed emergency blocks on Chinese clothing imports to protect Europe's senescent garment industry from cheap competition, raising the prospect of empty shelves in the lingerie stores of London, Paris and Milan. A delighted press, particularly in the UK, seized on what it called the 'bra wars', though in fact bras were a rather small proportion of the threatened garments. ('Why is it that British newspapers are so obsessed with women's underwear?' a European Commission official sighed plaintively to me while the dispute was raging. I was unable to enlighten him.) A patchwork compromise had to be sewn together.

In fact, a sufficiently determined lobby can believe, or at least argue, two opposing things simultaneously. A few years ago, American catfish farmers got cross when cheap Vietnamese catfish started entering the US market. After initial mutters that the imported catfish might contain traces of the Vietnam War defoliant Agent Orange (and whose fault would that be, exactly?), the farmers hired lawyers and lobbyists who convinced lawmakers to force the Vietnamese to stop calling their catfish catfish, on the grounds that it was a different family to, though in the same *Siluriformes* order as, American catfish. The Vietnamese relabelled their exports as *basa* or *tra* (meaning, in Vietnamese, catfish). American consumers, amusingly, appeared to regard the newly renamed catfish as a fancy imported premium product, and sales continued to thrive.

Undeterred, the US catfish farmers changed their strategy. Their lawyers successfully secured import duties on Vietnamese catfish on the grounds that they were being 'dumped', or sold at unfairly low prices, in the American catfish market. To do so under US trade law, they needed to prove that Vietnamese catfish were a 'like product' to American catfish, having previously spent many thousands of dollars to establish that Vietnamese catfish were not, in fact, catfish.

It's not all quite so amusing. Trade lobbies have more serious impacts, such as threatening the future of the planet. Global production of ethanol and other biofuels has surged over the past few years as the world seeks solutions to oil shortages and the carbon emissions that come from burning fossil fuels. But only some ethanol, such as the sugarcane variety produced in Brazil, is likely to do much good. Ethanol produced from corn, as it is in the US, is expensive and inefficient. It may in fact even emit more carbon than extracting and burning gasoline. The American corn ethanol industry is kept in business by generous subsidies and high tariffs which keep out cheaper and more environmentally friendly Brazilian imports. Iowa, the centre of that industry, punches above its weight when it comes to setting policies by being the first to choose presidential candidates in the state-by-state primaries. Genuflecting before the ethanol subsidy programme is a ritual that nearly all presidential candidates undergo as the price of trying to get their campaign off to a flying start. (One exception, to his credit, was John McCain.)

In some ways, the Peru example is a slightly unusual one, as it involves farmers from rich countries losing out. Generally, farming is the most protected of all industries. Cotton is one of the most extreme examples. There are probably no more than 10,000–20,000 cotton farmers in the US, out of a population of 300 million. But the sector, depending on what happens to cotton prices, gets up to $4 billion a year in federal payouts and has managed to resist almost all attempts by other countries to put limits on its subsidies. Indeed, protecting American cotton farmers has been one of the cornerstones of US trade policy for many years. Their disproportionate influence would be breathtaking, were it not so painfully familiar from repeated episodes throughout history.

In some of these cases, the debates have been going on for centuries and continue to distort global markets today. The combatants sometimes change sides, a pro-free-trade industry becoming protectionist as its interests shift. But over time, the arguments employed and the ability of small lobbies to punch way above their weight have an eerie similarity.

The basic theory that explains why small lobbies can outmanoeuvre bigger ones owes a great deal to the theorist Mancur Olson, who developed it more than forty years ago. Broadly speaking, the relevant part of the theory goes like this. When many individuals have a similar interest, it makes sense for them to band together to get what they want. But because there are so many of them, it is hard to get them organized. The temptation is for each member to rely on the next to do the work for her. And if everyone does this, nothing gets done. However, when the benefits of organizing are captured by a relatively small number of members of a group, it becomes easier and cheaper to motivate them into forming an effective lobby. Such groups have also become adept at joining with others to form coalitions. This explains why lobbies of producers are generally much more powerful than groups of consumers. For the latter, the benefit of lower prices is spread across everyone who cares to make a purchase; for the former, the gains from higher prices are captured only by a few.

Like many Europeans, I grew up watching repeated episodes of direct action by French farmers complaining about the threat to their livelihoods. With a flair for theatre that suggests many have in fact missed their métier, the farmers have repeatedly blocked or set fire to trucks containing imported lambs from Britain and dumped tons of surplus vegetables in village squares as a protest against low prices. I have yet to see, and nor do I ever expect to, a mass demonstration of French consumers marching down the Champs-Elysées chanting in unison (in French, obviously): 'What do we want? Somewhat cheaper sugar! When do we want it? Phased in over a seven-year period!'

Just as Olson's theory predicts, within the farming community it is the concentrated lobbies that have the clout. This is on open display in the so-called 'Doha round' of trade talks, which were launched in 2001 in the eponymous capital of the Gulf state of

Qatar and stuttered painfully in the years following, with agriculture proving a particular stumbling-block.

It has been calculated that the effect of reforming farm subsidies in the Doha round of talks would cause an average fall in the overall household income of Japanese farmers of just 1.4 per cent, and in the US it would be statistically indistinguishable from zero. For most farming households, agriculture is actually a sideline – they derive most of their income from other work. But those losses would be concentrated in the big farms which scoop up most of the subsidies and the benefits of trade protection, and which have the money and the clout to organize politically. Agricultural liberalization would cut the income of the wealthiest 10 per cent of American rice farmers by 19 per cent, and the wealthiest 10 per cent of cotton farmers by 10 per cent. Moreover, because the value of the subsidies is reflected or 'capitalized' in the land the farmers own, their removal would also seriously reduce the value of their assets, by 26 per cent for the rich rice farmers and 12 per cent for cotton growers. Subsidies and protection have a ratchet effect: once they are given it is hard to take them back.

International trade has often been the ground on which these fixtures are fought out. Historically, import tariffs are generally one of the earliest types of levy that governments have managed to exact, with income and sales taxes following later. It is easier to tax goods passing through a port than it is to keep records of the incomes of everyone in the country, still less of every time something is bought or sold in an entire economy. But in rich countries that original justification has long since ceased to wash. Tariffs in most economies have become explicitly protectionist, raising the price of cheap imports to prevent higher-cost domestic producers from being undercut.

So what are the reasons why tariffs persist? One is simply the effect of inertia: once protection is in place, it is politically painful to remove it. Both domestic producers and those, like the Peruvian farmers, that have privileged access usually argue vociferously against across-the-board reductions in tariffs. Another obvious reason is that they are specifically what lobbyists ask for. Because tariffs can be varied between goods they are an effective way of targeting protection at a particular industry. And it is easier for that industry to defend the continuation of a tax that raises government revenue than a public subsidy that evidently gives it away.

So what kind of industries tend to get protected? Intriguingly, they tend to be those that are failing, not those that are succeeding. When I took over as trade editor at the *Financial Times*, it struck me after a short while that covering most of the highest-profile international trade disputes – textiles, clothes, shoes, steel, sugar – was a little like touring a retirement home peopled with the decrepit has-beens of European, American and Japanese farming and manufacturing, who spent their time doddering about complaining at the insolence of the young foreign whippersnappers pushing them aside.

This seems odd. It has often been remarked that governments trying to 'pick winners' to support with public money frequently pick badly. But such an unerring tendency for rich countries to support failing industries with tariffs suggests that, rather than governments picking losers, it is losers that somehow manage to pick government trade policy.

Somehow, declining and shrinking industries seem to lobby harder for protection than do expanding and successful industries. Perhaps the best explanation lies in exactly what the returns for those industries are in expending time, effort and money in doing so.

Trade protection creates economic rent, a concept we encountered in the oil and diamonds chapter, by holding domestic prices above world market levels. In expanding industries, new companies will enter the market if prices are kept high and compete away the rent of the incumbents. But in declining industries where it costs companies a lot to enter the market – setting up steel plants, investing in research and development, building brand loyalty through advertising and so on – the existing companies can appropriate some of that rent. And in some industries, like sugar farming in Europe, governments stop other domestic producers entering the market by means of quotas or other restrictions.

Steel producers protected with tariffs can enjoy a few more years churning out profits. Software houses protected with tariffs would merely encourage a lot more people to set up software houses. In fact, this asymmetry is so pervasive that protecting losing industries rather than successful ones is written into the rules that govern world trade. Under the laws of the World Trade Organization, the Geneva-based body that provides a negotiating chamber and a court of appeal for the rules of international trade, governments have several tools to protect their industries. They can use special import tariffs known as anti-dumping and countervailing duties (the refuge of the American catfish farmers) if those industries can show they are being seriously damaged by subsidized or unfairly low-priced competition from abroad. They can impose emergency quotas or 'safeguards' through duties or quotas (the resort of the European bra-makers) if there is a sudden flood of imports. No similar support is possible for exporters that might be expanding more quickly if trading partners were trading more fairly.

So industries that will fight hard for protection tend to be ones in which import penetration (the share of the market taken by foreigners) is increasing. Employing a lot of unskilled workers who might find it hard to get jobs elsewhere also helps, as they will all tend to vote solely on whether they are being protected. And once an industry does have protection, it tends to lobby harder to keep it, since the alternative is to undertake costly adjustment as it is undercut by cheaper imports.

This explains why certain industries ask for protection: it does not quite address why they get it. Success depends on their level of organization and their ability to threaten governments with political pain if they are betrayed. That in turn often depends on how many companies are in the industry and how geographically concentrated they are. It can also depend on how well a sectional special interest can pass itself off in the theatre of press and public opinion as having the country's interests at heart.

Farmers tick many of these boxes. To fulfil the last criterion, they have become adept at wrapping their cause in the flag of nationhood and appealing, however misleadingly, to traditions of rural life. National identity often lives in the landscape. The hymn 'America the Beautiful' celebrates 'amber waves of grain'. The French farmers, adept at scooping up big chunks of the European Union's generous farm subsidies, appeal to their country's reverence for the *terroir* in which the roots of their food and wine traditions are deeply sunk, even though the typical French subsidy recipient looks out on to a giant flat fertilizer-soaked agro-industrial wheat farm in the Paris basin, not a dreamy panorama of misty lavender fields in Provence. The Japanese have an attachment bordering on the spiritual to the geometric beauty of the rice terraces that elegantly contour the green hills of their country's interior.

There are, too, more prosaic reasons for farmers' power. As we saw in the water chapter, they can claim, sometimes even with justification, that keeping some food production at home will help protect the country in case a war or some other disaster cuts off imports. They are also often very good at lobbying, frequently being concentrated in ways that maximize their power, and adept at building coalitions.

The US cotton interest, for example, has power beyond its size partly because it is spread among a number of smaller Southern states. Since each state has two senators, regardless of size, cotton commands a disproportionate bloc in the Senate. In 2006, ten Southern senators wrote to the US trade representative's office threatening to vote against any deal in the Doha round that made radical changes in the US cotton support programme. The six states they represented have a combined population of less than 33 million. California, by contrast, where many of the asparagus growers live, and which receives a disproportionately small share of government farm subsidies, has just two senators for 36 million people. American cotton growers are part of a powerful coalition with other heavily subsidized farmers. They have also managed to co-opt many US textile producers. In theory, the textile interests should prefer cheaper imported cotton to the expensive domestic variety, but they have been bought off through a special government compensation programme.

Indeed, the textile and clothing industry is not far behind farming in its ability to stage protracted defences of an uncompetitive position. Mass-production clothing is cheap to set up and employs a lot of unskilled labour. It is also ferociously competitive and hence even small shifts in costs or efficiency can put a whole industry rapidly at risk.

So it is not surprising that the modern debates about free trade more or less began with an antecedent of the bra wars, the 'Calico Law' controversy that dragged on for decades in the late seventeenth and early eighteenth centuries. It set English textile and clothing manufacturers against importers and provoked the most extraordinary political and intellectual ferment – particularly remarkable since formal theories of free trade were not worked out until a century or so later.

At the time, one of the dominant beliefs about trade was 'mercantilism' – broadly, that exports were an intrinsic good as they strengthened the country, earned money in the form of precious metals from abroad and helped build up the naval expertise on which an island nation depended. Modern-day economists would shudder at this, arguing that exports are a necessary evil. What matters is what we consume, not what we make, and exports are merely the good stuff we have to sell to foreigners in order to pay for what we want in return. It doesn't benefit the Chinese to ship iPods to America rather than themselves using them: they do it to earn dollars to import the oil and aircraft and so on that they need. However, this was a time when trade often followed the mail-gloved strong arm of the state, and the distinction between the military navy and the merchant navy was less clear than it is now. Without a functional international market in place it was more justifiable to think of exports as evidence of strength. The argument about their importance in building up shipping was later accepted even by Adam Smith, generally a staunch supporter of free trade.

For England to expand its trade in the middle of the seventeenth century, for example, required the Lord Protector, Oliver Cromwell, to eschew the standard practice of conducting wars against religious opponents. He launched instead the first in a series of sea-battles against the Dutch, the other big Protestant power in northern Europe, to keep open trade routes in the North Sea and the English Channel for English merchants to exploit. These were accompanied by the Navigation Act, the first in a series of laws that aimed to boost the English navy at the expense of the Dutch, who at this time, with a better fleet and system of trade finance, offered shipping and credit on better terms. Among other things, the laws required that all goods shipped to and from England's colonies be carried in English ships. Sugar, tobacco and other colonial products destined for foreign markets had to be taken to England first and taxed there before being taken on.

But the logic of mercantilism went beyond merely encouraging English shipping and trade to arrive at an absurd conclusion. The wealth of England, as we saw in the chapter on water, had largely been built on wool. As the seventeenth-century poet John Dryden wrote:

> Tho' Jason's fleece was fam'd of old,
> The British wool is growing gold.

But wool would not last for ever. In the seventeenth century, the East India Company, a trading concern that would later run India as a contracted-out British imperial possession, first tried and failed to break the Dutch stranglehold on pepper imports from east Asia. It then turned what started as a sideline into one of their main operations – the import of cotton cloth, generally known as 'calico', from India. Unsurprisingly, once people had the feeling for cool smooth cotton rather than hot and itchy woollens, particularly underwear, they went mad for it. Calico from India and linens from elsewhere, such as continental Europe, became fashionable.

Comfort and style were also cheap: clothes made of Indian calicoes were a third or a sixth of the price of wool. In 1620, the East India Company imported 50,000 pieces of calico in total; by 1690, it was bringing in 265,000 neckcloths alone from just one of its three main producing areas, Madras.

Indian silk cloth also began to threaten the livelihoods of the weavers who imported silk thread to work themselves. The most visible were the Huguenots, French Protestants escaping religious persecution who had become one of the East End of London's many successive waves of immigrants. Towards the end of the seventeenth century there were around 100,000 of them in Spital-fields, an East End neighbourhood today being swallowed up by London's financial district.

Big Wool and the silk weavers swung into action, and the last three decades of the seventeenth century witnessed a furious campaign of petitions to Parliament, endless polemical pamphlets and, increasingly, mass demonstrations. The East India Company fought back with its own torrent of propaganda. And all of them insisted vehemently that they alone had the national interest on their side. A tract of 1896, poetically entitled 'An English Winding Sheet for Indian Manufacturers', complained of the calico trade: 'In the end it must produce (except to the patentees) empty houses, empty purses, empty towns, a small, poor, weak and slender people, and what can we imagine the value of our land?'

The last point was a key one. The woollen industry scores well on the metric of what makes an industry likely to get trade protection: a substantial but often geographically concentrated and well-organized set of workers, with few immediate opportunities for employment elsewhere. But its lobbying power was improved by connections to a group who had more political clout: the better-off types who owned the land on which sheep were raised and who had lent money to the weavers. Local gentry and weavers were often bound together by links of debt, employment and, sometimes, marriage. Younger sons of local gentry were often apprenticed to master craftsmen. If the wool industry went down, landowners would get hurt along with it.

The counter-lobby, meanwhile, had to overcome awkward charges of self-serving hypocrisy. The East India Company must have struggled to keep a straight face when arguing that what was good for the Company was good for the country. Sir Josiah Child, a politically well-connected grandee at the Company, periodically unleashed his own volleys of rebuttal to the weavers' arguments, speaking in the name of free trade. He claimed in a polemic of 1681, pointedly entitled 'The East India trade most National', that the petitions against Indian textiles were the work of malcontents with a personal grudge against the Company or who had been bribed by merchants doing business with Turkey or other countries disadvantaged in the English market.

But the Company was itself a monopoly, having exclusive rights to trade with the East Indies (south and east Asia), and being owned by a limited number of 'joint-stock' investors. Indian calicoes imported by the East India Company may have been cheaper than British wool or cloth from Turkey, but they still enjoyed freedom from competing English importers in Asia. As John Cary, a mercantilist writer, argued: 'The proposition that trade should be free, I allow, if it is thereby meant that trade should not be monopolized by Joint Stocks.' An association of linen drapers who dealt in Indian calicoes also pushed for free trade, and were less vulnerable to accusations of hypocrisy (if not thinly disguised self-interest), but it was the East India Company that took the lead in lobbying.

Parliament at this time was dominated by the landed gentry, but some were amenable to persuasion, and Sir Josiah spread money liberally around the more malleable members. The East India Company accounts for 1691 showed a remarkable special item of £11,372 for 'secret service', a euphemism for the greasing of palms.

Thus a pattern emerged that would be repeated hundreds of times in trade disputes down the centuries. Two groups of producers, one with an interest in cheap imports and one acting in defence of domestic production, argued for their particular interest and each claimed that it was identical with that of the nation as a whole. For the wool and silk weavers read today's South Carolina textile producers, or European sugar farmers, or Caribbean banana growers. For the linen drapers and the East India Company read Wal-Mart, or the Brazilian ethanol industry, or the US fruit companies Del Monte and Chiquita. The voices of the consumers who had to don woollen underwear (and today's equivalents who have to buy overpriced bras, sugar and bananas), if indeed they were raised, were barely heard.

Workers and landowners with their livelihoods at stake have a way of making sure they get attention. The composition of the protectionist alliance met two of the conditions that make trade lobbies effective: it was concentrated enough to campaign well, but broad enough plausibly to claim widespread support. Their first big victory was a resolution by Parliament in 1678 commanding all English people to wear only woollen apparel during winter, defined as the period between All Saints' Day (1 November) and the Annunciation (25 March). And if it was hard to force the living to wear wool, the dead would complain less: all corpses for burial, Parliament said, must henceforth be wrapped in woollen cloth.

The East India Company, which had close links with the Crown, lost one of its most important champions when King James II, the last of the Stuart house of monarchs, was deposed in 1688. Sir Josiah was a Tory, a party that had emerged out of the supporters of the monarchy, and the Company was widely regarded as a Tory stronghold. So when the opposing Whigs won power in Parliament in 1695 the Company's enemies were both economic and political. Petitions from around the country poured into Parliament: the silk weavers of Canterbury, the wool weavers of Norwich (who claimed that 100,000 people depended on their industry), the yarn makers of Cambridge. A bill of 1696 prohibiting 'all wrought silks, Bengalls, dyed, printed or stained calicoes of the product of India or Persia or any place within the charter of the East India Company which shall be imported into this kingdom' did well in the House of Commons but died in the upper House of Lords, dominated by Tory magnates.

After another bill was drawn up in 1697 and once again stalled, the protectionists' anger got personal. A demonstration of Spital-field weavers managed to force its way into the lobby of Parliament, and on its way back to east London tried to break into East India House, the Company headquarters in Leadenhall Street in the City of London. Three were jailed. In March, a deputation of 3000 weavers threatened Sir Josiah's own house in Wanstead in east

London, and in April another demonstration outside East India House ended in a riot and the building was again attacked.

In 1700, a bill was finally passed that banned the wearing of manufactured silks or printed or dyed calicoes from Persia, China and the East Indies. Some elements of the free-trade coalition, such as traders who bought calicoes for re-export to Europe, were placated by the creation of a system of bonded warehouses. Peace returned and all was well with the woollen industry. Or rather, in another pattern to become wearily familiar in trade disputes, it wasn't. No sooner had one hole in the dyke been stopped up than another one sprang. Because imports of plain cotton cloth were still allowed, as a petition to Parliament in 1703 plaintively explained, the Act 'hath rather occasioned the figuring, printing and staining of calicoes here in England to the detriment of our woollen manufactures'.

An excise duty, or sales tax, on printed cottons and linens was imposed, and then doubled. But still the imports kept coming and the wool and silk weavers suffering. Without the East India Company to blame, they were reduced to venting their fury on the consumers themselves, who had failed dismally to change their predilections as required. The summer of 1719 witnessed numerous incidents of 'calico-chasing': gangs of weavers roaming the streets of London, tearing cotton clothes off the backs of hapless female passers-by and triumphantly parading their captured trophies round the streets on the tops of poles.

The onslaught of petitions started up again, pinging into Parliament from all corners of the country. Most likely there was some surreptitious central coordination by the well-organized London weavers: the wording of the complaints was suspiciously uniform, and some emanated from towns with no weaving industry at all. Still, it worked. The 'Calico Bill' passed in 1721 showed just how ridiculous a law a truly determined lobby could achieve.

It banned not just the importing but the wearing or use in furniture or furnishings of all printed, painted or dyed calicoes – except, as a concession to consumers, those unfashionably dyed all blue. It would be tempting to record this for posterity as the all-time historical high-water mark for textile protectionism, were it not outdone by an even more draconian law in France at the same time that made the smuggling of contraband textiles a capital crime on the third offence. Three strikes and you're dead.

I said at the beginning of this chapter that political protection can defy market forces for decades, or even centuries, if the lobby backing special treatment is sufficiently strong. But, particularly when an overwhelmingly superior product comes along, it finds it hard to do so for ever. So it was with woollens. The ban on imported manufactured cottons merely set English printers to work on linen or fustian (a linen–cotton mix): Scottish linen-makers had managed to get an exemption for their product in the Calico Bill.

And in a fine example of necessity being the mother of invention, the compulsory wearing of hot heavy clothing spurred the development of spinning machinery for English manufacturers to make their own cotton cloth. Twelve years after the Act was passed, John Kay made a significant breakthrough in weaving technology with the creation of the flying shuttle. Within fifty years of that, a trio of inventions – the spinning jenny, the spinning mule and the water frame – were on the way to mechanizing textile production. British manufacturers could now beat handmade Indian cloth on grounds of cost as well as political expediency.

They also became adept at mechanizing the printing of cotton. Appropriately enough, one of the first great factories for calico-printing in Lancashire, which would rapidly become the world centre of the industry, was set up by one Robert Peel. It was his grandson of the same name who, as prime minister in the middle of the nineteenth century, came under the influence of England's new weavers – this time the free-trader cotton kind rather than the protectionist wool variety – to execute one of the most dramatic moves in trade policy in history.

The repeal of the Corn Laws in 1846, as we saw in the chapter about the US and Argentina, was a defining moment. Britain turned away from centuries of propping up its landowners and towards supporting its industrialists. As G. K. Chesterton described in his gloriously nutty narrative poem of English history as witnessed by the disenfranchised poor, 'The Secret People', the political eclipse of the landowners was so rapid as to seem inexplicable:

> . . . the squire seemed struck in the saddle; he was foolish, as if
> in pain, [. . .]
> We only know the last sad squires rode slowly towards the sea,
> And a new people takes the land: and still it is not we.

A lavish system of support for agriculture was rapidly withdrawn. Such a dramatic transformation necessarily involved creating an overwhelming force to shift a previously immovable interest. One of those theatres of war, the sugar industry, remains a battleground for trade politics today, of which more later.

The repeal of the Corn Laws is one of those turning-points that seems so inevitable in retrospect – Britain was rapidly industrializing and becoming the workshop of the world – that it is worth recalling just how remarkable a political act was the actual decision. The Corn Laws were repealed in 1846 by a Conservative prime minister whose party had come to power in 1841 publicly united in a desire to protect landowners. Only a third of the Conservative Members of Parliament actually voted for the repeal bill when it came before them, and the bill relied on support from the Liberal opposition. The government fell within a month and left the Conservative Party divided over trade for decades. Why did it happen?

The short answer is because Peel feared the alternative was revolution. The landowners were a powerful lobby, and well ensconced in the House of Lords, which had the power to block legislation. But the brilliance of the campaign for repeal was to knit together an alliance of interests that seemed not merely to possess serious firepower within a newly changed political system but to have created an unnerving threat to overthrow it.

The purpose of the Corn Laws, various versions of which were passed in the seventeenth and eighteenth centuries, was to regulate the price of food in such a way that farmers could always make a living but the poor could always afford to buy it. ('Corn' in this context is employed in the traditional British usage meaning all bread grains like wheat and barley, not maize.) But its overall effect was generally to hold prices up, benefiting the landowners. At the beginning of the nineteenth century, agricultural protection looked fairly secure. A new version of the law passed in 1815 in response to a drop in food prices – itself influenced by the end of the Napoleonic wars, which had damaged international trade – banned grain imports when the domestic price fell below 80 shillings a quarter (28 lb). The government of the time had more than the usual interest in protecting the landowners, from whom they had borrowed heavily to fund the military campaigns.

But rapid change in the British economy was compressing the landowners into a minority. Accelerating industrialization in the nineteenth century led to extraordinary growth in population – and a population who increasingly lived in towns and wanted cheap food rather than living in the countryside and wanting high farm gate prices. The population of Britain increased from 12.6 million to 18 million between 1811 and 1841, and the country, which had ceased to be self-sufficient in food from the 1760s, grew further beyond the capacity of its farmers to feed it. Their employers, particularly the cotton textile mills, had a vested interest in lower food prices, as it meant their employees could buy the same food for lower wages, and more generally in spreading the doctrines of free trade, as they were the most competitive textile exporters in the world.

The political framework was also changing. The Great Reform Act of 1832 increased the parliamentary seats allotted to industrial cities and swept away many of the 'rotten' or 'pocket' boroughs – constituencies with small and easily bribed electorates which could in effect be bought and sold, and which tended to rest in the control of local landowners. Particularly in the cities, evangelical Christian movements were also pushing for religious and political change, and would provide a bountiful fountainhead of reformist fervour.

The lobby that began pressing for reform got support from both the middle classes who owned and ran Britain's growing factories and the working classes who laboured in them. It was led by the Anti-Corn Law League, a pioneering national-level political pressure group. In organization and tactics, the League was way ahead of its time. Like so many trade lobbies to come after it, it may sometimes have masqueraded as a consumer-focused campaign wanting cheaper food for the poor. But it was a producer interest – the manufacturers, and particularly the cotton textile owners – that provided its core leadership, its money and its organizational clout. Founded in London in 1836 as the Anti-Corn Law Association, it had by 1838 found a natural home in Manchester, the centre of the textile industry.

The two main leaders of the League were later to become some of the most famous advocates for free trade in history: Richard Cobden and John Bright. Cobden, who pursued the campaign against the Corn Laws from a prominent position in Manchester political life – he became Member of Parliament for Stockport in 1841 – was credited by Robert Peel with the repeal of the laws, 'acting, I believe, from pure and disinterested motives'. But, as textile manufacturers, Cobden and Bright were brought to the campaign by a very particular commercial interest. As we have seen, the ideal trade lobby is one that is sufficiently well concentrated to be able to campaign coherently, yet sufficiently broad – or capable of portraying itself as such – to pass itself off as representative of the nation. The Anti-Corn Law League was a very good example.

In its vanguard were the textile manufacturers of Lancashire. Textile mills clustered in the county for a variety of reasons. It was convenient for the great port of Liverpool, which enabled cotton to be brought in and clothing shipped out. It was near the Lancashire coalfields, which provided fuel for the steam-powered looms that replaced water-powered weaving. And the damp northern climate helped prevent yarn from snapping as it was being spun. As the total number of power looms doubled in England between 1835 and 1850, Lancashire's share increased from 67.5 to 79.1 per cent. By 1846, 70 per cent of the League's donations above £100 came from Lancashire.

But export-oriented industries as a whole were broadening and spreading around the country. As the Industrial Revolution progressed, demand soared for semi-finished manufactured goods, such as iron bars and girders, that acted as inputs to other industrial processes. And as industrialization and the railway boom began to be exported elsewhere, such as North America and continental Europe, so did the components needed for construction. Published directories of city-dwellers for the period show that all occupations were spreading out across many urban centres, with the exception of one: landowning.

The stark division between landowners and industrialists was in any case something of a caricature. One of the reasons that Britain's aristocracy has endured for so long, without any of the messy unpleasantness that accompanied the decapitation of its counterpart in the French Revolution, is its ability to adapt. The British nobility had as long ago as the sixteenth century started investing in industries outside its traditional agricultural interests, including the mining of coal, lead and salt, and taken advantage of the transport opportunities provided by the canal system to sell raw materials such as timber and gravel over longer distances.

For most, this remained a sideline to their main activity of farming, or at least collecting the rent from tenant farmers. But diversification accelerated markedly in the nineteenth century, not least because of the growing sophistication of financial markets. The Bank of England, at that point a private entity, had been created in 1694 to help the government borrow money to fight the French. Trading in stocks boomed in the 1830s and 1840s as controls on companies setting up and selling shares were lifted, and the new railway companies took advantage. Somewhere around a fifth and a quarter of share offers in the 'railway mania' investment boom were taken up by landowners. Indeed, railway companies wishing to avoid landowners objecting to their planned routes often found it prudent to reserve a certain portion of each new share offer to buy them off. So even though the House of

Commons (and even more so the House of Lords) remained dominated by aristocrats, some had taken a stake in the country's economic future rather than clinging exclusively to the rewards to be had from owning its economic past.

The Anti-Corn Law League used a combination of propaganda and aggressive campaigns of electoral manipulation that would have done credit to any modern Washington lobbyist. It made thousands of objections to the registration of known protectionist voters when the electoral rolls came up each year, and registered its own supporters as the number of eligible seats and voters increased after the 1832 parliamentary reform. By canvassing support in the urban constituencies where its backing was strongest and reporting the results back to its headquarters, the League often had a better idea of the electorate's views than either of the two main political parties.

And it used every line of rhetoric it possibly could to promote free trade. For those who would benefit directly, like the cotton manufacturers, it appealed to self-interest. For those, like tenant farmers and agricultural labourers, who might have been tempted to see the issue as one of the countryside against the city, they argued that the effect of the Corn Laws was merely to raise the price of land and thus their rent. And for those who might have lost out financially, it invoked morality and Scripture. It was wrong on principle, it said, to support an aristocratic monopoly. John Buckmaster, a free-trade agitator who toured country towns and villages trying to recruit farm labourers and craftsmen to the cause, followed a prototype 'What would Jesus do?' campaign. 'If the Corn Laws had been in evidence when Jesus Christ was on earth,' he rather presumptuously declared, 'he would have preached against them.'

Perhaps the League's most important success was to win over the temporary allegiance of the 'Chartist' movement. Working-class protestors were part of the coalition of the disenfranchised that had managed to force the 1832 Reform Act through Parliament, by adding the force of mass meetings and even violence against property to the cause. Nottingham Castle, property of the Duke of

Newcastle who had initially opposed parliamentary reform when the bill reached the House of Lords, was burned to the ground by an angry mob in 1831. But unlike the leading lights of the League, the working and lower-middle classes remained literally unenfranchised by the Reform Act, failing the property qualification still required to have a vote.

The Chartist movement, named after its charter of demands, emerged from 1838 to push for deeper electoral reform. It demanded equally sized parliamentary constituencies elected by secret ballot and a vote for all adult men. While they too were instinctively and viscerally opposed to the aristocratic monopoly of the landowners, the Chartists did not wish merely to replace one class of overlords with another. Their suspicions about the motives of the League were aroused when many of the textile magnates who backed it nonetheless resisted the Factory Acts, which shortened hours and restricted child labour in the cotton mills.

In 1842, the Chartists called a series of industrial actions called the Plug Strikes to try to induce the industrialists to support them. The League responded that they should concentrate on the issues on which they agreed. In an address 'To the Working Men of Rochdale', trying to persuade them to return to work, John Bright argued that the Chartist leaders were imperilling progress by asking for too much. 'For four years past they have held before your eyes an object at present unattainable and urged you to pursue it,' he said. 'Your first step to entire freedom must be commercial freedom – freedom of industry.' The League argued vehemently against the idea that lower food prices would merely be used as an excuse to lower wages. They got enough support to carry the day. The backing of thousands of voteless citizens might not have been the determining factor in shifting the vote in the House of Commons. But it may well have played an important role in persuading the Lords, for whom the memory of the disturbances around the Reform Act were still vivid.

Meanwhile the opposition to reform, the Anti-League (also known as the Agricultural Protection Society), came much later onto the scene than the League itself, not emerging until 1844. Loyalty to the Conservative Party and a reluctance to campaign openly against Robert Peel restrained the protectionists until it became clear that he was irrevocably decamping to the free-trade side. And organizationally they were no match for the free-traders. By 1845 the League had an annual fund of £250,000, while the core of the Anti-League, the Essex Agricultural Protection Society, had raised just £2000.

Protection for farmers was in fact gradually reduced over some years, but the repeal in 1846 sticks in the history books as the pivotal moment. The final push was helped by a disastrous harvest in 1845 and famine in Ireland, which required emergency imports of grain and finally got the message through to the Commons and the Lords that continuing to protect landowners ran an increasingly large risk of serious unrest. When matters came to a head, Parliament chose the certainty of limited damage if it repealed against the uncertainty of what would happen if it did not. Revolutions and rebellions spreading across Europe in the 1840s showed what happened when hungry and vulnerable emerging working and lower-middle classes demanded power and did not get it.

According to Richard Cobden (admittedly not an unbiased source), Peel reacted with something like satisfied vindication when news arrived in the House of Commons in 1848 that France had erupted in a second revolution that overthrew the restored monarchy and once again instituted a republic. That, Peel reportedly responded, was what came of ignoring entirely the wishes of those who did not have a vote: 'It was what this party behind me [the Conservatives] wanted me to do in the matter of the Corn Laws,' he said, 'and I would not do it.'

To succeed, the free-traders had a series of formidable lobbies to overcome. Sugar planters were one, whose demise is a fine example of how trade interests can endure at length but not necessarily for ever. Like so many other industries that proclaimed the contribution they made to the nation, the rise of England's Caribbean sugar industry took place almost entirely under the wing of the state. The great sugar aristocracy of Britain got fat on artificial financial sweeteners. Historically, Islamic conquest had spread the cultivation of sugar from the ancient growing grounds in India and the Tigris–Euphrates valleys to Sicily, Cyprus, Rhodes and north Africa. Later, during the era of European empires, sugar plantations went further west and south, searching out the tropical heat and water in which the crop luxuriates. It was carried to the Canary Islands and the Azores and, finally, taken to the Americas. By 1516 the Caribbean colony of Santo Domingo was shipping sugar back to Spain. The harvesting of the crop requires large amounts of labour, and sugar also took with it slavery, first to the Mediter-ranean and then, notoriously, to the Caribbean.

Having previously taken a refreshingly direct but not indefinitely sustainable strategy of stealing sugar from Spanish ships through state-licensed piracy, England used its naval and military power to create its own sugar islands in the seventeenth century. It seized Jamaica from the Dutch and drove Portuguese sugar out of the northern European market. Oliver Cromwell, he of the militarist mercantilism, was so delighted to hear of the capture of Jamaica that he took the rest of the day off.

But just as the Indian cotton business preached free trade while instituting a monopoly, so did sugar. In fact, it created two. In 1660, sugar from the Caribbean was made an 'enumerated' commodity, which could not be exported directly from the colonies to conti-nental Europe or North America but had to be landed (and taxed) in England first. The colonies were also dissuaded from processing the sugar themselves by prohibitive tariffs on refined sugar, as opposed to the raw treacle-like molasses, and from making manu-factured goods that would compete with English exports. Thus the trade went: slaves from Africa to the West Indies, sugar from the West Indies to England, finished goods from England to Africa and to the colonies.

Since they were at this point highly competitive, the growing lobby of sugar planters were all for being able to sell their produce to any market they could find. The governor of Barbados in 1666 argued: 'Free trade is the life of all the colonies . . . whoever he be that advised his Majesty to restrain and tie up his colonies is more a merchant than a good subject.' (An interesting distinction.) But the temptation for England to extract profit from the colonies was too high and the pressure from the sugar refiners of Britain, centred in London and Bristol, too great.

Our friend Sir Josiah Child from the East India Company popped up again, this time with arguments that made it clear that the interests of colonies should be subservient to the centre: 'all Colonies or Plantations do endamage their Mother-Kingdoms, whereof the Trades of such Plantations are not confined by severe Laws, and good execution of those Laws, to the Mother-Kingdom.' Apart from a small concession in 1739, when they were allowed to export directly to ports south of Cape Finisterre in Spain, all sugar had to go via England. The Crown also excluded Scottish ports from the colonial trade, one of the reasons why the Scots, after trying and failing to set up their own New World colonies, were forced to merge their kingdom with England. After the Act of Union in 1707 the trade was permitted and Glasgow acquired a thriving sugar-refining business.

In compensation, the West Indian colonies were given their own monopoly – an almost complete control of the British market with much lower import duties than sugar from elsewhere. The state further helped them out by increasing demand. From 1731 sailors in the Royal Navy were given a daily ration of rum, which rose to a pint a day by the late eighteenth century, a practice not abandoned until the 1970s. Generous allocations of sugar were later given to the impoverished inhabitants of government-run almshouses.

So instead of being allowed to engage in free trade, the Caribbean colonies were channelled down a particular route. They pumped out sugar and other enumerated crops like tobacco for which their British market was protected, and were discouraged from trying anything else. As time went on the sugar plantations began to lose their competitive edge, as monopolies tend to, and their relative prices rose, as monopolists' prices tend to. Rising prices did not much affect their sales in the protected domestic market but did help lose Britain some of the French sugar market as France decided it needed a Caribbean sugar industry of its own.

The argument can plausibly be made that, early on, the mercantilist creation of the sugar islands did indeed help strengthen the British nation, not least in expanding its fleet. Relying on a military opponent like Portugal, Spain or the Netherlands for sugar supplies would have meant placing Britain at the mercy of a monopoly whose profits could be used to attack British ships. And some research suggests that, at least initially, sugar islands like Jamaica paid for themselves by providing centres for smuggling and plundering Spanish ships.

But as cheaper sugar became available from around the world, particularly Latin America, in the eighteenth century, the question increasingly arose: just whom did this arrangement benefit? That it enriched sugar landlords with plantations in the Caribbean, and the sugar refiners and rum distillers back in Britain, is certain. That it benefited the nation as a whole became an increasingly untenable argument.

By the end of the eighteenth century, probably 8–10 per cent of the total income of the English came from activities in the West Indies. But that did not mean that the nation as a whole was better off. The costs were the alternative uses to which the heavy investment in the Caribbean could have been put, the higher price of sugar at home and the burden of maintaining what by 1763–75 was an average of nineteen warships and between three and seven regiments of soldiers in the Caribbean.

That the English paid over the odds for sugar was not in doubt. The average price of sugar in London in 1765 was a third higher than in Nantes in France. When Britain briefly captured the Caribbean islands of Guadeloupe and Martinique from the French in 1759, the influx of cheaper sugar meant that the price of sugar in London fell by a quarter. The historian Robert Paul Thomas calculates the total profit from the British West Indies at £1.45 million a year in the 1770s. But the money it invested in the Caribbean could have raised a minimum return of £1.3 million if invested elsewhere. Together with an annual cost to consumers from more expensive sugar of £383,000 and the price to taxpayers of maintaining the soldiers and sailors at £413,000, the West Indian colonies had in fact become a drain on Sir Josiah's 'Mother-Kingdom'.

This argument took a while to sink in, thanks to the political power of the concentrated beneficiaries versus the diffuse bearers of the burden of cost. In the eighteenth century, the sugar lobby in England sprayed money around merrily on themselves and their cause. The lavishly wealthy West Indian planters, many of them absentee landlords who spent more time oozing through the salons of London than tramping the fields of Jamaica, became stock figures of eighteenth-century English society. Their sons filled the elite public schools of Eton, Westminster, Harrow and Winchester. A play opened in 1771 in London called *The West Indian*, which begins with a huge reception for a planter coming to England. One servant says admiringly: 'They say he has rum and sugar enough belonging to him, to make all the water in the Thames into punch.'

In the unreformed Parliament before 1832, political power was relatively straightforward to buy. Three brothers from the Beckford family, one of the great plantation-owning dynasties, were MPs at the same time in the eighteenth century. A London-based agent for the colony of Massachusetts reported in 1764 that fifty or sixty West Indian-influenced Members of Parliament held the balance of power in the Commons. In 1830, one West Indian planter spent £18,000 getting himself elected in Bristol. And like most landowners, the sugar planters were well represented in the House of Lords: Charles II had made thirteen Barbados plantation owners into baronets in a single day in 1661.

The undoing of the sugar lobby came when the costs of protection multiplied and their opponents started to organize. Sugar was originally a luxury enjoyed by the rich. But as the population grew and moved into the towns, the need for concentrated and non-perishable calories rose rapidly. Along with three other imported stimulants – tea, coffee and tobacco – it helped to fuel the workers of the Industrial Revolution. Sugar consumption per head increased fivefold in the nineteenth century, creating an enduring sweet tooth throughout the population. George Porter, a sugar broker, wrote of sugar in 1851: 'Long habit has in this country led almost every class to the daily use of it, so that there is no people in Europe by whom it is consumed to anything like the same extent.'

The cost of cosseting the West Indian planters continued to rise. New sources of cheap sugar – Hawaii, the Philippines, Cuba, Mauritius – multiplied, and British sugar lost yet more foreign markets. During the European wars of the early nineteenth century, Napoleon reacted to the British blockade of continental ports, which cut off sugar supplies from the French Caribbean, by planting sugar beet across northern Europe.

Expensive Caribbean sugar had become more than an annoyance. Because it made up a significant part of the working-class diet, wages had to be higher than they would otherwise have been to enable factory workers to eat. As such, it was one of the main targets of the industrialists, one of whose rallying-cries was a call for the 'free breakfast table' – that is, for British workers to be allowed to buy the cheapest food possible. One speaker in Parliament in 1844 estimated the cost of protected sugar to the country as £5 million a year.

It was not a coincidence that the same free-trade liberals who inveighed against the Corn Laws had also frequently supported the abolition of slavery, which was finally outlawed in the British empire in 1834. The attack on slavery was also an attack on the sugar monopolists. (Less honourably, the textile manufacturers benefited nonetheless from the continuation of slavery in the Southern states of the US, which helped keep their cotton imports cheap.)

Eric Williams, a historian who later became prime minister of the Caribbean nation of Trinidad and Tobago, said that by the late eighteenth century 'The chasm was yawning at the feet of the sugar planter, but, head held proudly in the air, he went his way mumbling the lesson he had been taught by the mercantilists and which he had learned not wisely but too well.' The sugar lobby had broken the cardinal rules of maintaining protection. It had threatened to become a serious drag on the whole economy, and had irritated a highly organized rival lobby – and a lobby of exporters at that. The abolition of slavery undermined the sugar business (though the slaveowners, naturally, were compensated from the public purse for the inconvenience suffered). Through an act passed in 1846, the same year as the repeal of the Corn Laws, the duties on sugar from all sources were gradually equalized, and later all sugar import tariffs were reduced.

And so today's world trade in sugar is a free market. Or at least it might have been, except that once more some tigerish competitors from an earlier era dug in their claws and transmuted into protected sloths in a later one. Those Napoleonic continental sugar beet farms are still with us. Indeed, they are now protected by tariffs and subsidies under the European Union's Common Agricultural Policy, despite the fact that their output is now wildly more expensive than cane sugar from Brazil, Thailand or Australia. They have also been joined by British beet sugar farming, which was rapidly expanded by state subsidy in the 1930s to bail out farmers hit by the Depression and to guard against a renewed blockade as the prospect of another European war loomed. Trade politics abounds in ironies, and one is that the same European Union credited with ending Europe's internal wars preserves the very sugar farms whose existence it should have rendered unnecessary.

Until some partial reform a couple of years ago, the price of sugar in Europe was three times the world average. (It is now merely twice.) And yet the EU exported far more sugar than it imported, massive subsidies dumping it cheaply on global markets. Also still with us are the sugar growers in Mauritius. Once part of a rush of low-priced sugar that undercut the Caribbean sugar islands, they themselves also cannot compete with Brazil and Thailand and now rely on preferential access to the European market, reflecting the fact that Mauritius, too, was a European colony. The red-ink profiles of European empires no longer sprawl across maps of the world, but their faded outlines can still be seen in the patterns of global commodities trade. The EU maintains an elaborate system of preferential access to its market for its former colonies – a way, perhaps, of assuaging its post-colonial guilt. The attitude might be summed up as: 'We're very sorry about those three centuries of imperial subjugation. Got any sugar?'

In the end, unlike in nineteenth-century Britain, it was not a consumer revolt or rival domestic lobbies that forced reform in the EU's sugar regime. The intractability of agricultural reform in wealthy countries reflects an odd dynamic. As countries become richer, they spend a lower proportion of income on food, and so the effect of artificially higher prices becomes less important to consumers. Had the sugar farmers managed to inflict serious damage on their economies and bring widespread inconvenience, as did the coal miners who made Britain shiver in the dark by forcing a series of power shortages during the 1970s, they might well have provoked the backlash that the coal unions eventually faced.

When a loaf of bread costs, as it did in England in 1800, a quarter of a day's pay for a construction labourer, people will riot when the price doubles. When it takes, as it does in Britain today, about ten minutes' work at the minimum wage to buy one, fewer people will notice. The EU Common Agricultural Policy is currently reckoned to cost an average family about a thousand euros a year – not negligible, but not enough to get them marching down the Champs-Elysées. No political party has been swept to power in Europe in recent times by promising to get tough with agriculture.

Nor are there very strong rival producer lobbies within the EU. Unlike the nineteenth-century textile magnates, no call centre or software house is going to argue that expensive sugar is significantly cutting into its employees' standard of living. Meanwhile, food companies receive some official EU compensation for the higher cost of using European sugar. And when the food industry, which uses sugar as an input, tried to discuss the need for cutting its price, the sugar lobby was right on hand to block them. Within the British Food and Drink Federation, an industry association, sugar beet interests managed to stop the organization calling for cheaper sugar. Jonathan Peel, the director of European and international policy at the FDF at the time, was a descendant of the same family as Sir Robert, and found it hard to replicate the success of his illustrious forebear. 'I remember thinking that not much had changed in 170 years,' he told me. Ludicrously expensive sugar is a luxury that EU consumers and taxpayers could quite easily have afforded to retain.

What helped to force reform was a new phenomenon: complaints from a lobby overseas – Brazilian sugar growers – who had recourse to the World Trade Organization. They obtained a WTO ruling that the EU tariff and subsidy regime was illegal under WTO rules. When the regime was partially reformed, though still leaving EU prices well above world levels, the clout of the European farmers relative to their former colonies was painfully evident. European sugar farmers were offered an estimated €6 billion as a buyout. The former colonies were given less than a quarter of that to help them adjust, with just €200 million in the first year.

The WTO's predecessor, the General Agreement on Tariffs and Trade, was created by a treaty signed in 1947, part of the apparatus of economic global governance designed after the Second World War. But even the far-sighted architects of that edifice had to cope with the effects of lobbying. As we have seen, two of its other main elements, the International Monetary Fund and World Bank, were created at a conference in Bretton Woods in New Hampshire. Why New Hampshire? To buy off the opposition of an isolationist senator from that state who might otherwise have opposed their existence. Trade politics really does get everywhere.

Litigation at the WTO also illustrates the vehemence and persistence with which vested interests will defend the economic rent they have been extracting. One of the most bitter disputes in world trade over the past few years was, literally, bananas. The low-cost 'dollar banana' countries of mainland Central America such as Ecuador, Honduras and Panama, favoured by the US, were up against the relatively picturesque but more expensive smallholder bananas from former European colonies in the Caribbean. Appropriately enough, the banana industry in the Caribbean was encouraged by European colonial masters as a replacement for the declining sugar industry. I once visited a former sugar mill in St Lucia that had finally ended operation in 1941, just as the severe restrictions on transatlantic trade as a result of the Second World War began to bite. It then became a banana plantation. It is now a museum.

The economic rent that the two sides were fighting over was considerable. The money to be made out of bananas was gigantic, and was reflected strongly in the lobbying power that each side could bring to bear. The remarkable story of United Fruit, the company that created and ran most of the banana plantations in Central America, has been well told. It managed to get a government overthrown (Guatemala in 1954) for the insolence of proposing to nationalize some unused land owned by United Fruit. The power of the industry has entered the lexicon: such countries are, of course, banana republics. For decades United Fruit operated almost as an alternative state within Central America, its ubiquitous power and presence earning it the local nickname El Pulpo ('the octopus').

On the European side was more than a guilty desire to help out former colonies. The companies that controlled the banana trade into Europe took a big cut on the way and thus appropriated much of the economic rent for themselves. The fact that two of the banana-growing islands, Guadeloupe and Martinique, are technically part of France and send delegates to the French national assembly also meant that Europe's most formidable agricultural lobbying country had a particularly strident dog in the fight. A fragile truce, with which no side was particularly happy, took the best part of two decades to emerge.

Working out the power of lobbies and who gets hurt by what has now become a science. Since the only sanction the WTO has for violating its rules is to place retaliatory blocks on imports, governments that have won cases will try to go after those interests that will inflict the most political pain on their antagonists. When the US was authorized to retaliate against the EU for its recalcitrance in reforming its banana regime, it decided in 1999 to threaten to block imports of Scottish cashmere. It calculated that the British interest in helping its banana-growing former colonies might be overcome by the need to save a symbolic endangered industry –

and one based in a country that voted overwhelmingly for the Labour government that had recently come to power.

Similarly, European retaliation for illegal US tax breaks went after oranges – a fruit grown in the famously marginal electoral state of Florida – and the politically and symbolically important target of Harley-Davidson motorbikes. When the tiny island nation of Antigua and Barbuda won a WTO case against the US for blocking online gambling services operated from the island, it threatened to ignore US copyrights and patents, thus arousing the wrath of industries like pharmaceuticals, movies and music that depend on intellectual property rights. Those industries happen to be some of the most active in America's trade lobby.

However much one side dresses up its arguments by appeals to the economics of free trade, and the other side to the need to keep poor workers in employment, preserve the countryside or keep the country self-sufficient, the outlines of their self-interest show sharply through. The Caribbean sugar interests went from being free-traders to protectionists as they lost competitiveness. The English textile industry oscillated from being protectionists in the calico wars of the eighteenth century to free-traders in the battle over the Corn Laws in the nineteenth only to return to protection-ism in the twentieth century as it was once again undercut by cheap clothing from Asia. The effects of these distortions are evident on every supermarket shelf and market stall in Europe, America and Japan.

Good advice to any foreign agricultural lobby trying to get access to the markets of the rich countries would be to threaten to grub up the existing crop and plant coca instead. Alternatively, let it be known that your country is a hotbed of Islamist radicalism. Pakistan, as a reward for being a US ally, was surreptitiously given the same anti-narcotics trade deal as Peru, before India spotted the subterfuge and complained.

And the coca trade is a good entry point to look at how trade has evolved to create the oddly unbalanced and far from flat world of the present day – and one in which the seamless free market of the economics textbooks fails, once again, to operate.

7. Trade routes and supply chains

Why doesn't Africa grow cocaine?

Less controversially: why doesn't Africa roast its own coffee, or make its own chocolate, or spin its own cotton? Notwithstanding what you have just read in the previous chapter, it's not much to do with international trade politics. But it has a lot to do with ports, payment systems and paperwork.

During a lull in the civil war in the west African state of Liberia in the early 1990s, a piece of graffiti to warm the heart of any management consultant appeared on a wall in Monrovia, the capital. 'War is over,' the slogan (prematurely, as it sadly turned out) declared. 'All we need is logistics.'

The anonymous author had a point. As with grain in ancient and modern Egypt, international trade can take resources from places of plenty to places of scarcity, and the exchange can enrich both sides of the contract. But we also saw in the last chapter on trade politics how the concentrated lobbying of entrenched interests can block and distort that process, and how much, even in the supposedly globalized world of today, governments can interfere in the process of commerce.

This chapter takes a closer look at the means by which that trade gets done and things get moved from one place to another: at the growth of supply chains and the transport and trading routes on which they depend. It also examines how even economies that ought to be able to specialize in particular products, given the resources with which they have been endowed, are unable to take advantage of them.

The traditional trade theory of comparative advantage starts off from a base of perfect markets, with all sides having complete information about what they are buying and selling, and in which economies can rapidly adjust to producing new goods in response to trading opportunities. In reality, the world doesn't work that way. In earlier centuries, it did so even less.

International trade requires several things: good communications, cheap and reliable transport, certainty about the stuff getting across borders and to the customer and about the price it will fetch when it does, and trust that the exporter will get paid. In earlier eras, when long-distance trade was a precarious and uncertain business, it often took the power of the state to ensure that all this happened, frequently by doing the trade itself or heavily underwriting those that did.

Such a benign, supportive environment for trade was often the exception rather than the rule in ancient and medieval times, and in Africa that too often remains the case today. Just as political interference can prevent comparative advantage in trade operating, so can the inability to get exports from source to destination. Basic cheap manufactured goods made in China and shipped across two oceans and around the world to ports in Spain can massively undercut the same products made just across the Mediterranean in Africa.

Similarly, contrary to some of the views of globalization's discontented, business often does not go where land is cheapest and wages lowest. Coffee beans grown in Africa for European markets are almost always taken to Europe before being roasted and ground for sale; cocaine, much of which is smuggled into Europe through trans-shipment points in west Africa, is grown and processed thousands of miles away in Latin America and then taken across the Atlantic.

Why? Because it is hard in Africa to overcome the technical and logistical difficulties of processing coffee and to achieve the rapid and reliable transport needed to get it to market before it goes stale. Simple cost advantage is often wiped out by much greater efficiency in making goods and getting them to market – and in particular in creating a surging torrent of commerce that sweeps new products along efficiently, reliably and inexpensively towards their destination. We all know the Chinese proverb about teaching a man to fish rather than giving him a fish. But to make him even better off, it will help if he can get that fish to market.

Advances in transport and telecommunications have enormously increased the opportunities on offer to developing countries to sell into a world market. But it would be a mistake to imagine that the inevitable result of this is to effect the 'death of distance' or to make the world flat. One of the more unexpected aspects of global trade over the past couple of decades is the resolute failure of distance to die. Economists have long been puzzling over the fact that, on average, the effect of distance on reducing trade has remained high. There remains relatively little trade between far-flung regions compared to that between close neighbours. There is also surprisingly little trade between rich and poor countries. Most trade today is in fact in fairly similar products and services between fairly similar countries, not between very different economies exploiting big innate advantages over their trading partners.

Advances in technology can help forge, extend and thicken supply chains. But it also takes human ingenuity beyond that of the inventor. It takes entrepreneurs to seize the opportunities that technology offers, and it takes governments to encourage, support and facilitate them, and when appropriate, as it often is, to get the hell out of their way.

How is it that these webs of production and commerce have been woven densely and firmly in some continents, like Europe, and yet have remained sparse and frail in Africa?

It has not always been so. As we have seen, trade in Europe received a severe blow with the collapse of the Roman empire, after which a coherent trading system was replaced with a politically fractured and shifting mosaic of city-states and kingdoms. These realms were neither large nor stable enough to secure trade routes. Since governments were not able to fulfil those functions, private clubs came in to fill the gap. When regional trade within Europe in grain, furs, timber and so on revived and grew in the Middle Ages, traders arrived at an ad hoc solution – a particular form of trading association known as a 'merchant guild' or 'Hanse', generally based in a particular city.

To begin with the Hanses provided armed protection, which fulfilled the most basic need of trade – getting the goods to the buyer securely without them being stolen on the way. As they developed, the merchant guilds expanded their role to become self-regulating clubs which negotiated with local rulers on their members' behalf, forging agreements on standard tolls and other fees to hammer out regular reliable trade routes. They also managed to wangle members particular trade privileges, which was a good incentive for other traders to join.

Urban air is particularly conducive to commerce and somewhat more protective of the rights of the individual. By the (admittedly pretty dismal) feudal standards of the day, with many Europeans tethered to the station in life into which they had been born, many of the Hanses were egalitarian. They governed themselves and had fairly open policies on running for office. Since the point of trade was to get stuff abroad, a group of the Hanses formed an international association called the Hanseatic League, which established control over trade in the Baltic Sea.

Lübeck, the German port on the Baltic, was the League's leading light, with the great ports of London, Cologne, Bruges and Novgorod (in what is now Russia) also particularly active. In fact, at its height the League acted rather like a state. Having established control over the narrow Danish straits and the overland route to the Baltic across the Jutland peninsula, it fought wars to prevent the Dutch and English threatening its privileged position. It also established colonies or *Kontors* in its leading cities, in which the capitalist breezes were particularly bracing; some of them were walled compounds with their own warehouses and living quarters for the merchants.

In Paris, a Hanse known as *les marchands d'eau* essentially controlled all trade carried on the city's waterways. This started out as a limited exclusive right to trade in fish and wine brought in on the Seine, both of which, then as now, Paris consumed in hefty quantities, or to tax foreign merchants who had the temerity to enter such trade themselves. Increasingly, though, the water merchants started regulating weights and measures and setting rules for the city's markets. Eventually the Hanse expanded into something somewhat resembling an alternative government for Paris.

As states themselves got better at regulating trade and suppressing pirates, the need for the Hanses diminished. The Hanseatic League in particular eventually succumbed to the envy of merchants excluded from it and the jealousy of governments such as the Dutch that wanted to collect tolls and monopolize trade themselves. This tension evident in the role of the League is one that we will see recur down the centuries. Like any other public service, the operation of a trading system was frequently a monopoly. Those with monopoly power often tend to abuse it, and the creation of a trading system or a trade route all too often was followed by an attempt to milk it for profits by keeping out competitors.

It was precisely this pattern which also saw the rise and then fall of the chartered trading company. We have already met the most famous – the East India Companies of the Netherlands and England, founded at the beginning of the seventeenth century. The former dominated the spice trade from east Asia for more than a century, while the latter ended up going well beyond simply being a later and longer-distance equivalent of the Hanses to become a privately held prototype of modern empire.

When it was set up in the seventeenth century, the East India Company was not just the only business that traded between Asia and Britain but the only business that was allowed to. The Company wanted a monopoly to ensure it had sufficient certainty of profit to make it worth making the effort and taking the risk involved in trading goods across thousands of miles. Trading with Asia involved great distances and high risks. It was too big and too long-term for the traditional traders.

The spice trade during the sixteenth century was dominated by the Portuguese, not least because their explorers had found routes around the Cape of Good Hope to India and then to east Asia. But as we will see in the chapter on corruption, they ran their trading empire badly. They used an inefficient distribution network of German, Spanish and Italian merchants and were vulnerable, as frequently happens in international trade, to newer, smarter and better-organized competitors.

Trading spices or other long-distance goods involved not just the risks of unreliable trade winds, storms and piracy but a danger of sudden falls in prices, rendering a trip unprofitable. Overcoming these risks required an operation of considerable size and reliability, good information and the ability to exploit it – and, critically, a monopoly of sales back home that would prevent it being undercut by an unpredictable glut on the market.

The East India Company, founded in 1600, was the latest and most ambitious of a series of English trading companies given a royal monopoly with a view to exploiting longer-distance commerce. The Company was run largely by the same clique of merchants that already ran the Levant Company, which was created to run trade with Turkey. The two initially shared the same governor, Alderman Thomas Smythe.

The first fleet of four ships departed for east Asia in 1601 with definitive evidence of a monopoly franchise – letters of introduction from Queen Elizabeth I asking local rulers, sovereign to sovereign, to trade with the Company. The sultan of Aceh, in what is now Indonesia, was their first successful contact, granting the Company trading rights and exemption from local customs duties. In the major trading city of Bantam, on the island of Java, it established the first English 'factory' – not a manufacturing plant but a permanent foreign centre for regular trade. Without a fixed trading post, merchants who visited only once a year and had to sail halfway across the world to get there would be at a bargaining disadvantage with local partners who would be able to drag out the negotiations as long as they liked, knowing that each day waiting for a deal would be costing their counterparts money.

The first Company expedition to east Asia returned with 500 tons of peppercorns, earning a knighthood for its commander. Throughout the seventeenth century the Company battled against its Dutch rival, which was created in 1602. But the Dutch East India Company proved to be very difficult to dislodge from its growing dominance of the spice trade. The Dutch had better ships and a much more developed financial system, which widened the pool of capital providers well beyond a narrow clique to encompass even quite modest investors. They could split their investments between many different ships, thus sharing the risk. They could borrow at much lower interest rates. They provided a sophisticated forward market that allowed merchants to sell produce at a guaranteed price in the future, avoiding the risk of sudden price changes.

In financial and logistical sophistication, the Dutch East India Company looked much more like a modern trading system. Yet it not only relied on a monopoly of demand in the domestic market but, through brutal use of military force, managed to establish the exclusive supply of spices from east Asia as well. (This story has been well told in the entertaining *Nathaniel's Nutmeg*.) Indeed, the history of trade routes and supply chains for centuries was not one of free agents operating in open markets, but of merchants exploiting military power and monopoly. For many trade routes and products, there was no alternative. Few companies operating without guaranteed markets would have put up so much money, men and ships for such far and uncertain trade. Any European power with a pretension to being a trading nation started incorporating its own. After creating their own East India Company in 1602, the Dutch created a West India version in 1621; the French created East and West Indies Companies in 1664 and a Compagnie de Sénégal to trade with Africa in 1672, the same year that the British Royal African Company was founded.

The state had to make a trade-off, judging the value of regular imports from a chartered company against the cost of granting that company a monopoly in the home market. Sometimes governments struck a balance by moderating the company's power with early versions of anti-trust law. The Hudson's Bay Company, for example, which traded furs from North America, could only sell the furs it brought back at small lots in fixed auctions, to prevent it manipulating the market by creating shortages and driving up prices.

Eventually, these institutions would outlive their value, as the cost of granting monopolies at home outweighed the benefits. But they endured for a remarkably long time. The British East India Company did not lose its monopoly over Asian trade until the nineteenth century. (A descendant of the Hudson's Bay Company is still in existence running a chain of department stores in Canada, though its grip on the North American fur trade is not what it was.) Over shorter distances, where the volume of private trade could build up to a critical competitive mass, they were superseded by what we might recognize as a more modern, free-market system of trade. Transatlantic trade was one of the first to resemble this, in the eighteenth century, with the exception of the longer routes to the north operated by the HBC.

Underlying this growth and change in supply chains and trade routes over the centuries, whatever form they took, technological forces were at work. Better trade and transport played an obvious role in shortening journey times and improving the flow of information between traders. But technological change was not, and is not, manna from heaven that equally benefits all societies and industries. It needs to land in the right environment, populated by clever business people who can seize and exploit its potential with governments to encourage them.

The nineteenth century saw the rapid growth of transoceanic trade in bulk commodities. It was this that essentially started the transformation that we saw in the water chapter which turned countries like Egypt from local breadbaskets to global consumers. The reason is not difficult to see: the railway opened up the Argentine pampas and the American prairie, and steam-powered ships radically decreased the time and cost, and increased the reliability, of long-distance sea travel.

The latter point perhaps deserves particular emphasis. One of the most frustrating aspects of sea transport before steam power was not the time but the uncertainty. Wind power is weaker than steam but it is also far more variable.

The influence of the wind on trade and commerce was graphically demonstrated by the nature of one of the earliest economic indicators used to steer the economy. To this day, in the ornate room in the Bank of England where the institution's governing

Court meets is a dial placed high on a wall and connected to a wind-vane on the roof. In the early nineteenth century, the direction of the wind was used to set monetary policy. If the breeze was blowing up the Thames and ships were able to come into port, the Bank would need to extend more credit (the early equivalent of cutting interest rates) to enable merchants to buy the arriving goods.

Just how much the inception of steam power changed the whole rules of the game is evident from the accounts of seafarers before it became widely used. Henry Wise, a chief officer of the *Edinburgh*, a ship in the East India Company's service, was so frustrated with the vagaries of the trade winds that in 1839 he published a collection of the logs of long-distance voyages undertaken by the Company's ships. The book was a thinly disguised excuse to propagate what was clearly a fervent one-man campaign to encourage the use of 'mechanical propellers', a technology whose widespread use was then in its infancy. 'The absence of any thing like practical detail in the various suggestions hitherto submitted for improving the communication with India, via the Cape of Good Hope, and the non-appearance of any work establishing the vast advantages of steam-power applied as an auxiliary aid to shipping, occasion this intrusion upon public attention' was his self-exculpatory introduction.

Wise's logs show that ships generally took between 100 and 130 days to sail from England to Bombay, with wide and unpredictable variations in journey time. Ships from Britain sailing south through the Atlantic round the Cape and to India followed the prevailing trade wind that blew from the north-east, which involved going well out of their way to the west, and then frequently spending days or weeks becalmed in the doldrums around the equator before picking up the southerly and westerly trade winds that would take them south and around the Cape.

'During most voyages to distant parts of the globe, contrary winds are less a source of detention than vexatious calms,' Wise wrote. He recounts the story of the warship *Coote* in the Company's service, which was resupplied with provisions by a steamer.

The *Coote* was heading to capture Aden, the Yemeni port that the East India Company seized as a base to suppress piracy on ships bound for India. The *Coote* had progressed only ten miles in the previous twenty-four hours, and had 200 miles still to go. As Wise pointed out, with propellers it would have been in Aden within two days.

Wise got his wish. Transoceanic shipping became steam-powered and this, together with the opening of the Suez Canal in 1869, utterly changed the pattern of long-distance shipping. Freight rates that were recorded over many decades, for commodities such as coal from the north-east of England shipped to London, allow us to make comparisons across time. They show a sharp decline from 1850 onwards, around the time that metal hulls and steam propulsion were widely introduced.

One of the effects of better transport is to create a more perfect market across a bigger area rather than one splintered by inefficient logistics. So the effect of cheaper shipping is very clear in the convergence of the prices of bulk commodities like wheat on either side of the Atlantic. In 1852–6, a bushel of wheat cost $0.85 in gold dollars in the wheat-selling city of Chicago, while the listed price in the importing city of London averaged $1.85. By 1895–9, when the railroads and steam ships had enormously improved the supply chain, Chicago wheat cost $0.70 to London's $0.83. By 1910–13, just before the First World War intervened to end the first great era of globalization, wheat was actually very marginally cheaper in London than in Chicago, $0.98 to $0.97. A single market had been created.

The technological breakthroughs that enable such trade to improve are often to do with information as much as transport itself. An economist's idea of paradise (pitiful but true) is one governed by the law of one price, where the prices of similar goods in different markets converge such that inefficiencies are driven out of the system. To get to this nirvana, information about prices in different markets is crucial.

In the right circumstances, information is money. There is an old story that the Rothschild European banking family made a huge amount of money out of the battle of Waterloo because their carrier pigeon system brought them news of Wellington's victory before anyone else in London had it, enabling them to snap up financial assets cheaply from their nervous owners. The story is largely a myth (the news actually came from newspaper reports in Brussels, and the Rothschilds lost money through miscalculating the brevity of the war). But the family certainly had a large and complex network of agents throughout Europe, which meant they were frequently ahead of anyone else with news, political or otherwise, that might affect asset prices.

The modern equivalent of the carrier pigeon and the Rothschild network is the mobile phone, whose cheapness makes it a far more democratic medium and one more likely to create an efficient market than entrench one participant in a monopoly. For years, development economists and World Bank officials had been coming back from Africa and India with starry-eyed tales about cellphones delivering efficiency gains by allowing farmers and fishermen to check on the prices at various markets before they sold their produce. Finally, someone actually went and collected data from the coastal fish markets in Kerala in south-western India – and, pleasingly, the anecdotes turned out to be accurate.

Before mobile phones, the prices Keralan fishermen could get at markets within 15 kilometres of each other varied from zero (that is, no-one was there to buy at any price) to 9.9 rupees per kilo. Mobile phones came to Kerala in 1997, and within four years most fishing boats had one: the base towers were planted so that mobile phone coverage extended 20–25 kilometres out to sea. Prices between markets rapidly converged. Previously, any given price was on average 60 per cent higher or lower than the average of all prices. After mobiles, that disparity declined to 15 per cent. Previously, 5–8 per cent of each day's catch was dumped because there was no-one to buy it: that fell to almost zero. The price of fish to customers fell by 4 per cent; fishermen's profits went up by 8 per cent. To use a ghastly cliché, the introduction of mobile phones was a win-win. Finally the familiar rhetorical question had an answer: this particular technology had a lot to do with the price of fish.

The internet has proved to be an even more powerful tool for matching buyers and sellers across the world and enabling trade links to be established. But the invention of a new technology does not automatically mean it is going to be used. There are frequently vested interests to be overcome in exploiting a new bit of kit to streamline and shorten supply chains, and it often takes an entrepreneur with an unusual degree of vision and persistence to overcome them.

The story of how the PC manufacturer Dell used the internet to create worldwide supply chains which can react so quickly to demand that each computer is assembled to individual order has formed the basis of a best-selling treatise on the flatness of the world. But more than a century earlier, another pioneering American company showed how a new technology needs imagination and entrepreneurial drive to transform a supply chain.

The railways and the telegraph, as we have seen, opened up the American Midwest and West and their vast plains and prairies as the source of grain and meat for America's industrialized east coast and then for the huge markets across the Atlantic in Europe. But for one particular comestible, fresh beef, it took a remarkable company to wrest those new technologies into a supply chain that could feed one of the biggest agglomerations of urbanized workers in the world.

GF Swift, once a minor-league Boston wholesale butchering company, built a continental economic empire by vertically integrating the entire supply chain, from field to fork. It not only shortened and regularized the time it took beef to travel but enormously accelerated the speed and quality of the information being passed the other way. The technologies that GF Swift exploited were complementary: transport and telecommunications. The telegraph and the railroad developed together, the lines running alongside one another. In 1849, the New York and Erie Railroad pioneered use of the telegraph to control operations.

Five years later it was standard practice among the railroad companies.

The technology, incidentally, helped to drive its own standardization, including one of the most fundamental of all measurements: time. In the middle of the nineteenth century, there were over 200 different local times in the US. Towns might be only a few minutes ahead of or behind the time in the next town along. Even the American railroad companies between them used about eighty different times, since journeys took so long that there was plenty of opportunity for people to change their watches. As railroad travel quickened and expanded, the potential for confusion increased, and in 1883 the railroads imposed a uniform time, with the four time zones that persist until today: Eastern, Central, Mountain and Pacific.

Prices as well as times converged. The same commodities increasingly cost the same in cities on either side of America, as they were later to do in cities on either side of the Atlantic. And commodity prices not only fell but became more predictable for both buyer and seller. Formal commodity exchanges grew up in Chicago that allowed forward sales – enabling farmers to know ahead of time what they would get for their grain and consumers to know what they would pay for it.

The railroads changed not just the volume but the orientation of US trade. Until then, it had generally gone north to south, being floated down the Mississippi. Goods bound for the east coast were often taken first to New Orleans – a diversion almost as dramatic as the pre-steam East India Company ships bound for India sailing most of the way west across the Atlantic first. But livestock was rarely transported by ship. Hogs were too difficult to manage and cattle too large and unwieldy. Cows bound for the east coast were herded a thousand miles on foot, a journey that started between late February and June in the Midwest and ended up with the cattle, often in considerably worse shape and fewer in number than at the beginning, arriving in east coast stockyards between April and August.

With the railroad, live cattle could be taken direct to the markets in a few days. But they still arrived, in the words of the Massachusetts Railroad Commissioners in 1870, at best 'panting, fevered and unfit to kill'. At worst, they said, 'a percentage of dead animals is hauled out of the car'. Transporting live cattle also meant carrying around worthless weight and space: 55 per cent of the animal was inedible. It also involved considerable inefficiencies of scale. Every town of any size, more or less, had to have its own slaughterhouse, from where the meat was distributed via local butchers. The supply chain was long and disjointed, and just as for the pre-mobile phone Keralan fishermen it was hard to match supply and demand.

In 1875, Gustavus Swift came to Chicago to set up a cattle-buying office for his Boston-based meat wholesaler. As he later wrote: 'I was determined to eradicate the waste of buying cattle which had passed through the hands of too many middle-men and against which too many charges had accumulated.'

Previous attempts to ship meat in refrigerated railcars had proved unprofitable. This was not particularly because the technology was inadequate but because they used the existing branch network of distributors, which was quite happy churning out profit from the system as it was and saw no particular need for speed. Swift set up his own branch distribution network, partly because he needed refrigerated warehouses, starting off by shipping to two businesses in Massachusetts.

His system had two features in common with Dell: one, a high volume of goods going through the system based on rapid transport and communications; two, a demand-pull rather than a supply-push system. Using the telegraph, orders placed by retail butchers were relayed to headquarters and to buyers at the stockyards for breeds, grades and quantities required each day. Cattle arrived at the stockyards by night, were bought in the early morning and were on the slaughterhouse floors no later than 11am. The telegraph balanced supply and demand in something quite close to real time. The magazine *Harper's Weekly* in 1882 published a story describing breathlessly how a side of beef left a Swift plant in Chicago hung on a hook and was transferred to a refrigerated railcar and thence to a freezer in a branch house in New York still hanging by the same hook.

The economies of scale and the elimination of waste more than offset the higher cost of refrigeration and Swift's considerable telegraphic bill. By 1880 he had twelve branches in New England; by 1884 it was the second-biggest meat-packing firm in the US; by 1903, after a series of mergers, it was the biggest meat-packing firm in the world. Before Swift started up, New York did the most slaughtering out of any of the US states, because that is where the consumers were. Afterwards, it was concentrated in the trade hub of Chicago. The city on Lake Michigan became what the poet Carl Sandburg in 1916 immortalized, with gusto if not metre and rhyme, as a city:

> Laughing the stormy, husky, brawling laughter of
> Youth, half-naked, sweating, proud to be Hog
> Butcher, Tool Maker, Stacker of Wheat, Player with
> Railroads and Freight Handler to the Nation.

Technology mattered, of course, but it would have been worthless without good management using information to increase speed, volume and efficiency. It also needed a government prepared to support the system, or at least not to get in the way. The eastern wholesale butchers tried to protect their cosy monopoly. They demanded laws requiring official inspection of cattle in the state in which the beef was to be eaten, to be conducted less than twenty-four hours before slaughter. Such a regime would have destroyed the high-volume hub in Chicago. In 1890, the Supreme Court declared such laws a violation of interstate commerce, and the market in chilled beef continued with the support of the highest court in the land.

Even when most companies will benefit from a new process, coordinating them into adopting it can be more difficult than it would appear. In the case of Keralan mobiles, it was relatively easy: no-one had a particularly strong vested interest in keeping the status quo, and a market or fishing boat beginning to use a mobile would find itself at a competitive advantage. But when a system is adopted that works only when everyone uses it, overcoming the 'collective-action problem' can be more difficult. Frequently, to unleash the power of technology and entrepreneurship to forge supply chains, governments need to allow competition, or indeed actively to create the circumstances for it.

Before the internet, one of the most rapid changes to the global economy and trade was wrought by something so blatantly useful that it is hard to imagine a struggle to get it adopted: the shipping container. Today's international shipping business is a resolutely unglamorous affair. Once it took a romantic struggle of sweating sailors and straining dockers to bring goods from Asia to Europe or from tropical zones to temperate. It has now become a cold-eyed, computerized business of mechanically shifting stacks of identical 8 x 8 x 20-foot metal boxes around the world, dehumanized by the unpoetic word which made it into the lexicon of our Liberian graffiti artist, 'logistics'.

Dull it may be, but it is also ruthlessly efficient. In the early 1960s, before the standard container became ubiquitous, freight costs were 10 per cent of the value of US imports, about the same barrier to trade as the average official government import tariff. Yet in a journey that went halfway round the world, half of those costs could be incurred in two ten-mile movements through the ports at either end. The predominant 'break-bulk' method, where each shipment was individually split up into loads that could be handled by a team of dockers, was vastly complex and labour-intensive. Ships could take weeks or months to load, as a huge variety of cargoes of different weights, shapes and sizes had to be stacked together by hand. And with valuable shipments passing through so many hands, pilfering was recognized as an unofficial part of dockers' pay.

Indeed, one of the most unreliable aspects of such a labour-intensive process was the labour. Ports, like mines, were frequently seething pits of industrial unrest. Irregular work on one side combined with what was often a tight-knit, well-organized labour community on the other. Often workers were organized into powerful unions with the ability to block up the bottleneck of global commerce. The violence, corruption and struggles for power in the New York docks depicted in the movie *On the Waterfront* were not all that far from reality.

In 1956, loading break-bulk cargo cost $5.83 per ton. The entrepreneurial genius who saw the possibilities for standardardized container shipping, Malcolm McLean, floated his first container-ized ship in that year and claimed to be able to shift cargo for 15.8 cents a ton. Boxes of the same size that could be loaded by crane and neatly stacked were much faster to load. Moreover, carrying cargo in a standard container would allow it to be shifted between truck, train and ship without having to be repacked each time.

But between McLean's container and the standardization of the global market were an array of formidable obstacles. They began at home in the US with the official Interstate Commerce Com-mission, which could prevent price competition by setting rates for freight haulage by route and commodity, and the powerful International Longshoremen's Association labour union. More broadly, the biggest hurdle was achieving what economists call 'network effects': the benefit of a standard technology rises ex-ponentially as more people use it. To dominate world trade, con-tainers had to be easily interchangeable between different shipping lines, ports, trucks and railcars. And to maximize efficiency, they all needed to be the same size.

The adoption of a network technology often involves over-coming the resistance of those who are heavily invested in the old system. And while the efficiency gains are clear to see, there are very obvious losers as well as winners. For containerization, perhaps the most spectacular example was the demise of New York City as a port.

In the early 1950s, New York handled a third of US seaborne trade in manufactured goods. But it was woefully inefficient, even with existing break-bulk technology: 283 piers, 98 of which were able to handle ocean-going ships, jutted out into the river from Brooklyn and Manhattan. Trucks bound for the docks had to fight through the crowded, narrow streets of Manhattan, wait for an hour or two before even entering a pier, and then undergo a laborious two-stage process in which the goods were first unloaded into a transit shed and then loaded onto a ship. 'Public loader' work gangs held exclusive rights to load and unload on a particular pier, a power in effect granted by the ILA, which enforced its monopoly with sabotage and violence against competitors. The ILA fought ferociously against containerization, correctly foreseeing that it would destroy their privileged position as bandits controlling the mountain pass. Thomas Gleason, president of the ILA, said: 'The container is digging our graves, and we cannot live off containers.'

On this occasion, bypassing them simply involved going across the river. A container port was built in New Jersey, where a 1500-foot wharf allowed ships to dock parallel to shore and containers to be lifted on and off by crane. Between 1963–4 and 1975–6, the number of days worked by longshoremen in Manhattan went from 1.4 million to 127,041.

Containers rapidly captured the transatlantic market, and then the growing trade with Asia. The effect of containerization is hard to see immediately in freight rates, since the oil price hikes of the 1970s kept them high, but the speed with which shippers adopted containerization made it clear it brought big benefits of efficiency and cost. The extraordinary growth of the Asian tiger economies of Singapore, Taiwan, Korea and Hong Kong, which based their development strategy on exports, was greatly helped by the container trade that quickly built up between the US and east Asia. Ocean-borne exports from South Korea were 2.9 million tons in 1969 and 6 million in 1973, and its exports to the US tripled.

But the new technology did not get adopted all on its own. It needed a couple of pushes from government – both, as it happens, largely to do with the military. Projects of huge help to private business several times had a military objective, or at least claimed a military pretext, not least because it was a way of allowing the federal government to play a leading role. The states may have claimed some jurisdiction over commerce, but the armed forces were indisputably a federal concern. The national interstate highway system, without which America would hardly be America, was introduced by President Eisenhower in 1956 as the National Interstate and Defense Highways Act. The ostensible rationale was that it would allow soldiers to be moved rapidly round the country, and the populations of large cities to be evacuated quickly in case of attack. During his days as an army general, Eisenhower had apparently been impressed by the autobahns built by Hitler to get the armies of the Reich rapidly around Germany.

As far as the ships were concerned, the same link between the merchant and military navy that had inspired the Navigation Acts in seventeenth-century England endured into twentieth-century America. To this day, a piece of legislation known as the Jones Act stipulates that all cargo being carried from one US port to another must be taken in US-built ships registered in the US and with a crew that is at least 75 per cent American – a restriction that America's partners in trade negotiations like to refer to when being lectured by Washington about opening their markets to US competitors. (Then again, the US navy does do everyone a big favour by patrolling the world's shipping lanes to try to keep them free of pirates.)

The government's first helping hand was to give a spur to the system by adopting it to transport military cargo. The US armed forces, seeing the efficiency of the system, started contracting McLean's company Pan-Atlantic, later renamed Sea-land, to carry equipment to the quarter of a million American soldiers stationed in western Europe. To begin with, ships on the return journey seem largely to have carried Scotch whisky, not least because of the invention of a stainless-steel tank container to carry it in bulk, which ended the problem of pilferage. One of the few benefits of America's misadventure in Vietnam was a rapid expansion of containerization. Because war involves massive movements of men and material, it is often armies that pioneer new techniques in supply chains. Napoleon was a logistical genius as well as a military one, though it was misjudging his army's ability to live off the Russian countryside that forced its disastrous retreat from Moscow in 1812.

The government's other role was in banging heads together sufficiently to get all companies to accept the same size container. Standard sizes were essential to deliver the economies of scale that came from interchangeability – which, as far as the military was concerned, was vital if the ships had to be commandeered in case war broke out. This was a significant problem to overcome, not least because all the companies that had started using the container had settled on different sizes. Pan-Atlantic used 35-foot containers, because that was the maximum size allowed on the highways in its home base in New Jersey. Another of the big shipping companies, Matson Navigation, used a 24-foot container since its biggest trade was in canned pineapple from Hawaii, and a container bigger than that would have been too heavy for a crane to lift. Grace Line, which largely traded with Latin America, used a 17-foot container that was easier to truck around winding mountain roads.

Establishing a US standard and then getting it adopted internationally took more than a decade. Indeed, not only did the US Maritime Administration have to mediate in these rivalries but also to fight its own turf battles with the American Standards Association, an agency set up by the private sector. The matter was settled by using the power of federal money: the Federal Maritime Board, which handed out public subsidies for shipbuilding, decreed that only the 8 x 8-foot containers in lengths of 10, 20, 30 or 40 feet would be eligible for handouts.

Containerization did not just carry existing cargo more quickly and cheaply: it catalysed a radical shift in the way that companies did business. One of the benefits of fast and reliable transport is that it enables companies to hold smaller inventories, or spare stocks, as they have more certainty about being able to get cargoes to where they need to be faster. In the 1980s, the Japanese, and particularly innovative companies like Toyota, pioneered what was known as 'just-in-time' production. Since the supply of inputs could respond quickly to shifts in demand, Toyota, rather than having a monolithic supply chain within a huge company, started to contract out its component manufacture to a variety of smaller, more nimble businesses.

The original Asian tigers, today joined in varying degrees by Thailand, Malaysia, Indonesia, the Philippines, Vietnam and of course China, now form what is essentially an internationally disaggregated manufacturing and assembly chain, sometimes known as Factory Asia. The cheap and rapid transport of components and goods between the countries, which are after all not all right on top of each other, has had a great deal to do with making it possible.

But why doesn't Africa do the same? As we saw at the beginning of the chapter, the continent is missing out on a lot of production and trade, and coca is one of the intriguing cases. Why do Africans, in fact, not grow coca and make cocaine? They certainly export it. The white powder that fuels Europe's media and financial services industries comes from Colombia, Bolivia and Peru, but much of it is smuggled out of the west African countries of Nigeria, Guinea-Bissau and Cape Verde.

Like coffee, coca grows well at high altitude, one of the reasons that so much of it is grown in the Andes. Africa already has large coffee-growing regions – Uganda, Ethiopia, Rwanda. So why does Africa not do the higher value-added parts of the supply chain – the production and intermediate transport? In the export trade to Europe, Africans are stuck doing the relatively low-paid and high-risk part of the supply chain, the final cross-border smuggling.

Management consultancy reports in an industry like cocaine are hard to come by – though, unlike the asparagus trade, we can rule out preferential tariff policy as an explanation. Natural environmental imperfection provides a minor reason: Africa has somewhat less good climatic conditions compared with Latin America and a relative shortage of large plateaus useful for growing coca. But the main explanation, according to the United Nations Office on Drugs and Crime, is that transport and logistics in Africa are so poor and the politics so unstable that it is more efficient to make cocaine in South America and transport it from there.

Coca does not have a quick return: it is grown on plantations that take several years to be raised to productive maturity. That, apparently, is too long a period to take the risk that political and logistical volatility will interrupt the business. (There are reports from the region that the opium poppy, which is much faster to grow and harvest, is beginning to be planted in west Africa.) In some ways, given how illegality multiplies the financial, logistical and human resource management challenges of production and transport, an absence of trust and reliability is even more crippling for an illicit crop than a legitimate one. As Bob Dylan said, to live outside the law you must be honest.

Now, no-one who has seen the way in which the cocaine trade has poisoned the society and politics of a country like Colombia would ever seriously suggest that growing cocaine for export would be a good move for Africa. But there are plenty of legitimate exports where bringing more of the value chain inside Africa would help in reducing poverty. One is coca's high-altitude companion, coffee. Africa exports lots of raw green coffee beans but makes relatively little roasted and ground, or instant, coffee itself. The same is true of cocoa: Africa has the world's two biggest growers of cacao, Ghana and Côte d'Ivoire, but the vast majority of their product is exported as raw green beans.

Andrew Rugasira, a Ugandan entrepreneur who started the 'Good African' brand of roasted coffee which has now found its way into British supermarkets, says that until he made them coffee to drink, some of the farmers from whom he bought his beans had literally no idea what the funny little things they produced were used for. Some thought they were bullets used by guerrilla armies in the ongoing conflicts in the next-door Democratic Republic of Congo. At this point they had been growing coffee for decades.

Searching for explanations, let us first rule out as a major reason the widespread but largely erroneous idea that trade policy is used to keep Africa poor. Import tariffs and subsidies can distort trade mightily, as we saw in the previous chapter, but these days they aren't a big deal for Africa.

It is widely believed that all rich countries impose tariffs on manufactured products from Africa but not on raw materials. One particular story that gets a good deal of play is that the European

Union lets in cocoa *beans* tax-free from Ghana but taxes imports of Ghanaian *chocolate*. Unfortunately, it is completely wrong. Because Ghana used to be a colony, it benefits from the special trade deal with Europe we encountered in the last chapter. Chocolate from Ghana enters the EU duty-free. Among the institutions and people I have heard or seen propagating this myth who should know better are the former British prime minister Tony Blair, the development campaign Oxfam, the UK's Department for International Development (who ended up having to pulp a large run of leaflets after the European Commission complained about the inaccuracy), the United Nations in its annual Human Development Report and, astonishingly enough, Alan Kyerematen, then Ghana's trade minister.

The real reason Ghana doesn't export more than a small amount of expensive high-quality chocolate is that it is prohibitively costly to do business there. It doesn't help that it's really hot in Ghana and chocolate melts in the heat: the cost of maintaining a refrigerated, or at least cooled, unbroken chain from factory to truck to port to ship all the way to Rotterdam is high. The refrigeration excuse, though, doesn't hold for coffee in Uganda or Ethiopia. There, the reason for the absence of more than the basic earliest stage of the supply chain is simply that the expertise, the finance and the logistics aren't there.

This is the stuff that really matters. A survey of villages in Uganda found that there was a clear link between access to logistics services like district markets, trucking companies and farm gate purchasers, and the likelihood of a village producing export crops – coffee, tea, cotton, fruit and flowers. And despite the concerns sometimes expressed about the dangers of farming for export rather than home consumption, villages producing such crops had lower rates of poverty than those who grew maize or bananas to eat themselves.

One of the more extraordinary ten days of my life was spent travelling around Africa in 2002 with the campaigning rock star Bono and the then US Treasury secretary, Paul O'Neill. When Bono and O'Neill talked to Africans, one of the most consistent complaints they heard was the difficulty of getting products to market along the continent's terrible roads. I still have my security pass from the trip, signed by Bono. He added a slogan for a putative campaign I would heartily have endorsed but which he thought might not fly with the general public: 'Rock Against Bad Infrastructure'.

When you look at the attempts to bring more parts of the supply chain into Africa, it is clear that these are the most important constraints on trade and production. Mali in west Africa, for example, is a traditional cotton-growing area, with near-perfect climatic and soil conditions. But apart from 'ginning' the cotton – a basic mechanized process for removing seeds and stalks – its attempts to go further up the value chain have struggled. I visited a cotton-spinning factory in Mali a few years ago and was told that the plant was running below capacity and was some way from making a profit. Labour was cheap but largely unskilled, and production was hobbled by unreliable and expensive power and difficulties exporting through either neighbouring Côte d'Ivoire, frequently rocked by civil conflict, or the overloaded port at Dakar in Senegal.

Being landlocked is a particular problem, which helps to explain why so many African and central Asian countries have difficulty achieving economic lift-off. Having to rely on neighbouring countries to truck out goods involves inevitable border delays and makes exporters vulnerable to conflict or other disruption in their transit routes. It is notable that the products that landlocked countries like Uganda and Zambia have begun successfully to export – fresh flowers and high-value vegetables – are often those carried by air. Each day's delay in shipping reduces a country's trade on average by 1 per cent, and by a striking 6 per cent for time-sensitive goods like perishable fruit and vegetables. One week longer to get your goods to market, and your country's ability to trade in high-value perishables is nearly halved.

It takes an average of twenty-four hours just to cross the border between Uganda and Kenya en route to the Kenyan ports like Mombasa, which then impose further delays. And as with the East India Company's ships sailing to Asia, it is not just the time but also the uncertainty that is so damaging to trade. Andrew Rugasira of the Good African coffee company reckons it takes a month to get his coffee from Uganda to Mombasa. Until valve technology was developed that allowed ground coffee to be bagged in a sterile atmosphere of nitrogen, thus stopping it going stale in transit, this in essence ruled out Uganda's being able to roast and grind its own coffee beans for export outside Africa.

It isn't just Africa, of course. Time and again across the developing world, the real constraints to competing with foreign producers are not trade policy but the lack of something to sell and the inability to get it to market cheaply. The plight of vegetable farmers in the Philippines is a case in point. A couple of years ago I visited the farmers, who grow garlic, cabbages, lettuce and other fresh produce high in the mountainous region of Baguio. They complained vociferously about cheap Chinese garlic, lettuces and carrots which, they said, were appearing in the markets in Manila and putting them out of business.

But in reality it appeared that a slow and expensive supply chain had more to do with their inability to compete than the threatened removal of protection by import tariffs. Unlike the markets of medieval Islam or the seventeenth-century Netherlands, the local wholesale distribution market for vegetables to which farmers trucked their produce had no forward prices, not even a day ahead. So no-one could be sure what price their produce would fetch when they rolled up with their lettuces. A shortage and hence high prices for lettuce one day would induce lots of growers to turn up the next with truckloads of lettuces, creating a glut and causing prices to fall.

There were few refrigerated warehouses and trucks, so the 'cold chain' so important to managing the supply of fresh produce was largely absent. There was no standardization of containers or cargo, so vegetables went through a laborious process of being unpacked and repacked by hand into plastic bags twice before being loaded into trucks, which then started a six-hour journey down winding mountainous roads to Manila. The effect of this on the battered vehicles was amply demonstrated by the dozens of repair garages by the roadside.

It was not surprising that a kilo of vegetables that cost two pesos at the farm gate had quintupled in price by the time it arrived at the market in Manila. Meanwhile, Chinese vegetables were arriving in Manila by sea in the ubiquitous standard container. The 40 per cent import tariff that the Philippines was imposing on some vegetables could not hope to compensate for the weaknesses in the supply chain.

Still, it is African countries that seem to suffer from weak infrastructure more than most: not just bad roads, but the lack of an efficient economic system. As we have seen, trade needs suppliers to trust that they will get paid, and legal and judicial systems that help rather than hinder business. A recent World Bank study which asked four big freight companies about trading times around the world found that three quarters of the delays in transport were administrative procedures – customs clearance, tax, cargo inspections and the like – rather than potholed roads or crumbling ports.

But how did African countries end up like this? Part of the answer is where they started off; part is how they got to where they are; and part is what they are doing, or not doing, now.

To begin with, it would be a mistake to think that all of Africa has always been undeveloped compared with the rest of the world. During medieval times, there were powerful empires in west Africa which traded salt, gold and slaves across the Sahara. An empire centred on what is now Mali built a spectacular Islamic university at Timbuktu that became a great centre of Islamic scholarship.

But the durability and reach of such civilizations were limited. As the physiologist Jared Diamond persuasively argued in his grand essay about why some people are rich and some are not, *Guns, Germs and Steel*, Africa had some intrinsic challenges when it came to development. The continent's north–south orientation gave it a huge variety of climatic conditions, which meant that crop types and technologies could not easily be transferred from one region to the next. The farming techniques of Mediterranean north Africa, even if they could be transplanted across the Sahara, do not work well in the semi-arid savannah grassland of the Sahel region at the desert's southern edge, still less the steamy tropical equatorial regions further down. And over much of Africa around the equator, diseases carried by the tsetse fly prevented the spread of domesticated animals, including the horse, which was the container ship of medieval transport in Europe.

Then came the impact of slavery and empire. As we have seen, particularly from the history of the East India Company, modern European empires often started off as trade routes and just growed. Having established territorial control well beyond simple trading posts, as we will see in the next chapter, the Company was essentially a contracted-out colonial power running India on behalf of the British Crown. Indeed, the growth of empire can be regarded as a coercive way of establishing a supply chain, often with the aim of affecting the balance of power between the parties as well as simply making transport easier. If granting a monopoly to a trading company was one way of securing the benefits of trade with a distant land, actually owning the place in question was an even more effective one.

The first great era of globalization, between 1880 and 1914, was also the age of what some historians have called High Imperialism – the apotheosis of the dominance of European colonialist powers over the rest of the world. During that time, a country that belonged to an empire had roughly twice the trade of those that did not. It does not seem to have mattered much whether the imperial capital was London, Paris, Berlin, Madrid or Washington DC. (The US, born out of a rebellion against an imperial power, had evidently forgotten its principles sufficiently by the end of the nineteenth century to have acquired a number of colonies, including the Philippines.) Using a common currency, belonging to a trading area with few blocks on imports and possessing a common language all contributed to easier trade.

But not all colonies were treated the same way, even within the same empire. Africa was never occupied to the same extent that Asian colonies such as India or the Dutch East Indies were. The tropical climate and the accompanying diseases were inhospitable to Europeans, the notable exception being right at the southern tip. South Africa, the one region of Mediterranean-style climate south of the Sahara, was heavily settled by the Dutch and then the British.

Yellow fever, malaria and other tropical diseases wiped out a large proportion of European solders and colonialists who tried to settle in sub-Saharan Africa. When, for example, the west African settlement of Sierra Leone was established as a home for freed slaves at the end of the eighteenth century, there were high hopes that it could form a thriving British colony. The requisite trading operation was formed, known first as St George's Bay Company and then as the Sierra Leone Company. It brought there a number of freed black slaves from North America who had fought on the British side in the American revolutionary war in return for their freedom.

But even compared with India, which came liberally endowed with its own supply of heat and mosquitoes and was not exactly a sanatorium for Europeans, conditions in tropical Africa were deadly. Nearly three quarters of the European settlers died in the first year of the Sierra Leone Company in 1792–3. An expedition by the Scottish explorer Mungo Park in 1805 to chart the course of the Niger river in west Africa ended up with a comfortable majority of the party dead before they had even completed the first overland part of the journey. The public back home were aware of the calamitous impact of Africa on health, and willingness to settle there was correspondingly lacking. One of the reasons that Britain developed Australia as a penal colony was that west Africa was considered and rejected as being too unhealthy, even for prisoners.

So instead of establishing large, permanent colonies, the dominant modus operandi of Europeans in Africa became to grab the resources and go. They had, of course, centuries of experience of treating Africa like this through the slave trade. The effect of the trade, apart from the disastrous impact on societies of taking away huge numbers of their young and productive members, was to encourage destructive and exploitative relationships between different kingdoms (to capture slaves to sell to the traders) and firmly to entrench European attitudes that Africa was a dark, primitive continent whose riches were there to plunder.

The functional names that were given to the colonies reveal this all too clearly: the Gold Coast (now Ghana); the Ivory Coast (still Côte d'Ivoire). The imperial 'scramble for Africa' in the late nineteenth century resulted in the competing European powers dividing the continent between them, rather than just trading gold, diamonds or slaves on the coasts as hitherto. But the mentality was often the same. Much of Africa was simply commandeered as a source of basic commodities for Europe. As well as the traditional metals and minerals, Europe imported the likes of groundnut oil from Nigeria for use as a machine lubricant and timber from Côte d'Ivoire. Perhaps the very worst case was the Belgian rule of the Congo in central Africa in the late nineteenth century – though it would be more accurate to say King Leopold II's ownership of the Congo, since it was a personal possession of the Belgian monarch rather than a colony of the state. Congolese were forced to produce rubber and, if they failed to meet their official quota, were mutilated or murdered. Several million are thought to have died.

The Europeans were there to extract, not to build. Compared with colonies like India, the railway and other transport infrastructure they built in Africa was woefully sparse. Nor was it just physical infrastructure of which Africa was relatively deprived. There was nothing close to the extensive and well-organized Indian Civil Service which recruited large numbers of locals and meant that India, whatever other problems it had, at least inherited a functioning state and bureaucracy when it gained independence. Whatever unhelpful effects China's recent activities in Africa have had in terms of propping up unpleasant regimes in Sudan and Angola, one of the reasons that some Africans have been prepared to give them the benefit of the doubt is that they have at least got some infrastructure built. In the 1970s, China constructed a railway more than a thousand miles long that connected landlocked Zambia with the Tanzanian port of Dar es Salaam. Zambia's usual trade route had been blockaded by the minority white regime in Southern Rhodesia. The Chinese helped out when, as a Zambian government minister once said to me, 'most of the world was looking the other way'.

And if anything, the weak social and legal infrastructure was a more damaging legacy than the physical one. As western Europe's rapid recovery after the Second World War showed, roads and factories can always be rebuilt as long as there is an invisible framework of education, the rule of law and a functioning economy to support the work. Without them, any amount of investment or aid poured in from outside will struggle to have much impact.

Britain transplanted its legal and political systems, along with many of its own citizens, into some of its colonies – notably Australia, New Zealand and Canada. From the beginning their administrations protected private property, had effective checks on arbitrary government action and did not put undue barriers in the way of people doing business. They have subsequently done much better than have those where colonists made the barest effort to export the imperial capital's economic and social development.

But lest we start throwing up our hands and concluding that geography and history are destiny after all, we must remember how spectacularly well Botswana did for so long despite an abysmally poor colonial inheritance of both social and physical infrastructure. Africa has been dealt a poor hand, but for the most part it could have played it a great deal better.

Roads and railways are expensive, and often require money from outside in the form of foreign investment or aid. But mobile phone coverage has spread rapidly across Africa, connecting businesses with customers, though many African traders continue to suffer from poor internet access. And improving ports and border crossings is often mainly a question of finding the political will to take on an entrenched customs bureaucracy that finds delaying trucks an excellent way of extorting bribes and doesn't want to lose it. Following the September 11 attacks on the US, there was much concern expressed that new security measures at ports and borders demanded by Washington would throw sand in the wheels of globalization and make it slower and harder to trade. In the event, border crossings on average across the world accelerated. Reformers in African countries and elsewhere accomplished reform by pointing at an external imperative: the need to meet US security standards. Those countries made choices, and the choices had good consequences.

Creating the conditions for supply chains to lengthen and trade routes to be established is neither easy nor routine. But it can be done. That Africa does not grow cocaine or make much chocolate or coffee owes something to geography and history; yet today it owes more to the inability of its governments to overcome them. It is entrepreneurial companies that exploit, and even create, such chains. But, as we saw from the history of the East India Company, or the containerization of world shipping, it often fell to a government to take the key decisions that allowed them to do so. Sometimes it has to take an active role. But often it just has to get out of the way. And this applies in particular to the bureaucrats who illicitly enrich themselves by intervening in the process of commerce.

8. Corruption

Why did Indonesia prosper under a crooked ruler and Tanzania stay poor under an honest one?

Here's a joke you hear in India. The chief minister of an impoverished Indian state goes on an exchange visit to an American city where the mayor, a wily old machine politician, shows him round. First the mayor points out a highway on the edge of town. 'See that?' he says. He taps his breast pocket and winks. 'Ten per cent.' Then he indicates a new baseball stadium. 'See that? Ten per cent.' And so it goes on. Finally he takes him under the portico of a grandiose City Hall. 'See that? Ten per cent.'

Next year the mayor goes on a return visit to India. The chief minister takes him up to his official residence, high on a hill overlooking the state capital. He makes a sweeping gesture over the city, taking in the miserable sprawling slums, the open sewers, the potholed roads, the abandoned factories. 'See that?' he says. He taps his pocket and winks. 'One hundred per cent.'

Abuse of public office is as old as public office itself. 'And thou shalt take no bribe,' God enjoins the Israelites in Exodus, 'for a bribe blindeth them that have sight, and perverteth the words of the righteous.' But there has been a particular surge of interest in corruption (a 'corruption eruption' as one commentator called it) in policy and academic circles over the past fifteen years. Development agencies like the World Bank rarely used to mention the term for fear of being accused of meddling in politics. Today their assessments of countries routinely include warnings about 'governance concerns', the currently accepted euphemism for bent officials on the take. Corruption is regularly cited as one of the reasons that poor countries stay poor.

Well, yes and no. As the Indian joke suggests, some kinds of corruption are worse than others. Some kinds are little more than a nuisance; others are corrosive. Some stop economic growth and investment dead; others are no more than a moderate headwind or, just possibly, a following breeze. Indonesia, which today has an annual income per head of over $3000, adjusting for different price levels, was ruled for decades by Suharto, an autocrat whose administration was notorious for bribery and cronyism. Meanwhile Tanzania, where the average annual income is less than $1000, remained desperately poor under a ruler who displayed great personal honesty and humility. Why?

First, let us sort out what we mean by the word 'corruption'. It can be very broadly defined as any abuse of position, whether public or private, for personal gain. Thus a procurement manager in a company who buys an unnecessarily expensive piece of kit because he has been bribed by the supplier might be called corrupt. But this might more properly be labelled fraud that rips off the company's shareholders rather than the general public. Drawing the definition like this would widen it out to include all sorts of white-collar crime. For our purposes, because we are largely interested in how governments and states have determined economic history, we can stick with the pithy description used by the World Bank: the abuse of public office for private gain.

Thus the United Nations oil-for-food scandal, involving the diversion of money from a UN-sponsored scheme that allowed Iraq to sell oil on the world market between 1996 and 2003 to buy food and medicine, was corruption; the accounting and business frauds that brought down the US energy company Enron were not.

Corruption arises because of what economists call 'principal-agent' problems, where one person or group of people – in this case, the electorate or general public – appoint another – here, civil servants or politicians – to carry out functions for them. If the principal cannot perfectly observe the actions of the agent, the agent has an incentive to act in his or her own interest instead. The public may want a government department to build a road as cheaply and efficiently as possible. But they may not notice the civil servant in charge awarding the contract to the expensive and inefficient company run by his brother-in-law, or the kick-back payment he gets in return.

Corruption is a form of self-interest that thrives on a lack of information and a lack of competition. Information can extinguish corruption by bringing the self-interest of the agents into plain view, thus eliminating discretion over the way they act. Competition can extinguish corruption by ensuring that those agents doing business expensively and ineffectively to benefit themselves are undercut by those doing it honestly and cheaply. The more monopoly and discretionary power that agents have over providing whatever service they are supposed to, and the less accountable they are, the more likely they are to succumb to corruption.

But rather than competition bringing down corruption, corruption is often allowed to prevent competition. Apart from the general moral and ethical arguments against bribery and dishonesty and the effect they can have in undermining general respect for the rule of law, corruption is generally bad for efficiency. It leads to decisions made by bureaucrats on the basis of what is good for them, not good for the economy. It directly affects quality of life by stopping public spending, whether on health, education or infrastructure, going where it is intended for. It loads heavy and often uncertain costs on business, making it hard for companies to plan ahead. It is especially bad for international trade. Controlling a border post is a particularly good way of extracting bribes: the exporter often has a lot to lose through delays, whereas the customs officer has authority to hold up shipments and all the time in the world to wait. And it rewards business people skilled in bureaucratic infighting or political manoeuvring rather than those actually good at running companies.

There is no doubt on the overall verdict: corruption is bad for growth. Standard measures of the perception of corruption within countries correlate quite well with national poverty. But within the broad brushstrokes of that overall picture there are some interesting fine details. In particular, a clutch of countries in east Asia have done well despite a long history of corruption. The most astonishing reduction of poverty in recent history has largely taken place in another east Asian country, China, which achieves no more than mid-table mediocrity in any international league of incorruptibility.

I heard a succinct explanation for this from a very senior official in the Indian government several years ago. I asked him why India attracted much less foreign direct investment than did China. Corruption, he said. I pointed out China's regularly poor scores in the corruption tables. (In the 2007 version of the 'corruption perceptions index' compiled by the anti-bribery campaign Transparency International, China and India are exactly as crooked as each other.) Yes, the official said, but the thing with China is there is only one political party to bribe.

If you are going to have corruption, best have it in as efficient and streamlined a way as possible. It is in this context that we will spend some time looking at the rule of President Suharto in Indonesia, not least because his name is pretty much synonymous with the 'crony capitalism' that has defined much of the economic rise of east Asia over the past forty years. It was, perhaps, the most striking example of how a corrupt, bloodstained dictatorship could nonetheless be an economically successful one. That Indonesia was corrupt under Suharto is not in doubt: Transparency International's inaugural ranking of countries in 1995 put Indonesia last out of the forty-one nations then surveyed, below China, Pakistan and India. But the country had got much better off despite it.

An army officer, Suharto seized the presidency with the support of the military in 1968. Indonesia, a mixed assortment of islands scattered around the equator rather unconvincingly masquerading as a unified country, was large, populous and ethnically and linguistically diverse. Colonized by the Dutch as part of their control over the spice trade, it had floundered around for its first two decades of independence. A weak and fractious parliamentary democracy was followed by the unstable dictatorship of Sukarno, the country's founding president.

As his apologists used to say, Suharto did at least bring order to Indonesia. But the collateral damage to life and liberty was heavy. On his way to power he used the army to conduct a vicious purge, killing hundreds of thousands of leftists. In a sinister echo of European fascism, Suharto then decreed that a 'New Order' of Indonesian government had begun. He proceeded to use the military and state bureaucracy to impose fierce discipline and centralized control over the country.

He created a de facto state political party, Golkar: all state employees belonged to one of its constituent bodies. Although he periodically held elections, Suharto in effect controlled the resulting Consultative Assembly and ruled by decree. He appointed all senior civil servants himself and kept close watch over them. His rule was not just modelled on the military but staffed by it as well. Former senior officers were often given roles as inspector-generals in public institutions and reported directly to him.

But rather than entangling the economy by misguided attempts to manipulate it, Suharto used much of the rope he had to tie his own hands. He adopted relatively orthodox economic policies that ended the hyperinflation that he had inherited in the late 1960s. He created a rule that the national government budget should balance. It was not quite as binding as it appeared: there were various ways to spend money that did not show up on the books. But it certainly guarded against the sort of wild spending splurges that destabilized superficially similar military dictatorships in, say, Latin America. He managed to attract foreign investment from abroad, partly by decreeing the free movement of capital across the country's borders. This reassured businesses, particularly Indonesia's talented but often unpopular ethnic Chinese trading community, that they could get their money out if they needed to, which gave them confidence to bring it into the country in the first place. The presence of cast-iron fire escapes makes even rickety buildings feel much safer.

The way such companies' interests were looked after shows how an efficient form of graft can operate. Foreign companies generally paid off a politically well-connected individual, often one of those former military officers or a senior ex-civil servant, to provide political protection for them by reporting back to Suharto any concerns they might have. Bureaucrats, usually for a back-hand fee, would then try to solve the problem. Corrupt, yes, but a systematic, organized form of corruption that acted as a network across which information could be passed and an early-warning system for investor discontent.

Meanwhile, the commanding heights of the economy were generally controlled by a network of favourites, the famous cronies, who had a mutually supportive relationship with the state. Suharto handed them juicy contracts and lucrative monopoly licences, and directed state-run commercial banks to lend to them. Few of his cronies would make it into anyone's list of the top 100 inspiring corporate leaders of the twentieth century. But from these clients he demanded, and got, benefits to the economy in return.

Suharto also undertook periodic demonstrations of presidential authority to show that he was keeping agencies and networks in check. In 1985, he disempowered the entire customs bureaucracy by decree when corruption in the docks became a serious problem, and handed the operation instead to a foreign company. The next year Indonesia's textile industry was jeopardized when the agency that held the government monopoly for importing cotton started trying to extract too many pay-offs. He fired the senior officials responsible and disbanded the monopoly.

For thirty years – a long time in government – the system worked fairly well. From being desperately poor, Indonesia grew rapidly and became a middle-income country. It reduced poverty and managed to avoid most of the traps into which many developing countries fell in their first decades after independence. It integrated into the global economy rather than trying the import substitution policies common in Africa and Latin America; it resisted skewing policies towards the cities at the expense of the countryside; it built up a good reputation in the global financial markets by repaying its international loans.

The former World Bank representative in Indonesia noted that Suharto was warned in the early 1970s by Robert McNamara, then World Bank president, that corruption threatened Indonesia's prosperity. The message was repeated in 1997 by the World Bank president of the time, James Wolfensohn. In response, Suharto pointed at the big gains in growth and income in the intervening quarter-century. His regime was brutal and corrupt, but it had produced results.

Other countries in east Asia had similar experiences. South Korea, for example, though it has more recently democratized and scores relatively well in current assessments of levels of corruption, achieved Western levels of income having been run by another authoritarian former general, Park Chung Hee. Park also maintained a network of favourites whose palms required regular applications of grease by anyone with whom they did business.

Korean businesses were backed with extensive government intervention, including state-directed lending, subsidies and selective tariffs on imports. Unlike Suharto, Korea also maintained strict limits on capital outflows and relied less on foreign direct investment to build factories. But like Suharto, Park subjected the favoured companies, gathered together into large conglomerates called *chaebols*, to the rigours of competition and inspection. The chaebols were heavily oriented towards exports, thus subjecting them to the competitive pressures of the global economy. Failing companies were allowed to shrink, not kept indefinitely on life support. Of the ten largest chaebols in 1966, only two were in the top ten by 1974. And like Suharto, Park collected detailed information on how the economy and businesses were doing through mandatory reports by the state-supported enterprises.

Moreover, Korea seemed to go one better than Indonesia in stopping bribes from actually influencing business decisions. Bribery in Korea during its rapid industrialization appears to have been largely an indiscriminate spraying round of regular payments known as *tukkap* (literally, 'money for rice cakes') to powerful bureaucrats and politicians – not particularly with the intent of swaying their minds on the viability of a particular project, but just to keep them happy. In the case of politicians, some of the money then appears to have been passed on to poorer constituents. The defence counsel for Korean corruption could well argue that in practice it functioned as an income support programme to supplement civil servants' notoriously low salaries and compensate for the absence of a large welfare state. Both problems were the result of the prevailing ideology of government in Korea at the time. Organized corruption thus quietly served a purpose that open public administration could not.

If corruption is stable and predictable enough, it essentially becomes simply a tax. And as the performance of western European social democracies shows, having substantial rates of taxation, as long as they are collected efficiently and predictably, is no block to getting rich.

Sadly it played no such role in Tanzania under Julius Nyerere, the country's first president. A former teacher, not a soldier, Nyerere came to power not long before Suharto in 1964 and ruled until 1985. Like Suharto, he presided over a new and geographically divided post-colonial country, Tanzania conglomerating the former German and British colony of Tanganyika on the African mainland with the Indian Ocean island of Zanzibar. If Suharto's posthumous reputation underrates his lifetime achievements, the opposite is true of Nyerere. When Suharto died in January 2008 he was widely described in the Western media as a bloodstained crook. When Nyerere died in 1999 a celebration of his life organized by the international debt relief campaign, Jubilee 2000, gathered tributes from across the world, from the then UN secretary-general, Kofi Annan, to the Chinese president at the time, Jiang Zemin. Nyerere's local diocese (he was a Catholic) started a campaign to have him beatified by the Vatican.

In terms of his personal conduct, much of the adulation is understandable. Nyerere was by all accounts a decent, honest, modest president, quite different from many of the corrupt and repressive 'Big Men' who ruled African countries in their first decades after post-colonial independence.

Yet under his rule, Tanzania was riddled with corruption, and Tanzanians ended the two decades of his presidency no better off than when it began. It is poignantly typical of him that, unlike his self-aggrandizing contemporaries, he pointed out his own failings. 'I failed,' he said in his valedictory speech as president in 1985. 'Let's admit it.'

Nyerere meant well. He was, however, horrendously misguided. His philosophy involved extending *ujamaa*, loosely translated as 'familyhood', into a principle of economic governance. In practice, as in many African countries, this meant trying to build up a self-sufficient economy behind high barriers to trade. It led to stagnation and inefficiency. Nyerere burdened Tanzania with price controls, foreign exchange rationing and hundreds of underperforming state-owned companies: it led to smuggling, corruption and a large underground economy.

And most notoriously, he swept up millions of smallholding farmers into large collectivized villages in the name of efficiency. A wide network of bureaucrats was created to supply them with seeds, fertilizer and other inputs and buy their output from them. Handing such power to officials who had little connection to the people they were supposed to be serving created a fertile environment for exploitation and corruption. However honest Nyerere was himself, his officials took wide advantage to extract bribes. Farmers reacted by retreating into semi-subsistence production and selling any surplus produce illicitly in a parallel market in which they could get higher rewards than the state price. After agricultural production collapsed, Nyerere was forced to abandon collectivization.

As one observer points out, Nyerere attempted to nationalize the villages: instead, he villagized the nation. His cadre of socialist state bureaucrats morphed into a cohort of self-interested local merchant-monopolists, their grabbing tendencies unmitigated by any ties of kinship or neighbourhood to the people that they were exploiting. The morality of the man at the top did not extend down to the officials executing his policies. Unlike Suharto, Nyerere had no means of getting his subordinates to do what he wanted them to. Tanzania's companies and bureaucrats were shielded from competition and held only weakly accountable to the president. Nyerere had a principal-agent problem on a nationwide scale.

The achievements of the two men stand in sharp contrast, and so do the ways their governments functioned. One obvious comparison is the case of the agricultural state marketing board. Marketing boards sound like a ferociously dull and technical subject, until you recognize that for many developing countries where farming remains a central part of the economy, they form an essential part of the supply chain. It is highly inefficient – and in the case of exports, pretty much impossible – for each individual farmer, particularly a small-scale producer, to sell her output at market herself. Enter the state-run marketing board, a common feature of most developing countries and still of some rich ones. The organization creates economies of scale by buying individual farmers' output and selling it on in bulk. It also frequently supplies inputs like seed and fertilizer.

Efficient in theory, marketing boards are also a superb opportunity for corruption in practice. (Nor are developing countries' marketing boards the only suspect ones: the Australian Wheat Board was accused of paying bribes to the Iraqi government as part of the scandal around the oil-for-food programme.) They are often monopolies by design, with farmers compelled to sell produce to them. Anyone running the state marketing board without proper supervision can set a price for farmers' output way below the market price and pocket the difference, or as much of the difference as is left after covering the marketing board's costs. Dismantling or privatizing the state marketing board was often part of the advice given to developing countries, particularly in Africa, by the International Monetary Fund and World Bank. Sometimes this ended up with a corrupt public monopoly being replaced with an exploitative private one, or with no supply chain worth speaking of, but that's progress for you.

In Tanzania, as we have seen, the state marketing boards were famously corrupt and inefficient. Along with the disastrous collectivization experiment, they managed to send the rapid growth in Tanzanian agricultural output in the 1960s into reverse. One of the best examples is the government monopoly on cloves, the sweet-smelling spice. In the middle of the nineteenth century, Zanzibar was the world's biggest clove producer. Sailors in the Indian Ocean could reputedly smell Zanzibar before they saw it, as the pungent scent drifted miles out to sea. But after independence, the state monopoly forced farmers to sell to it and gave them just 4 per cent of the world price, barely enough to cover their costs. Many either smuggled out cloves to sell on the black market at a higher price or simply gave up growing them altogether. Production dropped by more than half in the decade after 1965.

Cloves, coincidentally enough, are native to Indonesia. And in Indonesia, the marketing board for cloves became famous as an example of crony capitalism. It was run by 'Tommy' Suharto, one of the president's sons, who amassed a large fortune for himself in the course of operating it and other monopolies. When the Indonesian currency and economy imploded in 1998 as part of the Asian financial crisis, dismantling the clove marketing board was one of the key demands of the IMF in return for emergency loans to help the country. It was the best-known element of a long list of conditions that became a notorious symbol, even within the IMF, of heavy-handed micromanagement.

But though his control was exploitative, it was not devastating. The clove industry was milked but not destroyed. During the Suharto years, Indonesia remained – as it is now – by far the world's largest clove producer and exporter. There is a big difference in outcome between a form of corruption that regularly diverts a number of eggs from the golden goose to the dictator and his friends, and the kind that kills the bird.

Still worse is the kind of indiscriminate large-scale theft practised by dictators like Mobutu, whose mismanagement of Zaire made Nyerere's Tanzania look like Sweden in comparison. Countries like Mobutu's Zaire resemble rather episodes of the old TV game show *Supermarket Sweep*, everything that is not nailed down being whisked away. Any regime that looks unstable, as African and Latin American dictatorships often tended to be, is liable to grab as much as possible before being kicked out of office. In the words of Mancur Olson, the theorist whose account of interest groups we encountered in the discussion of trade politics, it is better to have a 'stationary bandit' with a longer time horizon, who wants to be able to continue extorting into the future, than a 'roving bandit' who just wants to plunder and leave. The other advantage of a dictator who thinks he is going to be around for a while is that most of the proceeds of corruption are kept and spent in the country. African autocrats, always with an eye to the exit, all too often transfer their loot to bank accounts in London or Switzerland.

For the efficient cream-skimming kind of corruption to work, a degree of central coordination seems to be necessary. Economic theory explains this as akin to a situation where each company in a set of companies has a monopoly in producing goods that complement those of the others. Imagine a frankfurter company, a bun baker and a mustard manufacturer which make the constituent parts of a hot-dog. If the companies are working cooperatively, each will set its prices relatively low so it makes a profit but does not kill off demand for the final product. But if they are operating independently, each will jack up prices much higher in the expectation that the others will as well. There is no point in the baker giving up profit by under-pricing buns when the demand for the assembled hot-dog is going to be reduced by the stratospheric prices of sausages and mustard.

Similarly, a set of agencies with the ability to extract bribes from businesses – say the customs service, the tax authorities and the electricity company – will charge lower rates if they are working together rather than independently. A lower rate of bribe means more businesses can flourish: that means more growth, and, ultimately, more bribe revenue collected. A centrally organized, cream-skimming bureaucracy wants the economy to grow quickly – it means more Mercedes and cocaine all round. A disorganized grab-what-you-can bureaucracy is reckless as to whether the economy grows or not.

Perhaps the best example of disorganized, decentralized corruption is India, where, as the Indian official quoted above suggested to me, there is a multiplicity of political parties and bureaucrats to placate. Like east Asian countries, it has a large and powerful bureaucracy, and in the first half-century after independence in 1947 the dominant belief in state intervention gave bureaucrats the ability to meddle extensively in the economy.

But as we will see at length in the next chapter, Indian politics came to be dominated by a series of divided, squabbling political parties, which often rely on electoral blocs defined by religious, caste or ethnic identity. The form of politics practised, though it often goes under the name of socialism, is essentially a form of 'clientelism' in which government spending and privileges such as jobs are directed towards key constituencies to buy their support. Enough people can be bought off this way to ensure there is not enough popular demand for the entire system to be overthrown.

In India, as Mark Twain said of the weather, everybody talks about corruption but nobody does anything about it. And despite a series of political bribery scandals from the 1980s onwards, and the dismantling of much of the system of government licences and rules that enabled bureaucrats to extract bribes, estimates of the amount of government money going astray in India remain staggering.

So why did east Asia tend to have one kind of corruption and Africa and Latin America different types? The answer appears to be the usual combination of legacy from the past and choice in the present. East Asian autocrats tended to inherit powerful state bureaucracies and rarely had much opposition from other sections of society, such as a strong class of landowners. This was not so in most of Latin America, where the need to buy off the traditional aristocracy led to fiscal irresponsibility and frequent changes of government.

The pattern is not uniform. It is a standard joke in Manila that the Philippines and Chile should really swap places – the former looks much more like a Latin American country and the latter like an east Asian one – and the way in which their respective dictators used to run them certainly bears that out. Augusto Pinochet, who seized control in a military coup in 1973, exerted an iron grip over Chilean politics and society that meant he could resist pressure to buy off interest groups. Thus he avoided the usual bugbear of Latin American dictators, runaway public spending followed by hyperinflation.

Ferdinand Marcos, who came to power in the Philippines in 1965, rarely had proper control over the country. Just as in

Argentina, the legacy of Spanish empire was a powerful landowner clique, while the half-century of American rule that followed it left the Philippines with some semblance of representative democracy but without a strong bureaucracy to run it. In 1959, a so-called '50–50' agreement gave the president and the House of Representatives the power to fill half the civil service posts each. Together with the fact that politics was dominated by a number of powerful and independently wealthy families, this was a perfect setting for disorganized corruption. After Marcos imposed martial law in 1972, the economy did in fact grow fairly well for a few years. But he never had a full grip over the country in the way that Pinochet or Suharto did. He faced the perpetual threat of revolts among the military as well as communist insurgency and Islamic separatist movements.

Business executives used to complain that, under Marcos, officials were not just corrupt but corrupt and incompetent: you could end up paying off dozens of them before finding one who could actually deliver what was promised. Marcos had a clique of cronies just like Suharto but his human resources skills were poor: he chose badly and was incapable of keeping them in check. One of his advisers subsequently remarked that Marcos had intended to create a Japanese-style elite: unfortunately, he said, he 'chose the wrong samurai'. Some of the Philippines' most prominent business empires collapsed in the turmoil of the 1980s as the end of Marcos's rule approached, and had to be bailed out at vast public expense.

Given how damaging it can be, it is remarkable how long corruption can continue. Unless there is a crisis, a gap can endure almost indefinitely between the public discourse of an honest, neutral civil service and the private reality of a set of self-enriching bureaucrats. What starts out as a rational, if dishonest, response to an opportunity to make money often becomes hardened into a dominant culture that can last for centuries. Indeed, it can become so firmly embedded and accepted as part of the system that in one sense it ceases to become corruption, and merely becomes a different set of norms about the way that a state bureaucracy operates.

Such was certainly the case with China. As we have seen, China has one of the oldest bureaucracies in the world, and one that has traditionally held an exalted and powerful social position. The Chinese bureaucracy became a qualified profession chosen by competitive examination more than a millennium before most other civil services. It observed a clear distinction between the public and private spheres and expected its bureaucrats to be independent and impartial. If there is anything that provides continuity through the upheavals of Chinese history, it is the role of the bureaucracy that brought the entire concept of Chinese identity into existence and continues to uphold it.

Yet throughout much of the last millennium – particularly what is called the 'late imperial' period of the Ming and Qing dynasties between 1368 and 1911 – the civil service was riddled with corruption almost by design, not because it was so well looked after but because it was so badly paid. The Chinese imperial bureaucracy provides an excellent example of how corruption can be institutionalized into a norm rather than an aberration.

At the beginning of the Ming dynasty, bureaucrats' pay was relatively generous, possibly because the founder of the dynasty had come from a poor peasant family and thus had long and painful experience of corrupt local officials pleading poverty while supplementing their salaries with bribery. But the effects of inflation, which came from printing too much of the paper currency in which officials were partly paid, eroded what their salaries were worth over time. By the eighteenth century, one governor-general noted for his frugality estimated that he required 6000 taels (silver ounces) a year for his expenses, yet his basic pay was 180 taels.

In other words, it was simply not possible to exist without exacting private payments. Bureaucrats extorted fees for carrying out the most routine of administrative tasks; they sold public offices and licences for money; they demanded illicit land taxes; they paid and received bribes (*huilu*) that were flatly illegal but could easily be described simply as gifts. And they passed the proceeds up the bureaucratic pyramid in what became a permanent system of routine extortion.

Those who tried to live without doing so were regarded as merely eccentric. One such was Hai Rui, an official in Jianguan province in the sixteenth century. Accounts of the time show that his self-denial, which included eating meat just once a month, became famous. He ambitiously attempted to impose the same rigorous standards on what was then the wealthiest, politically best-connected and fiscally messiest province of all, by refusing to levy a large number of fees that were technically illegal but had become custom and practice. This merely irritated his fellow bureaucrats. He stands out in the accounts of the time as a pious and provocative troublemaker, not a brave man of principle.

His own description of the provincial officials' triennial trips to the imperial capital to pay off their superiors drips with scorn: 'when the time has come, the provincial officials load their carts with the silks and money they will present to the officials in the capital,' he wrote. 'From top to bottom everyone profits, and those who suffer from it are the people.'

The logical thing to do, of course, would have been to regularize the side-payments or increase bureaucrats' pay. But that would have meant raising taxes. It was too much, apparently, to give up the widely held ideal of an ascetic, devoted bureaucracy. Instead, the system carried on in a state of organized hypocrisy.

So how does the tolerance of norms change? When does the way things have always been done start becoming the way of the past? Often it is when a regime or a system has failed to deliver what it was supposed to. People will put up with corruption as long as it works. Indeed, they may simultaneously realize that such behaviour is at odds with the stated principles of government, yet shrug and tolerate it indefinitely. But they will still often continue to recognize that there is a gap between the principles and the practice, particularly if they can observe that such a gap is much smaller in other countries. And when the system fails to deliver, that gap can rapidly become unsupportable.

This is certainly true in the case of Suharto. He had long faced down demands for more honesty and openness by delivering enough growth and stability to satisfy all but the minority of voluble democracy enthusiasts and other malcontents.

But in 1997 east Asia was swept by a financial crisis that started with the collapse of the Thai currency and rapidly spread, like a virulent disease, to South Korea, the Philippines, Indonesia and beyond. Crony capitalism got a lot of blame for having created the conditions that led to crisis. In particular, corrupt and opaque policymaking cliques in many of the region's countries had let problems mount up with state-supported companies and state-guaranteed debt that did not come to light until they reached crisis point.

Suharto's virtues suddenly became vices. The collapse of Indonesia's currency and the economic implosion that followed severely diminished his personal authority and, because it was so centralized in him, public confidence in his entire regime. Many of the gains in income and wealth were rapidly reversed. The open capital markets that had built investors' trust that they could get their money out proved remarkably helpful when it came to, well, getting their money out. Whether justified or not, the IMF's insistence on Suharto dismantling some of the more egregious examples of cronyism such as the clove monopoly undermined him.

Less than a year after the Asian crisis began, he was forced from office. The damage wrought by the crisis took a decade to repair. Suharto's defenders would say that Indonesia's slow and halting recovery merely revealed how much the country missed his regime. A more balanced verdict would also point at the intrinsic fragility of a state oriented around the personal rule of one man and his clique, and blame him for some of the subsequent dysfunctions as well as the collapse itself.

Similar cataclysms from elsewhere in history often involve heavy military defeat or the loss of empire. For one of the most famous examples of attempts to close the gap between the principles and the practice, we turn again to our friends at the East India Company. At the end of the eighteenth century in the House of Lords,

Britain's highest court, corruption was put on trial for seven years in the person of Warren Hastings, former governor-general of India while it was under Company rule.

The trial was technically an 'impeachment', a process – obsolescent in Britain even then – designed to remove officials from their posts. (Impeachments still persist in some constitutions: witness Bill Clinton's trial in the US Senate, triggered by the Monica Lewinsky affair.) It became much more than a question of personal morality: the impeachment turned into a battleground between competing norms of morality and probity. On one side were reformers who argued that the Company's actions were corrupt. On the other, the Company's defenders retorted that this was the way that things were done in Asia, and that in any case they worked. And the battle was symptomatic of a wider struggle in Britain against the deeply corrupt politics of the eighteenth century. It was given impetus by the loss of the North American colonies in the War of Independence.

First, a short digression about corruption and empire, which will also explain how the British East India Company got to run the subcontinent in the first place. Empires are particularly susceptible to corruption. They have monopoly and principal-agent problems in spades. Colonial officials are state bureaucrats who often wield a great deal of power over the economies that they are administrating, and are frequently a long way from the imperial capital in whose interests they are supposed to be acting. The British and Dutch East India Companies, as we have seen, took over from the Portuguese, who had constructed a trading empire through carving out footholds in various corners of Asia. Reading contemporary accounts of just how decadent and corrupt the Portuguese colonial officers had become, it is painfully clear why the British and the Dutch could take over in Asia.

Portugal had forged trading links with India towards the end of the fifteenth century through the explorer Vasco da Gama. By the middle of the sixteenth century it had established Goa on the west coast as a fort and trading post. Goa was run by a viceroy who answered to the king in Lisbon, and most of the senior posts were held by *fidalgos* – the sons of the Portuguese nobility, who also made up the officer class of the military. This proved to be an arrangement highly unconducive to honest and efficient government.

The trading posts of Portuguese Asia were intended to finance themselves through rents charged to locals and levies charged on traders passing through the ports, with only the hefty profits from the actual trading of spices taken by the Crown back in Portugal. Thus the colonial outposts were largely left to their own devices. For a contemporary description of the results we have the highly disgruntled accounts of Diogo do Couto, who arrived in Goa in 1559 as a mid-ranking colonial official and became the official royal chronicler of Portuguese India. Apparently an honest man himself, he became increasingly appalled by the outright theft and abuse he encountered.

By the very nature of the Goan colony, the Portuguese king had a principal-agent issue of spectacular dimensions. Each term of colonial office lasted for just three years, and since it was over a year's sailing time from Portugal, it was close to impossible to rein in a recalcitrant viceroy. On receiving an order from Lisbon, a viceroy could simply send a reply saying that the orders had been received and understood and of course he would like nothing more than loyally to implement the wishes of the Crown, but with the greatest respect, following whatever course of action was instructed would have an unfortunate side-effect detailed herein that he was sure the king's advisers had not intended and would wish to avoid, and how did they suggest that he proceed in light of this fact? By the time this had gone to Lisbon and a response come back, a new viceroy would be in place, who could set the clock back to the beginning by stating that he had not seen the original order, or claiming that the situation on the ground had now changed or that further details of the order had regrettably become necessary and could he be furnished with same by return of post?

In the copious free time left over from playing this elabor-ate game of I-can't-hear-you with their nominal sovereign, the viceroy and his senior officials were free to get on with the real business of the colony: extorting money from all and sundry and dressing up like idiots. Do Couto's descriptions of the pomp and ceremony of the colony are saturated with contempt. The viceroy ventured forth from his palace carried in a sedan chair, heralded by a fanfare of flutes, trumpets and drums and accompanied by a large retinue of flunkeys. As for the circle of hangers-on, do Couto says, their 'velvet capes, doublets and pantaloons of the same, silken hose, gold buckle hat, gilded sword and dagger, cleanshaven faces and high topknots, it seems to me, would have made the good king die of shame'. Meanwhile, the ordinary soldiers stationed in Goa slept in open boats and lived on rotten rice, salted fish and polluted water. Military discipline disintegrated: fencing schools became dance studios; impoverished soldiers of lower ranks were seen begging in the streets.

There was a variety of ways in which the rulers of the colony managed to enrich themselves. The most easily observed one was 'old debts' or *dividas velhas*. The viceroy could, nominally in an emergency, requisition anything he needed – grain, rice, timber – from local subjects in return for receipts which could later be cashed in. Getting these certificates redeemed proved to be impossible, and the victims had to sell them to the viceroy's favourites at a quarter of their face value. The warships, at least those that were kept in a functional state of repair, spent much of their time sailing up and down the coast shaking down the captains of forts and territories for money. And they charged passing ships so much for berths and provisions that traders would do almost anything to avoid having to put in at a Portuguese-held port.

It was a hell of a way to run an empire. Do Couto's account of the goings-on in Portuguese Asia – which he only managed to distribute after many attempts to suppress publication or steal the manuscript – was told in the form of an imagined dialogue between a veteran soldier who had served in Portugal's Indian colony and a fidalgo who had been its governor-general. At one point the soldier says of the neighbouring Indian rulers: 'If [they] did not have their hands tied, Gentlemen, I am certain this business would have been over long ago – thank God they are kept in rein by the Great Mughal, who menaces their kingdoms. We ought to say masses for his health.'

In the event, it was competition from the British and the Dutch that ensured Portugal would become an abbreviated chapter in the colonial history of Asia. What did for the empire was not just the actions of a few reprobates, but the perverse incentives of the entire system. A powerful nobility was spoiled and indulged and given a monopoly on the officerships of the military and the governorships of the colonies. Insulated from competition and accountability, it developed a collective culture of plunder.

The British East India Company was also involved in corruption and self-enrichment on a grand scale. But, like Suharto's regime, it did so as part of a system that largely worked. And like Suharto, though the corruption attracted disapprobation, it was not until it failed on its own terms that the Company was entirely relieved of its power.

By then, the Company had gone beyond simply operating trading posts and was starting to extend its control over more of the subcontinent. Its relations with the Moghul emperor of India, Jahangir, had been established when it impressed him by twice defeating a Portuguese force in battle, in 1613 and 1615. Jahangir allowed the Company to establish permanent trading posts. It got a further boost when Charles II married Catherine of Braganza in 1662. The bride came complete with the city of Bombay. Charles, not particularly impressed by his new possession, leased it to the East India Company for £50,000 and a rent of £10 per annum. The Company introduced judicial, fiscal and administrative institutions and collected land rent on its own behalf.

The warning by do Couto's old soldier, that it was only the power of Moghul rule that was keeping local Indian rulers in check, was borne out in the first half of the eighteenth century. Provincial governors or *nawabs* were establishing their own dynastic rule in parts of India, particularly in Bengal in the east. As the East India Company sought to extend its power over the subcontinent, it repeatedly had to pay them off to allow its trading activities to continue. When they became too demanding and troublesome it took more drastic action.

If there was a moment at which the Company stopped being an armed trading enterprise and became an empire, it was in 1757 at the Battle of Plassey. The new nawab of Bengal, Siraj-ud-daula, annoyed with what he saw as British abuse of trade concessions, attacked the Company's settlement at Calcutta. After trying to parley peacefully if craftily in the usual way, the local commander, Robert Clive, decided to negotiate by other means. Having bribed conspirators in the nawab's court, he defeated him in battle and installed one of his collaborators, Mir Jafar, on the throne in Bengal.

Thus was set the culture of the Company in its rule in India: bribery and conspiracy to exploit local internecine feuds, with the ultimate threat of military action kept in reserve. The Company in India was at heart a gang of traders on the make (and on the take), not a legion of imperial warriors. They were always happier to buy someone off than to send soldiers against him and more concerned with making money than fulfilling a principled mission to spread British ideas of civilization.

Mir Jafar showed his gratitude for being made nawab of Bengal by rewarding Clive and others with lavish presents. Clive received the right for life to receive rent from land in Bengal, a gift worth £27,000 a year. Through a treaty with the Moghul emperor in 1765, the Company gained the right to collect revenue as well as to dispense civil justice, thus increasing its resemblance to a state. The nawabs who nominally ruled Bengal thereafter were closer to being colonial employees than sovereign rulers, their reigns dependent on their ability to deliver stability and business for their employer. And they acted not just to boost the Company itself but also to perpetuate the thriving culture of British officials on the take.

One of the reasons, perhaps, that the East India Company's corrupt operations did better than those of the Portuguese lay in its personnel policy. While the Portuguese, as we have seen, doled out colonial offices to foppish sons of a decadent aristocracy, the

Company became a way for bright young men from more modest backgrounds to transcend their origins. Many were from Scotland, where opportunities for more conventional social advancement were limited by English dominance. In Bengal between 1775 and 1785, nearly half the men appointed to serve as 'writers', who kept accounts and corresponded with London on behalf of the Company, were Scots. Becoming a writer could be a very lucrative position indeed, and competition for the places was intense. Often they were simply put up for sale. Ostensibly, the employees worked for the Company, which was a contracted-out agent of the Crown. In practice, they could semi-openly make money on the side themselves. Not until the mid-1760s were Company officials even formally prohibited from using their position to trade on their own accounts.

There was a widespread attitude among its employees that, in the same way that the Company itself was given a monopoly in return for undertaking difficult and risky long-distance trade, so a lengthy stint in an uncomfortable and dangerous part of the world entirely justified their returning with more than a modest pension. Though better than the insulting pay of Chinese imperial bureaucrats, Company salaries were not particularly generous. One successful Company official was quite open on the subject: 'We are men of power, you say, and take advantage of it. Why, man, what is the use of station if we are not to benefit from it?'

But with political power comes responsibility, and when government in India (and elsewhere in the British colonies) failed, the culture of the colonial officials came under more scrutiny. Beginning in 1769, Bengal suffered a severe famine in which around 10 million people died – around a third of its total population. Debates abound to this day about the proportions of bad luck, callousness and incompetence which caused the catastrophe. But the disruption, combined with a general depression in trade in Europe, meant that the directors of the Company had to appeal to Parliament to bail it out from bankruptcy.

This gave Parliament the excuse to put the Company on a tighter leash and make it more accountable to the Crown and the wider public as well as its shareholders. Suspicion, no doubt mixed with envy, had grown of the vast fortunes that senior officials of the Company were bringing back. Robert Clive, who had returned to England, was cross-examined by a parliamentary committee about the source and legitimacy of his wealth. He argued that his personal reward had been comparatively small considering the service he had given the empire, culminating in a self-exculpatory climax that has passed into legend: 'By God . . . I stand astonished at my own moderation!'

But as hard as the principal pulled on the leash, the agent strained at it. Clive was not the last Company official in India to face criticism in Parliament on the grounds of greed and corruption. Warren Hastings, an experienced administrator who had joined the Company as a clerk at the age of eighteen, was made the first governor-general of India in 1773. His powers were balanced by a council appointed by government, a move driven through against fierce opposition by the Company's shareholders and their friends in Parliament. The move to regulate the Company also saw judicial officials sent out from Britain to administer the legal affairs of India.

But Hastings fought hard against those members of the council opposed to his rule, and succeeded in subverting the judicial oversight when a schoolfriend, Sir Elijah Impey, became chief justice. (Impey later named one of his sons 'Hastings'.) In one episode, Maharaja Nandakumar, an Indian tax official, accused Hastings of receiving huge payments from one of the widows of the nawab of Bengal. Conveniently for Hastings, Nandakumar was himself accused of forgery, tried with Impey as chief justice, convicted by an all-English jury and hanged. Accusations of corruption mounted, particularly by Sir Philip Francis, a member of the council who bitterly opposed Hastings, fought him in a duel and then left for London to whip up public opinion against him.

Francis's personal vendetta found a receptive audience in London. The reality was sinking in, especially after the surrender of the British forces at Yorktown in 1781, that Britain had lost its North American colonies. So on top of the Bengal famine and the near bankruptcy of the Company, parliamentary reformers had some supporting evidence for their argument that misgovernance was undermining the empire. In 1781, the House appointed a select committee to investigate the administration of justice in Bengal. By 1788, by which time Hastings had retired to London, it had accumulated sufficient evidence to attempt an impeachment.

The context for the impeachment was critical to understanding what was actually on trial. Eighteenth-century British politics was deeply corrupt. Robert Walpole, generally credited with being the country's first prime minister, presided over a ministry so steeped in bribery, chicanery, electoral malpractice and gerrymandering that he became known as the 'Grand Corruptor'. As we saw with the sugar lobby, parliamentary seats and influence were routinely bought and sold. It would be going too far, however, to say that this system had settled into being a widely accepted norm. Satirists such as the artist William Hogarth bitterly attacked the venality of politics. His series of four paintings *The Election* portrayed Britain as a broken-down coach that had ceased to progress because of rampant vote-buying. Reformist Members of Parliament like Edmund Burke and Charles James Fox drew parallels between the collapse of the Roman empire, rotted from the inside by corruption, and the weakening of the British colonies.

During the impeachment the competing sides put on trial the entire culture of the East India Company's operations in the subcontinent. Hastings's defence argued he had merely fallen into line with local practice. Hastings's chief counsel, the celebrated Edward Law, said of 'entertainment allowances' received by Hastings from the nawab of Bengal's widow that 'It is impossible for any persons to read any oriental history without knowing that custom has prevailed over the East, from the most ancient times to the present.'

Edmund Burke dismissed what he called this 'geographical morality'. Via a comprehensive tour of comparative jurisprudence, taking in Islamic and Hindu law in India and Turkey, the legal code of Genghis Khan and the difference between the Persian words for legitimate gift giving and a clandestine and corrupt bribe, he concluded in a grand peroration: 'Let him [Hastings] run from law to law ... follow him where you will; let him have Eastern

or Western law; you find everywhere arbitrary power and pecu-
lation of Governors proscribed and horridly punished.'

After an epic trial lasting until 1795, the impeachment failed.
Perhaps the implied challenge to the prevailing culture of Westminster was too much. To make his case that the Company was
violating established norms, Burke had to make the wildly uncon-
vincing claim that bribery and corruption were alien to British
political life.

Moreover, while there was growing criticism of the East India
Company's monopoly powers, the Company was nonetheless still
spreading British influence over a large part of the subcontinent and
generating trade and wealth. Unlike the officials of the Portuguese
empire, the servants of the Company were diverting for themselves
a portion of a growing pile of spoils from victory, not grabbing
what they could as the colonies went into decline. They were
skimming cream, not playing *Supermarket Sweep*. The Company
permanently lost its monopoly on trade with east Asia in 1834. But
it was permitted to continue running India until it had failed even
on its own terms, with a serious revolt of its own Indian soldiers
in 1857. (In Britain at the time, the uprising was called the Mutiny;
in India it is now frequently known as the Great Rebellion.)

Part of the reason, perhaps, that democratic reform in Britain
has always tended to be piecemeal is that there have been few
failures or disasters of sufficient magnitude to force rapid transformation. The loss of the American colonies was enough to put
Hastings, and by extension the culture of the East India Company,
on trial, but not to compel immediate radical change. Burke and
his fellow reformers also wanted stricter limitations on the ability
of the royal household to give out posts and sinecures to its favourites, which they said corrupted political life. But Burke argued for
gradual, organic reform, tweaking existing institutions rather than
destroying them in favour of new ones. He recoiled in horror from
the cataclysmic change that took place across the Channel in 1789,
where a true sense of crisis brought revolution, and the old forms
of institutionalized corruption came to a crashing end.

In the era before general modern taxation – income tax was

not introduced in Britain until 1798, to fund the wars against Napoleon, for example – the state had to find creative ways to fund itself. Selling offices was one of the most obvious. They brought both social prestige and monopolies of certain services or functions, such as the grain-milling we encountered in the chapter on cities. James I of England, who had difficulty increasing taxation with an uncooperative Parliament, created an entirely new category of hereditary 'baronets' to raise money. Meanwhile officers in the British army literally bought their positions, which raised money for military campaigns.

France had a similar system. But the disillusion set in earlier, particularly with the practice of selling military commissions to the nobility and then relying on the resulting officer class to recruit what were more or less private regiments. The feeble performance of the French army on the battlefields of the Seven Years War in the middle of the eighteenth century, particularly against the more professional Prussian armies, suggested that privately run regiments had been found wanting in the toughest possible marketplace. And the French Revolution itself in 1789 was in a sense a wider crisis of the French nobility, which had failed to restrain the monarchy sufficiently to deliver better government. Once the king had been overthrown, office-holding for money was immediately abolished and replaced, at least in theory, with state officials and army officers chosen on merit.

In Britain, exactly as the gradualist Burke would have predicted, change happened more slowly. As individual institutions showed they were not just corrupt but incompetent, they were reformed. A separate Irish Parliament in Dublin, if anything more venal than the Westminster equivalent, was abolished only in 1801 after a rebellion in 1798 showed it had manifestly failed in its task of keeping Ireland subservient. Britain's system of purchasing military commissions ensured that the army continued to be officered largely by the rich aristocracy. But the practice survived for longer thanks to British military successes in the wars of the eighteenth and early nineteenth centuries, culminating in the Duke of Wellington's victory over Napoleon at Waterloo in 1815 (very greatly helped, it must be said, by the Prussian professionals). Why change a winning team, even if the star players bought their places in the squad?

The gentleman–amateurish system lasted until the shambles of the Crimean War in the middle of the nineteenth century, in which the commanders' military and organizational incompetence was on spectacular display – most notoriously in the disastrous charge of the Light Brigade in the Battle of Balaclava, based on a misunderstood order. Wellington is credited with the (probably apocryphal) remark that Waterloo was won on the playing fields of Eton, one of the schools most favoured by Britain's aristocratic elite. A century later, George Orwell, himself an old Etonian and one of the most brilliant and trenchant critics of hereditary privilege, retorted that the opening battles of all subsequent wars had nonetheless been lost there.

Along with disillusionment with the performance of a corrupt regime must go the belief that a new system will actually be an improvement, fulfilling all the functions of the original and more. This is not always straightforward, and it is certainly not always cheap.

The shift to a professional civil service in the US is a case in point. The US developed into a vigorous democracy in the nineteenth century, at least for those white men who were allowed to vote. In the years after the Civil War ended in 1865, turnout at elections averaged 80 per cent of eligible voters, well above today's levels. But it was not always civic duty that took them to the polling station. A good number had either been bribed to vote or were after a job from the winner.

The US had been conceived as a decentralized agrarian republic. It was put together by a collection of states suspicious of each other and of concentrated power. It had little conception of how to cope with becoming a powerful urbanized nation with the active federal government needed to regulate a complex industrialized economy. For a start, it did not have a strong central bureaucracy. Beginning with the administration of Andrew Jackson, elected president in 1828 and the first to come from outside the east coast elite tradition of the Founding Fathers, American government worked on a 'spoils' system, with government jobs handed out to supporters of the ruling party. Similar systems operated at state and local levels, which helps explain the rise of corrupt but highly organized urban political machines that are still a feature of US city politics.

One of the most widespread and long-lasting corrupt uses of public office related to the postal system. Post offices functioned not just to distribute private mail but as circulation centres for newspapers, which were at this time heavily partisan and largely acted as mouthpieces for political parties. The local postmaster was a figure of considerable political heft. (Incidentally, such a role for the postal system, as a form of political patronage, endured in Japan into the twenty-first century: the Japanese postal bank is the biggest savings system on earth, and bosses from the ruling Liberal Democratic Party have long used it to fund pet projects.)

Eventually, beginning in the late nineteenth century, and in line with several European countries, the American civil service was professionalized and depoliticized. But this took several decades of campaigning, with voters having to overcome their instinctive suspicion of swelling federal bureaucracies. And along with the decline of the spoils system came a drop in election turnout, which averaged only around 60 per cent from 1920 to 1948. The spoils system may have been a corrupt, inefficient form of administration, but it made for a lively democracy.

Moving from a corrupt self-enriching bureaucracy to a professional, unbiased one can be expensive. In any system where public office is routinely used to extract illicit bribes, the official remuneration for that office, as in China during the imperial period, is frequently low. Honest civil servants need to be paid well. I have heard it said by Africans that the first thing their governments need to do to improve administration and tackle corruption is to sack half the civil service and double the pay of the remainder. This, though, is one of the reasons why reforming a corrupt bureaucracy is politically as well as managerially difficult. It is a tough sell, to say the least, to announce to taxpayers that civil servants are on the take and that they therefore need to be

paid a lot more, or that political parties are illicitly peddling influence and that they therefore need to be funded by the state. (Maintaining the prestige part of remuneration for public office can be
relatively cheap and easy, as evinced by the regular conveyor-belt of
knighthoods to senior British civil servants.)

Corruption is by definition part of a system, and systems evolve
for a reason. Corruption is not a good thing. But, depending on
its nature and the way it has come about, it may well be less
damaging than at first it appears. Julius Nyerere was fundamentally a decent man; there are far fewer people who will say the
same about Suharto. But though the latter's personal corruption
was one of the main differences between them, it remains the fact
that one enriched his country while the other helped to keep his
desperately poor.

9. Path dependence

Why are pandas so useless?

Giant pandas are incompetent, inefficient piebald buffoons, and we should end their public subsidies and let them die out. I once wrote that in the pages of an international newspaper, and outraged reader emails comparing me to a genocidal dictator flooded in for days. I stand by my views, however, and am now going to draw on them to create a slightly tenuous metaphor for economic development.

The giant panda's problem is that it went down an evolutionary cul-de-sac and has now found it too late to reverse. Of course, as panda apologists will quickly tell you, they are endangered because humans are encroaching on their locale. But that is the proximate, not the underlying, cause. Their real problem is that their incompetence at consuming and reproducing makes them hopelessly vulnerable. Pandas eat almost exclusively bamboo, which helps confine them to a narrow habitat and puts them at immediate risk from any change. Bamboo is in any case so low in nutrients that they have to spend up to sixteen hours a day chewing it – the equivalent of trying to subsist on sugar-coated cardboard. And, furthermore, they have a short digestive tract more suitable for a carnivore than a herbivore, so most of what they do eat goes through undigested. Finally, they are so bad at mating that pandas in captivity have to be shown panda pornography to get them to perform. (No, really.) The prosecution rests. Pandas are useless.

Contrast the panda with the domestic cat, a creature that has a clearly defined yet flexible business plan. Modern moggies are descended from African wildcats. These entrepreneurial felines emerged out of the savannah and bushland as hunter-gathering was giving way to settled farming techniques, including irrigation, in the 'fertile crescent' of north Africa and the Middle East several millennia ago. Recognizing that *Homo sapiens sapiens*, the dominant species, was going to be a lucrative customer on an ongoing basis, cats instantly spotted and filled a gap in the market. Grain cultivation and storage had created a business opportunity in rodent control in which they had a clear competitive advantage.

Spreading across the worldwide human client base, cats merged with local providers where necessary, interbreeding with the European wildcat to produce the tabby. And aside from developing some niche speciality products along the way like the deity service they delivered to the demanding ancient Egyptian consumer, they subsequently diversified into the increasingly popular domestic pet sector, in which they now have a dominant market share. (Those related enterprises such as the tiger that chose to ignore business reality and base themselves in a more hostile market environment have had a much harder time.) Domestic cats are highly efficient hunters and eat a wide variety of foods; they can survive in urban and rural environments; they can afford to spend sixteen hours a day sleeping rather than stuffing themselves with biologically inappropriate and increasingly scarce vegetation. They breed easily and effectively. They are solitary but adapt to living alongside other cats and humans. Unlike pandas, cats do not require any state subsidy to thrive. The case for the defence is incontrovertible. Cats are great.

This analogy is evidently self-indulgent and by no means precise. Societies are not species, and do not evolve in the same way through random variations in genes that get passed down the generations. They choose their paths, even if sometimes unconsciously. And those choices can be changed more rapidly than the hundreds or thousands of years that evolution takes. But in the same way that pandas could go down the wrong route and get stuck there, so can societies and their economies.

People have choices about the routes that they take. But this chapter seeks to show that having taken a particular path in the past – even for reasons that seemed sensible at the time – might make it harder to plump for the right option in the present day. It might also affect the outcome even if that option is chosen now.

This is a not a counsel of despair. It is a recognition of the difficulties that attend making choices. To govern is to choose: yet without being predetermined, those choices are conditioned on the decisions that others have made in the past. We have to make policies with the institutions of government, law, politics and culture that history and previous generations have bequeathed to us. We can seek to change them, but we cannot instantly wish new ones into being.

The idea that the routes open to us now depend on how we got here has a name: path dependence. Much traditional economics resembles physics. It seeks to apply universal laws drawn from repeated observations. Path dependence more closely resembles evolutionary biology – the role played by a sequence of events, some of which may come by chance. Hence the analogy with the panda.

Some of the best-known, and perhaps easiest to grasp, examples of path dependence lie at the intersection of economic history and technology. One of them has been used extensively in the preparation of this book: the standard QWERTY keyboard layout used in most of the Latin alphabet keyboards of the world. Remarkably enough, it is designed not to speed me up but to slow me down, and in particular to stop me hitting two keys in quick succession.

The QWERTY layout dates from the development of the mechanical typewriter in the nineteenth century. Specifically it appeared on the version invented by one Christopher Sholes and perfected by engineers from Remington, the company to whom he sold the design. Since the typebars on that particular model were prone to jamming and hammering repeatedly on the same spot if hit in rapid succession, the keyboard deliberately placed many frequently used letter pairs such that it was hard to type them rapidly. The other design criterion was to collect the letters of the word 'TYPEWRITER' on the top row – a help to salesmen keen to show off the new machine but without the patience to go beyond the hunt-and-peck school of typing.

Even at the time, faster keyboards were being developed for other mechanical typewriter models, which put more of the heavily used keys on the same row. Subsequently other layouts such as the 'Dvorak' system have been invented which are widely held to be faster and certainly more comfortable than the QWERTY layout. And yet QWERTY persists, thanks to the combined impact of so-called 'network effects' and inertia. Network effects, which we encountered in the discussion about the shipping container, involve the increasing returns that are reaped when everyone uses the same system. It is evidently more efficient for all typists to use the same keyboard since they only have to be trained once. And because the Remington design was dominant when the typing industry took off, that was the one it adopted.

Having started down the QWERTY path for perfectly logical reasons, people continued along it even when it had long ceased to fulfil its original function. The amount of investment and organization it would have taken to leap onto a different path was prohibitive. What is striking is perhaps not that QWERTY continued to persist through the era of mechanical typewriters used largely by professional typists with heavy investment in formal instruction, but that it endures today. This is an age of cheap, easily changeable computer keyboards on which most people teach themselves to type. The costs of changing are much lower. And yet QWERTY remains dominant.

Inertia has a great deal to answer for. Shifting wholesale from one system to another would take a good deal of coordination and the willingness on everyone's part to accept short-term losses – the cost of new keyboards and the time taken to learn them – in return for longer-term benefits. This is the kind of thing we have governments for, but as yet none has volunteered. If only the US military, while imposing the standard 8 x 8-foot shipping container, had sorted out keyboards while they were at it.

Now, if it is possible for an economy to get stuck in a rut with something as relatively discrete and testable as a particular technology, it is even easier for a country to adopt an economic system, or follow a particular policy, and stick with it though it appears not to be working. Path dependence can arise despite consumers and companies all acting rationally and doing the best that they can with the choices available to them. If we change that assumption as well, given the operation of politics and lobby groups, it becomes easier still to see how a wrong move might yet become self-reinforcing.

Cultures and institutions have a way of replicating themselves. Habits created by a particular environment endure even when the surroundings change. We saw in the last chapter how cultures of corruption can arise and become embedded in a particular society at a particular time. Only an eccentric would claim that certain peoples are born corrupt. But they can certainly carry with them particular conventions that they have learned from their milieu.

In one intriguing experiment, a pair of academics set out to discover whether acquired habits would persist even when incentives and the environment changed. Their laboratory was New York City, and their subjects the international diplomats at the United Nations there. As part of their diplomatic immunity, consular officials and their families were exempt from paying parking tickets – at least until 2002, when New Yorkers' famously short patience expired and the law was changed. The diplomats' incentive to obey the traffic laws was low. Between 1997 and 2002, some 150,000 parking fines totalling more than $18 million went unpaid.

It turned out that different nationalities used this free pass very differently. Countries like Nigeria which score badly on standard measures of corruption had many more unpaid tickets than the goody-goodies like Canada and the Scandinavians. Removing diplomats from their native habitats evidently did not change their ingrained instincts about obeying laws. Interestingly, the longer diplomats remained in New York the higher were their rates of violations, perhaps as they realized what they could get away with. Exposure to what was presumably, for poor-scoring nations such as Nigeria, a less corrupt environment than their home country (unless they encountered New York City politics) did not change their imported culture. Cultures are not endlessly immutable, or the national politics of countries like the UK would be as corrupt now as when parliamentary seats were openly bought and sold in the eighteenth century. But nor are they instantly malleable.

The institutions that make economies effective rely as much on attitudes and behaviour as they do on external structure. Many developing countries have democratic constitutions and judicial systems modelled on western European or North American models. In other words, they have consciously attempted to put themselves on the same path as economically more successful countries. Yet they have often failed, so far, to deliver the same results.

The rest of this chapter will focus on three of the big developing economies – Russia, India and China – as they shift in various ways further towards a market economy. First we will look at how Russia emerged from communism, and how that experience differed from that of other communist countries, including both China and nations from the Soviet bloc in central and eastern Europe. Second, we will look at how modern Indian politics and economic policy have evolved, and what difference that makes to the way in which they have reacted to market-based reforms. China again makes a useful comparator.

To begin with, let us look at the contrasts between countries exiting from communism. Natural experiments are rare in economics and economic history. There are not many opportunities to do direct international comparisons like the study of diplomats in New York City. But the global collapse or reform of most communist regimes in the last twenty or thirty years has provided something within hailing distance of one. A large set of countries has gone through the process of transition from a command to a market economy. Most, but not all, have gone through the parallel process of becoming a democracy: China and Vietnam are the glaring exceptions. There are some interesting patterns in the evidence to suggest how their history helped determine their future, both in the decisions that they took and in what happened as a result.

Now let us look at how Russia got to where it is. Politics and government in Russia have had two specific characteristics that go back to the medieval era and have endured throughout tsarism and the Soviet era into the present. First, there has been a dominant executive with not much in the way of checks and balances. Legislatures and the judiciary have been subservient to the central power. If they stuck their heads up, they tended to get them cut off. Second, the dividing line between power and property has rarely been clearly defined. The executive has often claimed both the absolute right to rule and the authority to appropriate assets as needed – indeed, not even to recognize that anyone but the sovereign can fully own property.

These features made Russia an ideal country for both monarchical autocracy and communism. They are, however, anathema to a market economy, where businesses want secure private property rights and the confidence they are not going to be interrupted by an unaccountable and arbitrary government.

Now that their empire is safely gone, we can happily blame this on the Mongols, whom we met in the chapter on religion, and a wholly owned subsidiary of theirs, the Tatars. The 'Mongol yoke' rested on Russia for around two and a half centuries after its creators swept in from the east in the first half of the thirteenth century. Interestingly, before the influence of the Mongols had shaped it, Russia's development of individual property rights and political pluralism was in some ways ahead of western Europe. A class of landowners, the 'boyars', had become the absolute owners of their properties and political power was balanced among a set of ruling princes with principalities clustered around Moscow.

The Mongols themselves had little truck with anything but supreme centralized authority. To make it easier to rule, they gave Muscovy (a duchy centred on Moscow) taxation powers and authority over the other principalities in return for loyalty and cash payments to their empire.

Even after Mongol influence diminished, the centralizing tendency remained, as with the Islamic empires in the Middle East. Russia became an authoritarian monarchy and, as it absorbed surrounding territories, an empire. Ivan III (better known as Ivan the Great) established a strong state by breaking the power of his brothers and other princes, and Ivan IV (the Terrible) confirmed the trend by being crowned Tsar of Russia in 1547. (In translation, incidentally, Ivan IV's epithet loses some of its original sense: it was intended to convey power and majesty as well as simply scariness.) He brought independent principalities under his control and ended the independence of the trading centre of Novgorod. As we saw in the chapter on Africa and cocaine, Novgorod had been part of the Hanseatic League and thus plugged into a western European network in which circulated dangerous ideas of commercial and political freedom.

The period of Mongol control disconnected Russia from western Europe at a time when the Renaissance fostered ideas of progress and intellectual diversity. Tsarism proved resistant to the ideas of political pluralism that grew after the Protestant Reformation. The version of Christianity it pursued, Russian Orthodox, was largely unaffected by developments in religious and political thought in western Europe.

While Europe was growing out of the feudal system in which land was held in return for services rendered to the monarch, and establishing the idea that individuals could own property outright, Russia was going in the other direction. Ivan the Terrible claimed ultimate property rights over all land for himself. In 1550, a new law code required landholders to provide military and administrative service to the Tsar. Hereditary rights were not respected: unhelpful boyars had their land confiscated and found themselves deported. The Tsar also seized and redistributed the property of any landowner who left for the less authoritarian Poland–Lithuania federation to the west.

The system was refined by successive Tsars, perhaps reaching its zenith under Peter I (the Great) in the eighteenth century. Peter divided the military and civil service into a total of fourteen separate ranks with promotion linked to service to the state and created the splendidly named Chancery of Confiscations to seize and redistribute land as necessary. According to contemporary accounts he made a point of underlining the reach of his personal authority by physically beating even senior members of his entourage who disappointed him. (Peter's constitutional strength was matched by his bearlike physique, and these assaults could apparently do serious damage.) While European contemporaries would describe themselves to their superiors as 'your obedient servant' – a habit that persisted for centuries in British letter-writing etiquette – Russian nobles would sign off addresses to the Tsar as 'your slave'. Prince Vasili III, who succeeded Ivan the Great, said of Russian society that 'all are slaves'.

Peter was keen to import technology from the West, such as modern shipbuilding techniques, to try to catch up with European progress. He was also keen on European art and dress, personally shaving the beards of some nobles and imposing heavy taxes on facial hair for the rest. But any concessions to Western-style political reform were slow, grudging and prone to reversal. He set up what was in effect a secret police force to spy on and control his own people, a function in which the Russian state established lasting expertise. Envying the advanced economies and technologies of the West while rejecting the political structures that went along with them was a painful ambiguity to which Russia would return.

Catherine II (another 'the Great'), who ruled at the end of the eighteenth century, was interested in modern political ideas. She corresponded with western European philosophers of the Enlightenment who were developing concepts of individual rights and limited states whose political powers were balanced between the executive, the legislature and the judiciary. But apart from a narrow Charter of the Nobility, she and subsequent Tsars did little to put such ideas into practice. Judicial decisions, rather than being the province of a separate legal body, were largely made by Tsarist state bureaucrats in the course of their work. Serfdom, which meant peasants owed direct allegiance to their master, was not abolished in Russia until 1861, centuries after it had died out in most of western Europe. The only real recourse that people had against Tsarist rule was violence and rebellion. It was once remarked that Russia's constitution was 'absolutism moderated by assassination'.

The only substantive political unit of Russian society below the Tsar was at a very low level – the *mir* or village commune that existed essentially to enable its members to survive by collectively banding together. Russia never developed a landowning or merchant class that was capable of organizing itself to significantly restrain the Tsar.

In England, for example, the monarch transmuted over the centuries from an autocrat to a figurehead through gradually increasing constraints on royal power. Notable landmarks included the revolt of the barons that led to the signing of Magna Carta in 1215 and the Bill of Rights that followed the overthrow of James II in 1688. Nothing comparable happened in Russia. Nor did Russia embrace the formal separation of powers between executive, legislature and judiciary enshrined in the French and US republican constitutions. Instead, after Tsarism collapsed in the Russian revolutions of 1917, autocratic executive power was transferred almost intact from tsars to communists.

Under Tsar Nicholas II in the early twentieth century, just as under Peter the Great, there had been some experiments with economic modernization. The rudiments of a market economy developed under some of the more reform-minded of the Tsar's prime ministers. But politically Russia remained largely an autocracy. The Duma, a parliament of sorts that had existed for centuries, was opened up to elections under Nicholas II, but he rapidly regretted allowing any challenge to his authority and repeatedly ignored and then disbanded it.

Russia's only real experiment with a freely chosen parliament was the Constituent Assembly. Elected in 1917 after the first (February) revolution had deposed Nicholas II, it had its first and only meeting in January 1918. By then, the 'Bolshevik' communists had already seized power in what was known as the October revolution but was in effect an armed coup. Vladimir Lenin, the Bolshevik leader, sent the assembly members home. And that, as far as parliamentary restraints on absolute centralized power went, was pretty much that.

After a brief 'democratic parenthesis' during 1917, autocratic centralism was restored. Private property once again became subsumed under the authority of the state, though the rationale was now provided by the ideology of Soviet communism rather than the supreme personal power invested in the Tsar. Any substantial institution standing between the Party leadership and the people was fiercely suppressed, with the exception of some entirely co-opted organizations like the official trade unions. The Tsar's 'Okhrana' secret police were reborn in an even more powerful and sinister form – first as the Cheka, then through a variety of name changes and formulations to end up as the KGB.

For a while, the communists were forced by events to permit a limited market economy to function. After 'war communism' – the centrally directed economic mobilization necessary to win the civil war that followed their seizure of power – the communists eased back, allowing small private enterprises to exist and peasants to sell surplus produce. But the usual pace of progress for building up agricultural surpluses to fund investment was not fast enough. The Soviet Union wanted to become a military-industrial power as rapidly as possible. The market economy also created a political danger. The growth of the *kulak* class of richer farmers was a threat to communist dominance. The result was forced state collectiviz-ation of farms and mass murder of those who opposed it, and the tentative growth of a class that might have asserted its rights against the state was savagely cut short.

Politically, the executive remained in charge, and the division of power between the legislature (the Supreme Soviet) and the government (the Council of Ministers) was merely decorative. The judiciary, which had begun to gain a measure of independence under Tsar Alexander II in the late nineteenth century, made sure to run its verdicts past local Communist Party bosses when any serious matter was involved. In one particularly blatant breach of natural justice in 1961, a sudden rash of illegal dealing in gems and foreign exchange enraged the Communist Party's first secretary, Nikita Khrushchev, who demanded examples be made. He ordered the death penalty to be introduced retroactively. Specu-lators were retried and executed.

Russia and the other republics that went to make up the Soviet Union – Moldova, Belarus and so on – were not the only communist countries in the region, of course. Soviet communism was forcibly exported by the Red Army in 1945 to a clutch of countries in central and eastern Europe – Poland, Czechoslovakia, Hungary, Romania and so forth. From the West, the bloc may have looked like an undifferentiated mass of grey, stultified nations. But their political and economic histories before the communist takeover meant that the ubiquitous hammer and sickle hid very different attitudes and experiences, which would re-emerge once the weight of oppression was removed.

The experiences of the former Soviet Union (henceforth FSU) republics and the rest of central and eastern Europe since communism collapsed there in the early 1990s have been the subject of intense debate. Much of it has centred on the question of whether the state controls of the command economy – bureaucrats fixing prices, directing factory output and running the banking system – should have been dismantled in a single big bang of 'shock therapy' or taken apart piece by piece. Underlying that discussion is the assumption that a single set of policies was appropriate for all countries – or indeed would have produced the same results had it been evenly applied.

But, in practice, the same kind of policy applied in different countries had varied outcomes. Shock therapy in some central and eastern European countries like Poland and the Czech and Slovak Republics produced relatively good results in a short space of time. By the mid-1990s they were back up above their 1989 level of national income and growing briskly. Similar reform in the Baltic states that had been part of the Soviet Union itself (Latvia, Lithuania and Estonia) led to sharper reductions in output: their gross domestic product dropped in the early 1990s by between a third and three fifths. Yet most FSU republics reformed much more slowly but still experienced big drops in output.

A comparison with the reform of centrally directed 'command economies' in east Asia – specifically China and Vietnam – also suggests that it is not the pace of change that matters most. China and Vietnam reformed in different ways. China started earlier, in the late 1970s, but went much more gradually. Vietnam had a big bang of liberalizing prices and allowing its currency to be freely changed for others in 1989. But both of them grew quite happily in the years immediately afterwards – both, in fact, far quicker than any of the central or eastern European or FSU countries.

What appears to be going on is this. How economies *initially* reacted to liberalization depended more on where they started from than how they did it. All economies under communism looked a lot different from the way they would under a market economy, because the market mechanisms of supply and demand were not allowed to function and prices were fixed. Shortages were managed through rationing and black markets, not through allowing prices to change. As a result, the economies' structures were often wildly different from those which a market would have produced. They had huge but inefficient manufacturing sectors as a result of massive centrally directed capital investment. Their service sectors tended to be small and feeble. Their banking systems, required to direct money where it was politically expedient rather than where it would best be used, operated more like bureaucratic accounting offices than providers of finance. These distortions were magnified by trade relationships among the Soviet bloc countries that followed administrative diktat more than comparative advantage.

That the economies were inefficient and distorted should have surprised no-one. But the organizational incompetence of enterprises under communism was higher even than many pessimists predicted. Many literally subtracted rather than added value by over-using subsidized materials like steel and cement to make goods worth less than the inputs that went into them. Even in East Germany, one of the better-off countries, the privatization agency that rationalized and sold off its big companies after unification with West Germany expected to make a profit of DM500 billion; it ended up making a loss of DM250 billion.

As it turns out, the economies that had the biggest distortions underwent the largest drop in output, as the most inefficient and unwanted parts of the economy imploded. The FSU countries were chief among these. After all, most central European countries had experienced some form of market economy before the Second World War until the Soviets invaded and turned them into satellite states. Most of the Soviet Union's economy, by contrast, had been subject to a hugely distorting and militarily oriented crash industrialization programme run by a dictatorship since 1917, and did not have much to build on even before that. It wasn't the speed of the policies that each undertook which proved the critical factor; it was the path that their economies had followed in the way up to starting them.

Even more interesting is what happened after the shock of transformation in the first half-decade or so after reforms began. This second, longer-term part of the reaction to change appeared to depend more on the quality of the institutions that supported the market economy than on simple government policies. The institutions that countries started off with – the rule of law, respect for property, a functioning bureaucracy, an appreciation of market economics – depended greatly on their history. What happened to those institutions also varied with the route that each of the governments took.

In the medium term after undertaking market reforms, China and Vietnam grew merrily, as did most of the central and eastern European nations. The Baltic states, whose highly distorted economies shrank rapidly in the first half of the 1990s, turned around in the middle of that decade and grew steadily thereafter, though they have more recently encountered the downside of market economics, being hit badly by the financial crisis that spread rapidly in 2008. Central and eastern European and Baltic countries have also made big strides in instituting democracy and the kind of institutions generally seen in successful market economies: stable, predictable and non-predatory taxation; functioning corporate law; the absence of widespread corruption; a general ease of doing business. Lest this be thought of as an argument for indiscriminately rolling back the state, they have also managed to keep government spending fairly high as a share of gross domestic product – and redirect it towards helpful things like health and education rather than spraying around subsidies to inefficient industries.

Those central and eastern European and Baltic countries had a variety of historical experiences before the Iron Curtain came down at the end of the Second World War. By no means were they a collection of liberal democracies with market economies. But many had experienced strong influence from Western powers – the Austro-Hungarian empire and the kingdom of Prussia, and before that a Polish–Lithuanian federation. They naturally looked to the West more than did Russia. And they had more experience of constitutional limited government and individual rights than those who had known mainly the rule of the Russian empire.

As well as starting off from a more helpful history, they also had a clear idea of where they were going: the European Union. The EU often does more good to countries when they are trying to join than once they are in. The prize is membership of a lucrative free-trade area and the seal of respectability that comes from membership. The hoops that countries need to jump through on the way include demonstrating economic stability, democracy, justice and the rule of law. Even if nations don't start off with good institutions, the EU provides a powerful incentive to acquire them. It had played the same role decades before in helping Greece, Spain and Portugal move from dictatorship to democracy.

The same, sadly, could not be said for Russia. It often shows little more desire to learn from Western institutions than it did during the centuries of Tsarism. It has little history of market economics to draw on. A story detailing this used to go round the Bank of England. The bank has a valuable but little-known unit that runs training courses for central bankers from around the world. It was particularly busy in the early 1990s when streams of officials arrived from the Soviet bloc with training in nothing but Marxist economics. When one such group came for their course, so the tale goes, they professed to understand perfectly the way that prices were set in a market economy by the intersection of supply and demand. But they still expressed disbelief that no government bureaucrat was required actually to post the price. How could prices just emerge without the state saying so? Eventually, according to the legend, the officials were taken to Smithfield meat market in the City of London to show them the magic at work.

Even after the initial shock of transition wore off, Russia has lurched from boom to crisis. It defaulted on its government debt in 1998, sending shockwaves around a world still being battered by the Asian financial crisis that did for Suharto. Its economy was run for a while by a group of oligarchs who, by exploiting weaknesses in the market system, enriched themselves enormously. The oligarchs have their defenders, and some may have done some valuable work in turning round crippled Soviet-era industries. But their disproportionate control over the economy, the corners that some cut to make their wealth and their intermittent interventions in politics invited a backlash against the whole idea of free-market economies and democracy.

That backlash has duly arrived in the shape of the policies implemented by Vladimir Putin, Russia's prime minister and former president. Just as Muscovy went in a different direction to western Europe, so Russia has parted company with its former satellites. Central and eastern European countries are mainly striving to become liberal democracies, but Russia has systematically sucked power back from independent institutions into the state. The press has been muzzled, bought off or intimidated into quiescence; non-governmental organizations have been hamstrung by rules strictly limiting their activities and their funding; provincial governors, who formerly enjoyed a lot of freedom to tax and run their regions, have been turned into Moscow placemen; the Duma, through electoral manipulation and constitutional manoeuvring, has been reduced to little more than a rubber stamp.

Sound familiar? Not for nothing has Putin been compared with Tsars of centuries past. A favourite comparison is with the hardline Nicholas I, who ruled in the first half of the nineteenth century. Putin himself has unashamedly claimed a Russian exceptionalism. He wrote in 2000: 'from the very beginning, Russia was created as a supercentralized state. That's practically laid down in its genetic code, its traditions, and the mentality of its people.'

Meanwhile, though incomes grew rapidly in recent years, much of the rise was linked to the run-up in energy prices that made Russia's huge oil and gas deposits much more valuable and bailed out its formerly bankrupt government. Some of the oil and gas money was recycled into other parts of the economy. But rises in income ran well ahead of productivity growth, suggesting that much of Russia's newfound prosperity rested on oil derricks and gas pipelines and was vulnerable to renewed weakness in energy prices. Even the oil and gas sector itself underperformed, and foreign companies that might have helped improve productivity were driven out. And as we saw in the chapter on oil and diamonds, the combination of a powerful unaccountable state and an abundant mineral resource is not one that generally ends happily for the country concerned. Under Putin, the energy industry has been clawed back towards state control.

Putin did at least bring order, if not law, compared to the sometimes chaotic rule of his predecessors, Boris Yeltsin and Mikhail Gorbachev. Accordingly, perhaps unfortunately for their future freedom and prosperity, Russians themselves have seemed reasonably happy with the centralization of power, though the lack of a free media and fair elections has made it hard to tell. They don't miss real democracy since, many would argue, they have never had it. Corruption is rife, but that is just the way things are done. Elections have been far from clean, but Putin and his supporters would probably have got re-elected even if they had been. Yet even optimists are doubtful, especially with lower energy prices, that Russia's unfamiliar market economy can coexist and flourish with an authoritarian government intent on taking control of yet more of the levers of economic power.

That, though, is precisely the trick that China has so far managed to pull off. Its one-party state has not proved inimical to rapid economic development. Compared with Russia, China's economic growth has been broadly based across the economy (though with the service sector still underdeveloped, a point we will look at later) and has involved massive gains in productivity. How has it managed to do it? The histories of China and Russia before communism had some similarities. Both had been aware of the influences of Western economies and Western ideas but had turned away from them. So when they both started edging towards modern market economics, what were the differences?

Part of it might be the way they went about reform. In retrospect, Russia may well have done it the wrong way round. The collapse of the Soviet Union began in the 1980s when Mikhail Gorbachev, then general secretary of the Communist Party, started with the political opening up known as *glasnost*. Only later did he go on to economic reform, *perestroika*. In the meantime, the Russian state was collapsing. Since 1917, Russia's bureaucracy had been in a mutual embrace with the Communist Party. Civil servants at almost all levels took instructions from political bosses. With the Party imploding, both institutions crumbled at once and the civil service could not be transformed into a modern, workable bureaucracy. In other words, the Soviet Union started off by damaging the institutions it already had, diminishing the likelihood that they could be rapidly transformed into better ones.

By contrast, China started with economic reform, and has gone much further down that road than it has with political liberalization. The Chinese Communist Party does not look like being threatened any time soon. So far, Beijing has managed to institute reform within the system without destroying the system itself. It has retained the one-party political structure and restricted public opinion and free expression. The events of Tiananmen Square in 1989 showed the strict limits on political pluralism. Since then there has been no serious organized threat to the integrity of the one-party state.

Meanwhile, the organization of the Chinese state has enabled it to coexist with a limited form of market economy. For one thing, compared with Russia it has devolved much more authority down to lower levels. Local party bosses and bureaucrats compete against each other to increase economic growth in their regions, and have had considerable leeway to do so. The huge burst of foreign direct investment that has flooded into China since the 1990s has been lured in by local authorities offering tax breaks, infrastructure, power and water supply. China's rapid growth was kickstarted by several regional 'special economic zones' where China's restrictive business and labour laws were relaxed. A few republics attempted something similar in Russia, but Putin's government reined them in.

The Chinese Communist Party and the state bureaucracy have an intertwined relationship similar to that in the Soviet Union, but with China's long history of competitive examinations, it is closer to a meritocracy than the Soviet system. China introduced a 'cadre responsibility system' where local governments and bureaucrats commit to performance-based contracts. The Soviet state and Party had a crisis of confidence as soon as they tried to reform. China's state apparatus is sufficiently confident of its own strength to effect limited market reform without provoking a complete collapse of the system.

Another great advantage China had, by historical accident, was its business-minded diaspora, particularly that in Hong Kong. We saw in the religion chapter how Chinese minorities often provided the entrepreneurial class in countries across east Asia. China may have been suspicious of Western influence, but Hong Kong provided a source of finance and business expertise that had a familiar – indeed, sometimes a family – face, particularly after the former British colony reverted to Chinese control in 1997. The foreign direct investment that started coming into China in the 1980s following the first moves to liberalize the economy owed much to personal links. A survey of Hong Kong subcontracting operations in China's Pearl River delta between 1986 and 1989 revealed that over half had either exploited family connections or were investing via companies already present in the area.

China was also fortunate in having models to follow in the region, giving it confidence that it could liberalize the economy while retaining political control. Taiwan, Singapore and Korea had all managed to enrich themselves while being run by autocratic states. As we saw in the previous chapter, all had the powerful bureaucracy typical of east Asian countries, which in the case of China had long predated communism.

The administration of Chinese law is opaque and can be heavily influenced by the interests of the local Party, as anyone trying to get a Chinese court to close down counterfeiting operations could tell you. But Beijing does not violate property rights in quite the same arbitrary large-scale fashion as Moscow. Foreigners investing in China complain about the thickets of regulations and bureaucracy, often designed to help Chinese companies at the expense of overseas businesses. But nothing in China has quite gone the same way as the foreign oil companies who have been unceremoniously kicked out of Russia. China has a way to go on the institutions front, but, as we saw in the previous chapter, Chinese corruption does at least appear to be of a relatively benign form. There remains only one party to bribe.

And so to India. In theory, India ought to be able to do everything China can and more. Like China, it has a tradition of a well-developed civil service, in India's case inherited from the British empire. It also has a reasonably good history of being a market economy. As we have seen, the British East India Company went there to trade with thriving local textile producers before it decided to run the place itself. British imperial rule may have stunted and distorted the Indian economy but did leave it with reasonably good infrastructure, particularly in the form of a fairly extensive railway network. And, of course, India is a democracy.

Yet it remains substantially poorer on average than China. And while India's recent growth rates have been impressive, they are nowhere near high enough to catch up with its Asian rival, not least because it has done much less to upgrade its infrastructure. India's recent experience suggests that democracy and bureaucracy can be ambiguous legacies, particularly in a society riven by social caste. Political pluralism can mean deadlock. And a bureaucracy without strong political leadership has a way of looking out for its own interests and resisting reform. It took India over forty years of independence and the imperative of a financial crisis to get around to undertaking its own package of liberalization.

Despite its relatively free press and open political system, India displays some of the same odd sense of disconnection as Russia and China between politics and the economy. In part, India's economy has modernized spectacularly. In particular, it has created what Russia and China have not – world-beating service sector enterprises, in India's case in information technology and the outsourcing of business tasks like accounting and data analysis.

Yet Indian politics, if anything, has gone the opposite way from the process of modernization in most democracies. The typical pattern, as happened with the spoils system in nineteenth-century America we encountered in the corruption chapter, is to start off with clientelism – 'what will you sell me for my vote?' Next comes ideology – 'who will make the country better off, especially for people like me?' Finally, it appears, we get to managerialism – 'who will most competently, and with the most winning smile and plausible manner, implement the set of policies on which all mainstream parties broadly agree, albeit none of them will publicly admit it?'

Far from being dominated by ideology, still less management, Indian politics has become ever more dominated by competing crowds of interest groups grabbing for the spoils of government jobs and public money. Recently, the number of such parties representing particular social castes has exploded. It is less a question of left versus right – or even, as we will see, rich versus poor – so much as every caste for itself. And meanwhile, this squabble over the spoils has helped dim the prospects for further economic liberalization, which most economists would agree has helped to put India on a path to greater prosperity. How did India get here?

Tempting though it is, not least because it would allow us to take one final swing at the East India Company, we can't quite blame the British for India's politics in the same way we can blame the Mongols for Russia's. The British empire intensified and formalized the fissiparous malignity of caste divisions that scars Indian society and retards its economic development, but it did not create it.

Caste is a vastly complex subject, not least because it has a variety of dimensions including religious, social, ethnic, historical and occupational. The word itself is a foreign import to India: *casta* had been used in sixteenth-century Spain and Portugal in botany and animal husbandry to denote species or breed. The term was carried to India by traders and became a loose expression that could refer to community, blood-line, birth-group or religion.

The system of caste owes a great deal to Hinduism, which divided society into four categories or varnas. But, as we saw in the religion chapter, modern caste divisions are not a straight reflection of Hindu teaching. As well as the broad varna classifications of Brahmin (priest and scholar), Kshatriya (warrior), Vaishya (merchant and artisan) and Sudra (manual worker), there are literally hundreds of sub-groups called *jatis*. Sometimes, but not always, they are based on or associated with a particular occupation. One jati might traditionally be goat-herders, for example, and have certain respected rights and privileges as such. While varna is mainly a spiritual identity, jati corresponds more closely to the actual concrete experience of life: the community you are born into; the job you are likely to end up doing; the background of the person you are supposed to marry.

We also saw in the religion chapter how self-interest managed to spread caste division throughout Indian society, taking it beyond its Hindu roots. Hinduism has at least four major rival religions on the subcontinent – Sikhism, Islam, Christianity and Buddhism. It is remarkable how the jati subdivisions that are supposedly ultimately derived from Hindu teachings have managed to penetrate all of them.

Sikhism, for example, was founded relatively recently, at the end of the fifteenth century. The founding Gurus of the religion rejected the authority of certain of the Hindu texts, and defiantly wove an explicit rejection of caste Hinduism into its practices. In place of the name that might identify a Hindu's caste, Sikhs all have the same titles: 'Singh' for men, meaning 'lion', and 'Kaur' for women, meaning 'princess'. Yet a quick look at contemporary Sikh matrimonial websites, the modern equivalent of the village matchmaker, will frequently find 'caste' listed as one of the attributes of the potential spouse. Many Sikhs identify themselves as 'Jat Sikh'. On one level this is a historical occupational classification: the Jats tended to be landlord farmers, and there are many Jat Hindus and Jat Muslims. But on another it is a social caste. Many Jat Sikhs will not marry a non-Jat.

Given its ancient provenance, the classification of the Indian population by caste obviously predated British imperial rule. So, in fact, did the exploitation of those divisions for administrative purposes. The Muslim Moghul emperors who ruled India until the eighteenth century developed the technique of grading subjects by skin colour: fair, 'wheaten' or medium, and dark. (These prejudices also endure in modern matchmaking.) After the Moghul empire declined, the rise of many smaller Hindu kingdoms to fill the vacuum increased the importance of caste distinctions. As we have seen, the fact that Brahmins had a monopoly on priesthood, and were far more likely to be literate, meant they were much in demand as clerics and bureaucrats. Even in the Sikh kingdom of Ranjit Singh in the north of modern India, Brahmins got preferment because of the ruler's need to record and administer his realm. Someone, after all, had to collect taxes.

But the hold of caste over Indian society increased under the British, especially after the Crown took over in direct rule in 1857. The East India Company, as we have seen, preferred to operate through manipulating and co-opting local rulers rather than outright military occupation. Dividing and ruling required relatively detailed knowledge of Indian societies to work out where to divide and how to rule.

In particular, the British found it useful to organize the military along caste and sometimes religious lines. Having been impressed by the fighting ability of the Sikhs when defeating the Sikh kingdom in the 1840s, the colonists promptly recruited them into the British army. They designated the Sikhs a 'martial race' and formed a Sikh regiment. (Some Hindu families would bring their eldest son up as a Sikh to ease his military career.) A regiment was also reserved for the Rajputs, a sub-group of the Kshatriya caste.

Increasingly detailed classified tables in the regular colonial census reported caste affiliations, standardized and cross-referenced on principles derived from zoology and botany. More and more, these classifications incorporated ethnic divisions. To its credit, the East India Company itself was not particularly obsessed with ethnicity and the purity of blood-lines. It permitted and even encouraged its own white officials to marry local girls, one of the best-known ways of making political and business contacts. (As the old saying goes: the son-in-law also rises.) Gradually, however, and particularly after 1857, unpleasant Victorian notions of racial differentiation crept in. Caste distinctions became ossified by the bogus but highly popular nineteenth-century pseudo-science of anthropometry, the biological classification of race.

H. H. Risley, one of the British empire's main propagators of this poisonous nonsense, divided India into seven races from the darker, 'primitive' Dravidians in the south to the paler, 'advanced' Indo-Aryans in the north. According to Risley, the social status of each group varied in direct inverse proportion to the width of their noses. (In Africa, similar tests helped to separate Hutus from Tutsis in Rwanda, and we all know how well that one turned out.)

By the early twentieth century, caste was sufficiently embedded in Indian society to infect the political campaign for independence from the British empire. True, many independence activists rejected the whole concept out of hand as a tool of colonialism. The campaigning *Indian Social Reformer* newspaper in 1930 urged its readers to refuse to give census takers the details of their caste. But in the jockeying for position among India's nascent political parties that led up to independence in 1947, caste identities often played a role. The Unionist Party, for example, which represented landed interests in the Punjab in northern India, rallied support by railing against domination by Brahmins.

Some of the most famous independence leaders also had an ambiguous attitude to caste. Outside the four varnas lay two other groups. One was the 'untouchables', today generally known as 'Dalits', a caste below the four others. The other was 'tribals', people outwith the caste system altogether. These two suffered the most disadvantage and discrimination. Historically confined to unpleasant, low-status jobs, often shunned by higher castes and denied access to village wells and other public places, they were also routinely deprived of education. It was estimated in the early twentieth century that only 0.13 per cent of Dalits were literate. The British had created an extensive Indian civil service, staffed for the main part by Indians, but it drew disproportionately from the higher and better-educated castes, further entrenching their privilege.

Mahatma Gandhi, the most famous independence leader of all, decried the concept of untouchability as a stain on Hinduism and renamed the caste 'Harijan', or 'Children of God'. But his solution was religious, not political: he aimed not to abolish caste but to raise up the status of untouchables within the faith. Gandhi still defended the concept of varna classifications for providing essential order to society. So-called 'uplift' campaigners claimed to be agitating on behalf of Harijans, but in practice often ended up hectoring them to clean themselves up and act more like their betters.

It is a painful historical irony that the man who may unwittingly have helped to entrench caste in the politics of independent India was himself a Dalit and bitterly critical of Gandhi on the issue. B. R. Ambedkar, from a modest background in the 'untouchable' Mahar caste, managed to overcome huge educational disadvantages to gain a doctorate from Columbia University in New York before returning to India. By the late 1920s, having become a provincial legislator in Bombay under the limited self-government permitted by the empire, he became one of the country's best-known independence activists. In 1935, by the Government of India Act, the last big gesture of devolution before the end of colonial rule, the British created separate electoral representation for minority religious communities. Ambedkar demanded, and got, the same for untouchables.

This necessitated a giant census exercise by the colonial authorities, which listed nearly 400 separate untouchable communities and dozens of tribal groups. From that colonial classification come the terms 'Scheduled Caste' and 'Scheduled Tribe', corresponding respectively to the 'untouchables' and the 'tribals', that pepper modern Indian political discourse.

At independence in 1947, the net results of India's history were twofold with regard to its economic and political future. One, a minority of Indians were literate; two, Indian society, apart from the divisions of religion and language, was splintered by hundreds of caste identities. The path India had taken to independence shaped the way it went thereafter.

The constitution of the new republic, which came into force in 1950, was drafted mainly on the lines supported by Jawaharlal Nehru, who became India's first prime minister. It was based on the rights of people as individuals, not as members of a community. The concept of untouchability was outlawed and, along with later legislation, this supposedly ended the physical segregation of Dalits. But with the best intentions, it left footholds that enabled caste divisions to predominate. The constitution, at Ambedkar's urging, enjoined the state to 'promote with special care the educational and economics interests of the weaker sections of the people, and in particular, of the Scheduled Castes and the Scheduled Tribes'. In practice, this meant they got reserved government jobs, places at higher education institutions and legislative assembly seats. It also entrenched the colonial practice of collecting vast amounts of data on caste, and required an official commission and commissioner for Scheduled Castes and Scheduled Tribes to be created.

Caste prejudice could not, in any case, be wished away by a written constitution, any more than the end of slavery in the US after the Civil War could instantly end discrimination against blacks. Attitudes, as they do, endured. The first commissioner's report in 1951 spoke disparagingly of Dalits in similar terms to the 'uplift' campaigners of previous decades: they were, it said, 'lazy in mind and body and callous to [their] own condition'.

The result of slicing up the population by caste classification and handing out benefits on that basis was, unsurprisingly, to encourage politics to align itself in the same way. To begin with, Nehru's broad-based Congress Party dominated post-independence politics. But when it began to falter from the 1960s onwards, a growing swarm of regionally based parties began to use caste as an electoral tool. Before too long, the exceptional privileges granted to the minority of scheduled castes and tribes started to edge towards becoming a norm for the majority.

At independence, there were fewer than 50 million in the Scheduled Castes and around another 25 million in the Scheduled Tribes, totalling around 20 per cent of the population. But continual agitations on behalf of other castes led to a huge new grouping, 'Other Backward Classes', being invented and positive discrimination being extended to them. The Backward Classes Commission in the 1950s identified nearly 2400 communities, another 32 per cent of the population, as victims of 'backwardness'.

Until the 1980s, the Indian economy generally crawled along at the wryly named 'Hindu rate of growth' of 3–4 per cent annually which did little more than keep pace with the rise in the population. Indian society was thus essentially a zero-sum game. Anything you got had to be taken from someone else, and the common good could go hang. It was an ideal ground for clientelist politics to flourish.

For many, politics became a game of cultivating 'vote banks' – electoral blocs defined by caste, religion or ethnicity. Any caste that got reserved jobs or reserved places at college fought hard to keep them; those that did not fought hard to get them. Forming state or even national governments often became a matter of piecing together temporary alliances of special interests. Frequently this meant cutting across income divisions: a successful coalition might well include a pincer movement of a 'high' and a 'low' caste ganging together against a middling one.

The effect of this system on redressing the enormous imbalances in Indian society has been at best minimal and more likely negative. The reserved jobs and college places tend to be scooped up by the most affluent within any given caste – the gloriously named 'creamy layer'. The allocation of jobs by politicians is a superb opportunity for corruption: many are simply auctioned off to the highest eligible bidder. Since government jobs are a source of power and money to politicians, the system creates a strong incentive for them to resist any attempts to make government run more efficiently, to allocate positions on the basis of merit or, heaven forfend, to privatize state-run industries. India's history has taken it down an economic and social path from which it is politically hard to leap.

Meanwhile, the country is far from creating the kind of society that would provide genuine opportunities for all regardless of birth. More Dalits – perhaps a third – can now read and write than the miserably low percentages before independence. But India's overall literacy rate remains low. The official rate is around 65 per cent, though many of those can probably do little more than write their names. Much of the money supposed to go to education gets siphoned off by a huge bureaucracy and a corrupt political class.

The contrast between India and China in this regard helps explain why, although both are becoming modern economic giants, their development is quite different. With a longer tradition of meritocracy and education, and with nothing like the same social stratification, China has got its literacy rate above 90 per cent. Its bureaucracy, though corrupt, appears to be relatively efficient in its corruption. The result is a broad-based surge of growth, much of which has taken place in the manufacturing sector. Initially in textiles and garments, China's extraordinary rise has more recently taken in electronics, computers and cars. Such production, particularly in the labour-intensive assembly part of the process, has created mass job opportunities even for the relatively unskilled. Hundreds of millions have been lifted out of poverty.

While China's leadership decided to start liberalizing its economy more or less of its own accord and at a time of its choosing, it took a crisis to get a comparable movement in India. A small group of reformers clustered around Manmohan Singh, the finance minister who a decade later would become prime minister, seized the opportunity of a balance of payments crisis in 1991. In a few days, they pushed through a series of changes, particularly reforming an extensive system of government licences for imports, exports and business operations which bureaucrats had used to extort bribes from companies.

Still, though India's growth rate has picked up, the nature of its history and its institutions has made the pattern and the distribution of that growth quite different from China's. India has found it hard to match China's prowess in large-scale manufacturing. Its transport and electricity infrastructure, thanks to the sclerotic and inefficient state, is poor. The most vibrant sector of the Indian economy over the past decade has been its famous software, IT and other outsourcing industries. Often relying on satellite communications and generating their own power, software companies have thrived by having almost nothing to do with the government at all.

This superior performance in services, incidentally, has long historical roots. Thanks to data kept by the British colonists, it is possible to undertake comparisons of relative productivity (output per head) in India and Britain in different parts of the economy going right back to the end of the nineteenth century. Back then, Indian manufacturing productivity relative to Britain was about the same as for services, about 15 per cent, while its agricultural productivity was a little above 10 per cent. Since then relative Indian agricultural productivity has collapsed to 1 per cent of the British level, the manufacturing productivity ratio has remained more or less constant and the service sector has gained ground. By the end of the twentieth century, Indian service sector productivity had reached 30 per cent of the British level. India, it turns out, was relatively good at doing services decades before there was such a thing as computer software.

But India's lopsided development means the gains have been very unevenly distributed. India's poor overwhelmingly work in its troubled agricultural sector. Even more so than in manufacturing, employees need good literacy skills to be able to participate in service industries. Just like the reserved jobs in the caste system, many of the gains from Indian growth go to the already well-off. The head of human resources at one Indian software company once said to me: 'The problem with the IT industry is that it makes the creamy layer creamier.' The extensive job reservation system run by the state may in theory discriminate against those from privileged castes like the Brahmins, but their historically superior access to education has still given them a powerful advantage.

For India to escape its current pattern requires it to break habits acquired through decades of independence and, before that, centuries of imperialism. The socialism written into the constitution has to mean a genuine extension of services and opportunity to everyone, not a political system dominated by the elites from hundreds of different social groups squabbling for official privilege.

As previously noted, India's history has left it with some big advantages over China and Russia. For one, it is a democracy. Very few countries have managed to become genuinely rich to western European or North American levels without also becoming democratic. India's democracy is very far from perfect, but it can improve without a revolution or some similar enormous political upheaval. If China, by contrast, is to become a democracy, it will at some point have to go through a traumatic change. The state bureaucracy will have to stay intact and functioning while its intertwined relationship with a single political party is unpicked. Other east Asian countries, like South Korea, have managed this fairly well. But there is no guarantee that China will be able to adapt its historical legacy in the same way. Russia, for one, made an utter hash of it. And Russia's experiment with democracy since 1991 has left many Russians distinctly underwhelmed by this newfangled Western import, and willing to accept traditional restrictions on freedom in return for traditional stability.

Though the giant panda is indelibly associated with China, the lumbering creature is perhaps not the best symbol that the country could choose. The unconscious process of evolution has taken the panda on a path to oblivion, at least without continuing public subsidy, which it cannot retread and from which it cannot leap. No country finds itself in as intractable a position. But many nations have gone down routes that they would not have chosen had they foreseen where they would lead. And even if many in the country now recognize what needs to be done to change direction, it still takes large amounts of courage, luck and strength to find a better path.

10. Conclusion

Our remedies oft in ourselves do lie

Our circular whistle-stop tour of the economic history of the world started off by asking why Argentina is not the same as the US and ended up with seeing how countries choose different paths and get stuck on them. The same patterns and same problems that we have seen throughout history are continuing to recur. And while they can be corrected, changing paths can prove to be dauntingly hard.

The last few years have given us a good example of how some of the lessons of history can and have been learned, and how some have not. Globalization, which seemed to be invincible in the twenty years after the fall of the Soviet Union as it did in the last two decades of the nineteenth century, proved to be all too vulnerable. And just as the first Golden Age nearly succumbed to its own excesses in the 1890s, so did the finance capitalism of the turn of the twenty-first century find one of its greatest enemies in itself. It was not a world war that brought a twenty-year run of almost uninterrupted growth to an end: it was the overconfidence that produced bubbles in house prices and financial markets across the rich world, most dramatically seen in the US and the UK.

As the credit crunch turned into a full-blown economic crisis, problems became horribly apparent in the financial institutions on whose operations the global economy depended. Finance can be extraordinarily destructive as well as creative, as evinced by the collapse of some of the oldest banks on Wall Street. Lehman Brothers, an institution dating back to before the American Civil War, was gone in a weekend, buckling under an unsupportable weight of debt. Lending, even between one bank and another, dried up rapidly as panic spread that the entire financial system was about to stop working. The UK experienced its first run on a bank since the nineteenth century.

The damage soon spread to the real economy. Countries around the world plunged simultaneously into recession. Unemployment rose sharply. Global trade went into freefall, the volume of international goods commerce dropping by more than a fifth in three months. Fears grew that the credit crunch was depriving the engine of commerce of its most basic lubricant – the trade credit that underwrites international transactions, a form of financial instrument used for a millennium. Beleaguered industries began to cry for import tariff protection against unfair foreign competition. Suddenly, several of the central aspects of globalization – the movement of goods, of services and of capital – were simultaneously under the most severe threat they had faced since the 1930s.

The parallels with the Great Depression were so obvious they could have been scripted. Fortunately, the reaction was not. True, there was – and almost certainly will be for decades into the future – a fierce debate about the detail of the correct response. The US Congress had to take two goes at passing their rescue package for America's financial system, the Troubled Asset Relief Program (Tarp), amid worries that taxpayer money was being wasted. The need to include fiscal stimulus in the arsenal of response remained controversial. The decision not to rescue Lehman Brothers with public money in September 2008, but subsequently to step in to bail out Citigroup and American International Group after seeing the havoc that the Lehman bankruptcy caused, was controversial. Some thought the federal government and the Federal Reserve were wrong to act too slowly; others thought they were wrong to intervene at all.

And yet the three big policy errors of the 1930s – maintaining a tight monetary policy for too long, trying to stick to balanced budgets, and resorting to the mass protectionism of the Smoot-Hawley tariff bill – were, at least for the first couple of years of the crisis, largely avoided. The world's central banks – and particularly the US Federal Reserve, whose chairman had the advantage of being a scholar of the Depression – rapidly cut interest rates to near zero, and started pumping more money into the financial markets, a sharp contrast to the adherence to the gold standard in the first few years after the 1929 stock market crash. Governments around the world allowed their public finances to go into deficit – and some enacted new fiscal stimulus measures – to keep demand going, entirely the opposite reaction to the balanced-budget orthodoxy of the 1930s. Such moves were not universally popular. But even economists arguing against an extra boost from big new tax cuts or government spending professed themselves grateful for the 'automatic stabilizers' – the reduced tax revenue and increased expenditure that kick in when an economy slows. As we have seen, those stabilizers had largely been absent during the Great Depression.

And while – as we will see – it proved impossible to prevent governments implementing protectionist measures altogether, the first couple of years of the crisis saw many fewer restrictions on trade than the destructive rounds of beggar-thy-neighbour tariff increases in the early 1930s.

In responding to the global financial crisis, the central banks and finance ministries of the world's leading economies may have discovered new mistakes to make, yet they did at least avoid the most basic of old ones. And as the Lehman episode showed, they did at least seem to have absorbed one of the most fundamental principles of all: be prepared to learn as you go along.

But crisis management is one thing: ploughing on with the slow grind of medium-term policy quite another. The first is much easier than the second, not least because taxpayers and voters are more forgiving of governments which are dealing with a clear and present danger. The exigency of the crisis brought the normally unthinkable, such as governments taking over major private financial institutions, into the realm of the possible. In areas of policy where the financial crisis and global recession did not engender the same sense of urgency, perhaps because the threat seemed smaller and further away, governments struggled to escape the constraints they had always bound them and the entrenched interests that pulled the bindings tighter.

One clear example of a missed opportunity was the failure to advance the further liberalization of world trade. That attempt had been dragging on for nearly a decade via the so-called 'Doha round' of global trade talks, named after the capital of the tiny Gulf emirate of Qatar in which they were launched in 2001. The Doha round was intended to continue the job of cutting taxes on imports on a multilateral basis – that is, involving all member countries of the World Trade Organization – that had been started after the end of the Second World War and gradually driven forward since.

In theory, and in the rhetoric of participants, the global financial crisis and recession gave new urgency to a deal, not least because the enhanced potential for protectionist sentiment in the downturn gave it a new imperative. An agreement to bring down the ceilings on import tariffs would, all agreed, send a powerful signal that the world was not going to repeat the mistakes of the 1930s. Never again would tit-for-tat tariff increases be allowed to worsen a global recession.

And yet a series of interminable negotiating sessions failed to achieve a breakthrough. When the trade ministers from the WTO's entire 153-country membership assembled for their biennial conference in Geneva at the end of 2009, all they could agree on was not to discuss the Doha round at the meeting – the rough equivalent at turning up at the Versailles conference in 1919 and refusing to talk about the war. At the end of the first decade of the third millennium, with the global economy having entered an 'information age' that was supposed to revolutionize the whole basis of human endeavour and wealth, and acting under the new imperative of a global slowdown and rise in protectionist sentiment, those ministers were still trapped in the snares with which economic history had bound them for decades.

The US representatives came burdened with the weight of the agricultural lobby, and most particularly the cotton farmers. We have seen how American cotton interests manage to wield a political cudgel whose size is way out of proportion to their importance in the American economy. Cotton is one of the few crops that substantially fits the arguments of development charities that Western agricultural subsidies substantially hurt the livelihoods of some of the poorest farmers in the world – the eleven million people who grow cotton in west Africa and are hurt by the hugely subsidized cotton dumped on the world market by farmers in the southern states of the US.

The US, with its cotton-growing states continually watching over its shoulder, refused point-blank to discuss the issue separately until an overall deal on cutting farm subsidies and tariffs had been agreed. It was clear that the US farm lobby could continue to block any deal with which they were not happy. American farmers would not accept cuts to their subsidies without getting more access to export markets, particularly in countries like India and China. Seventeenth-century mercantilism was alive and well. The future of the global trading system was held to ransom by a sector that produces less than 1 per cent of the US's national income and employs less than 2 per cent of its workforce.

Meanwhile, over in talks on the industrial goods trade, Argentina showed what happens when you mollycoddle manufacturers for more than a century. Argentina still maintains high external tariffs on manufactured goods, and Buenos Aires argued vociferously against a deal that would have involved reducing the world's industrial tariffs.

In the meantime, many countries' main priority was to retain the right to defy the logic of comparative advantage. Nations such as Indonesia and the Philippines, with large populations and a shortage of land and water, have traditionally imported many staple foods, particularly rice. But their response to the shortages and stratospheric prices of the global food crisis of 2007–8 was to fight ever harder to retain the right to block imports in the future as part of a drive for national self-sufficiency. Unlike the crises of the 1840s which led to the repeal of the Corn Laws, countries did not seize the chance of the first twenty-first century food crisis permanently to reduce their agricultural protectionism.

Other food importers have taken a different route. Bypassing the trade talks altogether, the likes of Saudi Arabia leased large tracts of land in Africa to grow grain for themselves. They, at least, had grasped the logic of importing water from abroad. It was a shame they chose to do it in a way that resembled the imperial land-grabs of the nineteenth century, if not quite ancient Rome's policy of invading its main food supplier and exacting grain through forced taxation.

Meanwhile, India insisted on the need to retain agricultural import tariffs to protect the incomes of small farmers. Yet in reality, those smallholders are routinely pushed aside by the larger, more influential farmers who hoover up most of the subsidized water and power provided by the state. Corruption, and a political system that hands out benefits to the best-organized rather than the most deserving, has frequently left them bereft. Trade policy is a rather minor part of what is keeping Indian farmers poor.

And Russia was not in the talks from the beginning. Its isolation from the post-war economic order, wearyingly typical of the country's past, had kept it out of the WTO even though smaller and poorer countries had joined. In 2008 the WTO welcomed its 153rd member, the tiny west African nation of Cape Verde. (Population: 420,000. Main export: cocaine. They don't grow it, however.)

All of these problems have something in common: they involve an entrenched interest, or an alliance of them. Mancur Olson, who invented the theory of interest groups that we came across in the trade politics chapter, went on to argue that such factions have the capacity permanently to slow the ability of countries to adopt new technologies. Thus they can reduce economic growth. (Imagine the effect on world trade if the US longshoremen's unions had actually managed to stop the shipping container being adopted altogether.)

Such groups have a powerful interest in pushing policy debates away from anything that would entail their making sacrifices, even if there is widespread agreement that change of some sort is needed. If they are strong enough, they can bring all economic development to a halt and even send it into reverse. For a good example, we can take one final dip into history and look at the attempts of the Spanish empire to reverse the waning of its strength and influence. Once the biggest power in Europe, dominating trade with the Americas, Spain was increasingly shoved aside in the seventeenth century by quicker, smarter traders from the Netherlands, part of which had declared independence from Spain at the end of the sixteenth century. Spain was aware of its plight as its prestige decayed. But it appeared paralysed when it tried to throw the process into reverse.

From a distance of four hundred years and more, the causes look fairly obvious. A bloated aristocracy was living off rents and preventing more productive uses of land and labour. The largest landowning families had a long-established business of rearing sheep for high-quality merino wool, made particularly lucrative by a government monopoly. Small farmers were discouraged from planting and enclosing arable land in case it disrupted the grazing. This, together with controls on food prices, led to a general drift of the population out of the countryside and into the towns, though there was not enough work for them when they got there.

When the international market changed and the demand for such wool dropped, it was even less sensible to favour traditional forms of agriculture. Yet still the landowners clung to their privileges. Meanwhile, rather than nurturing its entrepreneurial class, Spain expelled it. The 'Moriscos' were Moors left in Spain from its time as part of the Islamic world, who had converted (perhaps rather nominally) to Christianity. They were skilled artisans and farmers. Unlike the sheep-grazers, they practised more labour-intensive forms of agriculture like the cultivation of vines, sugar and mulberries. But they were kicked out of Spain early in the seventeenth century amid the suspicion that they were secretly undermining Christendom.

Heavy taxes were exacted to fund increasingly unprofitable wars and imperial operations overseas. The monarchy, while living in profligate luxury, became the first serial defaulter in history, prefiguring the behaviour of its colonial offshoot Argentina. King Philip II defaulted on Spain's debts four times during his reign in the sixteenth century. The literature of the time, particularly the classic *Don Quixote*, reflects a society with a large gap between its inflated image of itself and the increasingly desperate reality.

It was not as if everyone was ignoring the crisis. A group of reformers called the *arbitristas* wrote stacks of policy documents with a range of suggestions. Some were sensible, such as a limit to the number of days that the extravagantly expensive royal court could sit in session. Some were understandable but misguided, like banning exports of raw materials and imports of manufactured goods to help domestic industry. And some verged on the surreal. A kind of proto-government policy unit, the Junta de Reformación, in 1623 recommended to the king that he prohibit the teaching of

Latin in small towns, to prevent peasants getting ideas above themselves and moving to the cities.

Yet there was not enough willpower to follow through with any of the suggestions. As a symbol of willingness to reform, the royal court adopted a mode of ostentatious austerity after the Junta made its recommendations. Yet just a few months later, those hair shirts were discarded in favour of silk as a lavish reception was arranged for a visit from the Prince of Wales. Perhaps the only lasting success of the reform movement was the widespread abandoning of the expensive and cumbersome ruff collar. That might have saved the nobles on laundry bills: it was not enough to save an empire. When it came down to it, the aristocracy would not give up enough of their privileges to preserve the system that had made them rich. As one contemporary observer said of reform: 'Those who can will not, and those who will cannot.'

But before we start drawing contemporary policy lessons from history, are we even right in suggesting that countries can turn themselves round quickly with the right policies? This book suggests that yes, they can.

Not everyone agrees. A huge amount of effort has gone into investigating why Europe, and specifically England, was the first country to enter the Industrial Revolution, and by doing so to achieve the first substantial sustained growth in average incomes for its citizens in history. The recent account by the historian Greg Clark suggests it was the process of higher-quality human capital spreading itself through the population over the generations. Richer and better-educated people had more children, and so gradually the attributes that make people suitable for industrialized economies – hard work, rationality and education – became widespread. This suggests that such a process cannot be forced, or changed by better policies from the top. It is simply a matter of waiting for higher-quality human capital to emerge.

Clark's book was a remarkable contribution to the sum of knowledge. In particular, it accumulated a large pile of evidence to support the thesis that human life on average (in terms of income, life expectancy, calorie intake and so forth) had not substantially improved for millennia before the Industrial Revolution. Increases in any given society's income had been followed by increases in population, making each individual no better off. Paradoxically, the biggest boost to per capita income in Europe before the Industrial Revolution were the plague outbreaks of the mid-fourteenth century, which made labour scarcer by reducing the population and hence increased the incomes of those that survived.

It is an interesting thesis. But the contention that the dissemination of different attitudes and, possibly, genes throughout the population sparked the Industrial Revolution doesn't do much to explain what has happened since – and most particularly in the past fifty years. The remarkable post-war performance of the Asian tigers happened in the form of sudden take-offs in growth. China's high growth can be traced pretty directly to the market-based policy reforms it initi-ated in 1979. It seems somewhat implausible that a sudden outbreak of cultural or genetic diligence had much to do with it.

Countries close to each other, with similar social histories and natural endowments, have performed very differently. Botswanans today are more than ten times richer than Sierra Leoneans. Yet forty years ago both were low-productivity agrarian societies. Both were part of the British empire. Both had very low rates of education. (In fact, if anything Sierra Leone had seen the advantage of an influx of relatively well-educated immigrants from North America.) Yet one used its diamond wealth to create the fastest-growing economy on earth for thirty years; the other squandered it to become the poorest nation on the planet.

This book is not a detailed instruction manual on economic policy. There are dozens of those already in existence. In any case, giving finely tuned advice on precisely what should be done with import tariffs, tax rates or anything else is impossible. That way lie mistakes like the micromanagement of Indonesian clove marketing boards by the International Monetary Fund. I don't know what the exact answers are, and anyone who claims she does should not be trusted. In general, the more that development economists have looked at the questions, the less precise and doctrinaire their advice becomes.

But certain basic ideas command wide acceptance. Don't cut yourself off from the rest of the world. Plan ahead for cities, but don't force them, and don't give them more power than they warrant. Try to let your economy do what it is best at, and support it where possible without trying to force it down a predetermined path. Don't obsess about religious belief, but watch for elites using it to further their own temporal ends. Stop overweening governments from ignoring property rights and the rule of law. Learn from the examples of those who stopped oil and diamond money poisoning their economy and their politics. Call the bluff of small interest groups who say they represent the whole country – and that can include bankers. For very poor nations, worry less about trade policy and more about customs procedures. Concentrate on rooting out the forms of bribery that will do the most damage, and worry less about corruption that is moderate and predictable. Be aware when your country is getting stuck on the wrong path and be alert for opportunities to shift it. And above all, be prepared to learn along the way.

So what is it that sends countries down the wrong route? Part of it is genuine differences of opinion, among outside observers as much as within the country concerned, as to what the right choices are. The import substitution policy, which we encountered in the first chapter, continued to be followed for decades in Africa and Latin America even when it appeared not to be producing results. Some people still argue in favour of it as a development strategy. And, as we have seen, the response of the US and other governments and central banks to the global financial crisis was contested, with some economists arguing that fiscal stimulus would be ineffective and some saying it needed to be much bigger.

Many countries, of course, are run by people who aren't particularly bothered about whether the population as a whole become better off, or how widely the gains are spread, so long as they get to run them. For reasons we have seen, natural-resource economies are particularly susceptible to this. There is not much that anyone outside can do about this except try to stop their own companies and banks operating in that country from making things worse.

Even if politicians within the country do see the need for change, they often find that taking the right decision is politically too difficult or goes against the grain of the way things have always been done. You can stand for election in India promising to end the entire system of caste preferences in jobs and education, and to promote a more equitable system of public services for all. But you will struggle to overcome what is now an established system of politics oriented around handing out favours to particular electoral blocs.

Following prescriptions like those above is not easy, or everyone would have done it. Often it can be exhaustingly difficult. Nor is it something that can automatically be done by presidential or prime ministerial decree. Achieving sustainable change in policy means bringing public opinion with you – even, often, in autocracies – and that requires political skill as well as technocratic expertise. Florence during the Renaissance did not just produce highly talented bankers – it also spawned the statecraft of Niccolò Machiavelli which told politicians the tricky means by which to get things done. Sometimes it takes a subterranean path to reach the light. What is politically possible varies enormously between countries, and between different times in the same country. India's balance of payments crisis in 1991, though obviously not a good thing in itself, opened a very narrow window of opportunity that some clever reformers could exploit.

Often, taking the right path is more than one country can do on its own. When countries like Egypt cling to a substantial degree of self-sufficiency in food, it may not be economically efficient. But to rely on international markets involves a great degree of trust that those markets will always be able to supply what they need. In the 2007–8 food crisis, for example, international rice and wheat prices shot higher as traditional exporting countries, including Argentina, put blocks on exports to keep food at home. For countries like Egypt to embrace freer trade and carry on importing water embedded in food means someone else has to carry on exporting it. And the traditional producers could not be relied upon.

Argentina was not the only agro-exporter to put blocks on sales abroad. Grain producers like Ukraine and rice-growers like Vietnam also did so. Unlike ancient Rome, invading Ukraine and extracting grain from it by force is not an option for modern Egypt. Politicians might want to make the right decision for the long term, but they also need to maintain their short-term popularity. And making a country vulnerable to a food crisis in the interests of future efficiency is not a great platform on which to stand for re-election.

This is why we have international institutions like the WTO: to enable countries to make the right decisions collectively when it is hard for them to do so individually. The ancient Romans could make decisions about food supply only within the seas and territory that they controlled and inside the effective range of bulk food trade. Today that range has increased to encompass the entire globe. Yet the institutions that are intended to run and regulate the world economy have not kept pace with the growth of trade and technology. Within its jurisdiction the WTO has far less firepower than the Hanseatic League, let alone the Roman empire. And of course, the WTO, and the other institutions of international economic government that were created to match the globalization of the world economy, are not fulfilling their potential. Even had it been passed, the Doha round would not have stopped agricultural exporters cutting off supplies to the world markets during the food crisis.

The global financial crisis might conceivably have boosted the power of global institutions by opening up the potential for a fundamental reordering of worldwide economic governance. After all, it was the Great Depression and the Second World War which begat the International Monetary Fund, the World Bank and the General Agreement on Tariffs and Trade, the forerunner to the WTO. But despite much rhetoric to this end, there were few early signs that the twenty-first century crisis would similarly help a new world order to be created. The Group of Twenty (G20) of the world's leading economies convened a meeting of their heads of government in Washington in 2008 as the crisis was raging. The leaders solemnly promised, among other things, to refrain from undertaking protectionist actions. At the time, I predicted the pledge would hold for about a week, a forecast I was told was unduly cynical. In fact, it turned out to be naively optimistic. The truce lasted all of 36 hours before it was broken by Russia (Moscow once more displaying its traditional attitude to the rule of law) saying it would go ahead with raising import tariffs on cars.

The G20 did agree to put more money into existing institutions, such as the IMF, and encouraged member governments to think of how financial regulation might be changed in future. But of a new world economic architecture – a global financial regulator, a mechanism to manage exchange rates – there was little sign. The Stanford economist Paul Romer is credited with the aphorism that 'a crisis is a terrible thing to waste', a slogan much quoted around Washington policy circles as the financial turmoil raged. If so, the first couple of years of the global financial crisis were a squandered opportunity as well as a near-catastrophe in their own right.

Even the existence of institutions does not guarantee they will be used properly. The financial crisis itself was not primarily caused by a failure of global regulation; it was caused by a global failure of regulation. That is, national regulators and national policymakers had lots of tools to stop fantasy financial assets being created, given ludicrously unrealistic prices and sold on. In a whole string of countries, they chose not to use them.

A few years before the Spanish monarchy's effort to arrest the decline of its empire ended in nothing more than the abolition of the ruff collar, William Shakespeare wrote these words:

> Our remedies oft in ourselves do lie,
> Which we ascribe to heaven: the fated sky
> Gives us free scope, only doth backward pull
> Our slow designs when we ourselves are dull.

The difficulty of getting on the right track and then staying there does not diminish as the world economy gets larger, more integrated and more complex. If anything, it is the opposite. Nations that have risen, like the US, can make mistakes that will cause them to fall back again. Argentina could have been like the US, but if it does not address the flaws that have brought its financial system into crisis, the US could end up like Argentina. Globalization increases the potential rewards for countries that can get their policies right but makes more obvious the gaps between them and those that cannot. The experience of history should lead us to hope and strive to make the world better, not to despair and resign ourselves to fate.

Selective bibliography and notes

Throughout the book I have made use of a number of excellent histories of economics and trade, among them the following:

Ronald Findlay and Kevin H. O'Rourke, *Power and Plenty*, Princeton University Press, 2008 – particularly interesting on how the Mongols were good for trade.

Greg Clark, *A Farewell to Alms*, Princeton University Press, 2008 – a brilliant and thought-provoking book, whose conclusions are discussed in the final chapter.

David Landes, *The Wealth and Poverty of Nations*, W. W. Norton, 1998 – including a good account of the way Argentina went wrong.

William Bernstein, *A Splendid Exchange*, Grove/Atlantic, 2008 – a huge breadth of colour and detail.

Figures on gross domestic product and other economic data are generally drawn from the invaluable work by Angus Maddison, collected in *The World Economy*, published by the Organization for Economic Cooperation and Development in 2006, and *Contours of the World Economy*, Oxford University Press, 2007.

Preface

The opening anecdote on Franklin Delano Roosevelt is from Arthur A. Sloane, *Humor in the White House*, McFarland & Company, 2001.

1. Making choices

The brilliant observation about debtors and creditors going in opposite directions after the First World War is from Jeffry Frieden, *Global Capitalism*, W. W. Norton, 2006, with valuable insights also from Albert Fishlow, 'Lessons from the Past: Capital Markets during the 19th Century and the Interwar Period', *International Organization*, vol. 39 (3), 1985; and Stanley Engerman and Kenneth L. Sokoloff, *Factor Endowments, Institutions, and Differential Paths of Growth among*

New World Economies, National Bureau of Economic Research Historical Working Paper no. 66, 1994.

I relied on various histories of Argentina, including Carlos Waisman, *Reversal of Development in Argentina,* Princeton University Press, 1987; Leslie Bethell (ed.), *Argentina Since Independence,* Cambridge University Press, 1993; Roy Hora, *The Landowners of the Argentine Pampas,* Oxford University Press, 2001; and Roberto Aizcorbe's robust polemic *Argentina, the Peronist Myth,* Exposition Press of Florida, 1975. Paul Blustein's highly entertaining and meticulously researched *And the Money Kept Rolling In (and Out),* Public Affairs, 2005, is the best explanation of how Argentina lurched into crisis in 2001.

Details on the single global market in commodities are from C. Knick Harley, 'Transportation, the World Wheat Trade, and the Kuznets Cycle, 1850–1913', *Explorations in Economic History* (17), 1980.

2. Cities

Edward Glaeser's work on cities provided much of the inspiration for this chapter, notably Alberto Ades and Edward Glaeser, 'Trade and Circuses: Explaining Urban Giants', *Quarterly Journal of Economics* (110), 1995; Edward Glaeser and Janet Kohlhase, *Cities, Regions and the Decline of Transport Costs,* Harvard Institute of Economic Research Discussion Paper no. 2014, 2003; Edward Glaeser and Joshua Gottlieb, *Urban Resurgence and the Consumer City,* Harvard Institute of Economic Research Discussion Paper no. 2109, 2006.

Other classics in the field include Paul Krugman's work on economic geography, such as 'The Role of Geography in Development', presented to the World Bank's Annual Conference on Development Economics in 1998, and a paper by J. Bradford DeLong and Andrei Shleifer, 'Princes and Merchants: European City Growth before the Industrial Revolution', *Journal of Law and Economics* (36), 1993.

Figures on city growth are from the United Nations' *State of the World's Cities Report 2006/7,* Earthscan, 2006.

The role of London in the English Civil War is described in Conrad Russell (ed.), *The Origins of the English Civil War,* Palgrave Macmillan, 1973; Thomas Cogswell, Richard Cust and Peter Lake, *Politics, Religion and Popularity in Early Stuart Britain,* Cambridge University Press, 2002; and Peter Ackroyd's wonderful *London: The Biography,* Chatto and Windus, 2000.

3. Trade

The concept of virtual or embedded water, one of the best single ideas I have ever come across, was invented by the academic Tony Allan, and is explored in various papers, including '*Virtual water': A Long Term Solution for Water-Short Middle Eastern Economies?*, School of Oriental and African Studies, 1997. A World Bank report from 2007, *Making the Most of Scarcity*, produced by a team led by Julia Bucknall, provides a comprehensive assessment of water management, including virtual water trade, in the Middle East and north Africa.

Estimates of nations' water use and the food trade came from A. K. Chapagain and A. Y. Hoekstra, *Water Footprints of Nations*, UNESCO-IHE Research Report Series no. 16, 2004; Charlotte de Fraiture, Ximing Cai, Upali Amarasinghe, Mark Rosegrant and David Molden, *Does International Cereal Trade Save Water?*, International Water Management Institute Research Report no. 4, 2004; and Hassan Hakimian, 'Water Scarcity and Food Imports: An Empirical Investigation of the "Virtual Water" Hypothesis in the MENA Region', *Review of Middle East Economics and Finance* (1), 2003. More detail also in the United Nations Human Development Report 2006, *Beyond Scarcity: Power, Poverty and the Global Water Crisis*. The analysis of Australia is by John Quiggin, *Key Issues in Australian Water Policy*, Committee for Economic Development of Australia, 2007.

The explanations of grain production and trade in ancient Egypt and Rome rely on Peter Garnsey and C. R. Whittaker (eds.), *Trade and Famine in Classical Antiquity*, Cambridge Philological Society, 1983; Karl Butzer, *Early Hydraulic Civilization in Egypt*, University of Chicago Press, 1976; B. G. Trigger, B. J. Kemp, D. O'Connor and A. B. Lloyd, *Ancient Egypt: A Social History*, Cambridge University Press, 1983; and John Baines and Jaromir Malek, *Atlas of Ancient Egypt*, Facts on File Publications, 1980.

Details on trade in medieval and early modern Europe are from Norman Gras, *Evolution of the English Corn Market from the Twelfth to the Eighteenth Century*, Harvard University Press, 1915; and two papers by Meir Kohn, *Trading Costs and the Pattern of Trade in Pre-Industrial Europe*, Dartmouth College Department of Economics Working Paper no. 00–06, 2001, and *The Expansion of Trade and the Transformation of Agriculture in Pre-Industrial Europe*, Dartmouth College Department of Economics Working Paper no. 00–13, 2001.

The idea of Europe using trade with the Americas to abolish the land constraint, and the calculations of the 'ghost acres' added thereby, are from Kenneth Pomeranz, *The Great Divergence*, Princeton University Press, 2000.

4. Natural resources

The original paper showing that natural resources are generally bad for your health is by Jeffrey Sachs and Andrew Warner, *Natural Resource Abundance and Economic Growth,* National Bureau of Economic Research Working Paper no. 5398, 1995.

Much of the material on Zambia comes from reporting trips to the country, and I am grateful to Beverley Warmington of the Department for International Development and Dipak Patel, the former Zambian trade minister, for their time and expertise.

The paper comparing São Tomé and Principe and Cape Verde is by Pedro Vicente, *Does Oil Corrupt? Evidence from a Natural Experiment in West Africa,* Oxford University Department of Economics Discussion Paper no. 317, 2007.

For the remarkable story of Botswana, I relied on the following: Scott Beaulier and Robert Subrick, 'Mining Institutional Quality: How Botswana Escaped the Natural Resource Curse', *Indian Journal of Economics and Business,* 2007; Scott Beaulier, 'Explaining Botswana's Success: The Critical Role of Post-Colonial Policy', *Cato Journal,* vol. 23, 2003; and Daron Acemoglu, Simon Johnson and James Robinson, *An African Success Story: Botswana,* MIT Department of Economics Working Paper no. 01–37, 2001.

For a comprehensive tour of how natural resources have helped to debase several African countries, see the excellent account by Nicholas Shaxson, *Poisoned Wells,* Palgrave Macmillan, 2006.

John Steinbeck, *The Pearl,* The Viking Press, 1947.

5. Religion

Max Weber's various writings can be found in the following collections: Stephen Kalberg (ed.), *The Protestant Ethic and the Spirit of Capitalism,* Oxford University Press, 2001; Stanislav Andreski (ed.), *Max Weber on Capitalism, Bureaucracy and Religion,* HarperCollins, 1983; Sam Whimster (ed.), *The Essential Weber,* Routledge, 2004.

For commentaries on Weber and the Protestant ethic, see S. N. Eisenstadt (ed.), *The Protestant Ethic and Modernization,* Basic Books, 1968; Gordon Marshall, *In Search of the Spirit of Capitalism,* Columbia University Press, 1982; R. H. Tawney, *Religion and the Rise of Capitalism,* Harcourt, Brace and Company, 1926.

Details on the tenets of Islam and their effect on growth are from Maxime Rodinson, *Islam and Capitalism,* Pantheon Books, 1974; Timur Kuran, 'The

Economic Impact of Islamic Fundamentalism', in the collection edited by Martin Marty and R. Scott Appleby, *Fundamentalisms and the State*, University of Chicago Press, 1993; Timur Kuran, *The Islamic Commercial Crisis: Institutional Roots of Economic Underdevelopment in the Middle East,* University of Southern California Center for Law, Economics and Organization Research Paper C01–12, 2002; Subhi Labib, 'Capitalism in Medieval Islam', *Journal of Economic History* (29), 1969.

The groundbreaking study on the recent relationship between Islam and growth is by Marcus Noland, *Religion, Culture and Economic Performance*, Institute for International Economics Working Paper no. 03–8, 2003.

For Hinduism and growth, and an economic explanation of slavery, see J. S. Uppal, 'Hinduism and Economic Development in South Asia', *International Journal of Social Economics* (13), 1986; and Evsey Domar, 'The Causes of Slavery or Serfdom: A Hypothesis', *Economic History Review* (30), 1970.

A broader assessment of the impact of religion and culture on growth is in Deepak Lal, *Unintended Consequences*, The MIT Press, 2001.

The story about the apparent laziness of Japanese workers appears in Jagdish Bhagwati (ed. Gene Grossman), *Essays in Development Economics: Wealth and Poverty*, The MIT Press, 1985.

An account of how ethnic and religious minorities dominate business in many developing countries is in Amy Chua, *World on Fire*, Doubleday, 2002.

6. Politics of development

The classic paper on the operation of interest groups is Mancur Olson, *The Logic of Collective Action*, Harvard University Press, 1965. The insights about failing industries capturing government policy are from Richard Baldwin and Frederic Robert-Nicoud, *Entry and Asymmetric Lobbying: Why Governments Pick Losers*, National Bureau of Economic Research Working Paper no. 8756, 2002; and Lael Brainard and Thierry Verdier, *The Political Economy of Declining Industries*, National Bureau of Economic Research Working Paper no. 4606, 1993. Calculations on farming winners and losers in trade talks are from Thomas Hertel, Roman Keeney and Alan Winters, 'Why WTO agricultural reforms are such a good idea – but such a hard sell', posted on the VOX-EU blog http://www.voxeu.org on 22 October 2007.

On the textile trade and mercantilism, see Adam Smith, *The Wealth of Nations*, Book 4, ch. 2.24, Penguin Classics, 2004; P. J. Thomas, *Mercantilism and the East India Trade*, P. S. King & Son, 1926; and Pietra Rivoli, *Travels of a T-Shirt in the Global Economy*, Wiley, 2005.

For a superb account of how the Corn Laws were repealed, see Cheryl Schonhardt-Bailey, *From the Corn Laws to Free Trade*, The MIT Press, 2006.

On the history of sugar and protection, see Sidney Mintz, *Sweetness and Power*, Viking Penguin, 1985; Robert Paul Thomas, 'The Sugar Colonies of the Old Empire: Profit or Loss for Great Britain?', *Economic History Review* (21), 1968; and Eric Williams, *Capitalism and Slavery*, Chapel Hill, 1944.

On bananas and United Fruit, see Peter Chapman's robustly political *Jungle Capitalists*, Canongate Books, 2007; and Steve Striffler and Mark Moberg, *Banana Wars*, Duke University Press, 2003.

7. Trade routes and supply chains

The story about the Liberian graffiti was recounted to the author by the redoubtable Mark Huband, formerly of the *Financial Times*. The helpful explanation of why Africa doesn't grow cocaine came from an interview with Antonio Mazzitelli of the West Africa regional office of the United Nations Office on Drugs and Crime on 11 June 2008.

On the East India Company and the spice trade, see Desiree Marie Baumann, *The English East India Company in British Colonial History*, Verlag Die Blaue Eule, 2007; Giles Milton, *Nathaniel's Nutmeg*, Penguin, 2000; and Henry Wise, *Analysis of One Hundred Voyages to and from India, China &c*, J. W. Norie and W. H. Allen, 1839.

On the shipping container, see the classic work by Marc Levinson, *The Box*, Princeton University Press, 2006.

On GF Swift and the beef trade, see Gary Fields, *Territories of Profit*, Stanford University Press, 2003.

On Keralan fisherfolk and mobile phones, see Robert Jensen, 'The Digital Provide', *Quarterly Journal of Economics* (122), 2007.

On Eisenhower and highways, see Henry Moon, *The Interstate Highway System*, Association of American Geographers, 1995.

For the impact of empire on infrastructure and trade, see Daron Acemoglu, Simon Johnson and James Robinson, 'The Colonial Origins of Comparative Development', *American Economic Review* (91), 2001; Kris James Mitchener and Marc Weidenmier, *Trade and Empire*, National Bureau of Economic Research Working Paper no. 13765, 2008; and Jeffrey Sachs, *Common Wealth*, Penguin, 2008. For the geographical origins of African underdevelopment, see Jared Diamond, *Guns, Germs and Steel*, W. W. Norton, 1999.

Much of the work on the costs of distance and poor logistics comes from a large body of work conducted under the auspices of the Doing Business project at the World Bank, notably Simeon Djankov, Caroline Freund and Cong Pham, *Trading on Time*, World Bank Working Paper no. 3909, 2006; and Jean-François Arvis, Gael Raballand and Jean-François Marteau, *The Cost of Being Landlocked*, World Bank Working Paper no. 4258, 2007. See also Jorge Balat, Irene Brambilla and Guido Porto, *Realizing the Gains from Trade: Export Crops, Marketing Costs, and Poverty*, National Bureau of Economic Research Working Paper no. 13395, 2007; and Anne-Celia Disdier and Keith Head, *The Puzzling Persistence of the Distance Effect in Bilateral Trade*, Centro Studi Luca d'Agliano Working Paper no. 186, 2004.

8. Corruption

The biblical quotation on corruption is Exodus 23:8, American Standard Version. Theories of corruption from Andrei Shleifer and Robert Vishny, *Corruption*, National Bureau of Economic Research Working Paper no. 4372, 1993; and Robert Klitgaard in Richard Zeckhauser (ed.), *Strategy and Choice*, The MIT Press, 2001. Other illuminating insights, including the role of Suharto, are in Raymond Fisman and Edward Miguel, *Economic Gangsters*, Princeton University Press, 2008. For an account of its rising prominence in politics and policy discourse, see Moisés Naím, 'The Corruption Eruption', *Brown Journal of World Affairs*, 1995.

The stories on corruption in the East India Company, the French military and late imperial China are by Vinod Pavarala, William Doyle and Pierre-Etienne Will, all in the fascinating collection edited by Emmanuel Kreike and William Chester Jordan, *Corrupt Histories*, University of Rochester, 2004.

Details on corruption in Indonesia and elsewhere in east Asia are from Michael Rock and Heidi Bonnett, 'The Comparative Politics of Corruption: Accounting for the East Asian Paradox', *Comparative Studies of Corruption* (32), 2004; Andrew MacIntyre, 'Investment, Property Rights, and Corruption in Indonesia', and Ha-Joon Chang, 'State, Capital, and Investments in Korea', both in J. E. Campos (ed.), *Corruption: The Boom and Bust of East Asia*, Ateneo de Manila University Press, 2001; and Andrew MacIntyre, 'Funny Money: Fiscal Policy, Rent-Seeking and Economic Performance in Indonesia', and Paul Hutchcroft, 'Obstructive Corruption: The Politics of Privilege in the Philippines', both in K. S. Jomo and Mushtaq Khan (eds.), *Rents, Rent-Seeking and Economic Development*, Cambridge University Press, 2000. A defence of Suharto is from Dennis de Tray, 'Giving Suharto His Due', posted on the blog of the Center for Global Development at http://blogs.cgdev.org, January 2008.

Various analyses of Nyerere's rule in Tanzania are in Michael Hodd (ed.), *Tanzania After Nyerere*, Pinter Publishers, 1988; Nyerere's own admission of failure is from Karl Maier, *Into the House of the Ancestors*, John Wiley & Sons, 1998.

The riveting tale of Portugal's colonial misadventures in Goa is told in George Davison Winius, *The Black Legend of Portuguese India*, Concept Publishing Company, 1984.

The US spoils system of the nineteenth century is described by Peri Arnold in Seppo Tiihonen (ed.), *The History of Corruption in Central Government*, International Institute of Administrative Sciences, 2003.

9. Path dependence

The famous QWERTY keyboard paper is by Paul David, 'Clio and the Economics of QWERTY', *American Economic Review* (75), 1985.

The story of the New York City parking tickets is in Raymond Fisman and Edward Miguel, *Cultures of Corruption*, National Bureau of Economic Research Working Paper no. 12312, 2006.

China's successful route towards a market economy is explored in Shuhe Li and Peng Lian in J. E. Campos (ed.), *Corruption: The Boom and Bust of East Asia*, Ateneo de Manila University Press, 2001. Russia's shakier journey is in Stefan Hedlund, *Russia's 'Market' Economy: A Bad Case of Predatory Capitalism*, Routledge, 2000; and the more optimistic Anders Aslund, *Russia's Capitalist Revolution*, Peterson Institute for International Economics, 2007. The two countries are compared by Jens Andvig in Susan Rose-Ackerman (ed.), *International Handbook on the Economics of Corruption,* Edward Elgar Publishing, 2007.

Comparisons of transitions out of communism in central and eastern Europe are by Richard Ericson and Vladimir Popov, both in Michael Cuddy and Ruvin Gekker (eds.), *Institutional Change in Transition Economies*, Ashgate Publishing, 2002; and Martin Myant, Frank Fleischer, Kurt Hornschild, Ruzena Vintrová, Karel Zeman and Zdenek Souček, 'Successful Transformations?', *Journal of Comparative Economics* (26), 1998.

Details on India's economy and caste system are from Susan Bayly, *Caste, Society and Politics in India: From the Eighteenth Century to the Modern Age*, Cambridge University Press, 1999; Edward Luce, *In Spite of the Gods,* Little, Brown, 2006; and Stephen Broadberry and Bishnupriya Gupta, *Historical Roots of India's Service-Led Development*, Warwick University Economics Research Paper no. 817, 2007.

10. Conclusion

On the eclecticism of modern development economics, see Dani Rodrik, *One Economics, Many Recipes,* Princeton University Press, 2007.

The account of the reform effort that resulted only in the abolition of the ruff collar is from Jan de Vries, *The Economy of Europe in an Age of Crisis 1600–1750,* Cambridge University Press, 1976.

Index

Alan Beattie was b   r in 1971. He   iat   ollege,
Oxford, with a degree in   tory and took   aste   nomics
at Cambridge. Beattie worked as an econ   t at t   nd and
then joined the *Financial Times*   1998. He has b   editor
of the *Financial Times* since 2004.